Religion and the
American People

by John L. Thomas, S.J.

Religion and the
American People

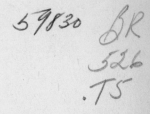

The Newman Press, Westminster, Maryland
1963

Copyright © 1963 by THE NEWMAN PRESS. *Library of Congress Catalog Card Number:* 63–12247. Printed in the United States of America.

In memory of Ben Gaffin

Preface

The aim of this book is to describe and analyze some of the more significant aspects of religion in mid-century America. Hence the term *religion* in the title is meant to be broadly descriptive rather than pretentiously comprehensive. Although the findings reported here were furnished by the most complete and extensive research on American religious beliefs, practices and attitudes conducted to date, their scope and quality are necessarily conditioned by the limitations inherent in the procedures through which they were obtained. Moreover, the phenomenon of religion is so puzzlingly complex in nature and so amazingly diverse in manifestation, while its varied historically organized expressions are so inextricably interwoven with other cultural elements, that adequate analysis of even one specific "faith" in a given period and place would constitute a formidable challenge. Considering that religion in America is profoundly pluralist, regionally diversified, and peculiarly open to cultural conditioning by reasons of its original transplantation, non-establishment and lack of speculative bent, it should be obvious that the aims of the present study must be relatively modest.

On the surface, at least, religion in American history appears to be characterized by a rhythmic ebb and flow of vitality. The last great wave, popularly associated with the name of revivalist Billy Graham, stimulated numerous observers to offer their interpretations of what they assumed to be a revival of religion, or of interest in religion, during the past two decades. Unfortunately, owing to the lack of adequately representative data, their comments and conclusions can be regarded as little more than perceptive insights or educated guesses. Since the research reported here used a carefully constructed national sampling procedure designed to yield results comparable to a fully random sample, it should go far toward supplying the empirical referents needed for reaching more balanced conclusions.

Much contemporary research and discussion related to religion places primary emphasis on the manifest or potential stresses and strains resulting from the competitive coexistence of organized religious groups under conditions of pluralism. While I do not question the validity of this concern, and indeed have devoted an entire chapter to an analysis of the findings in this regard, I feel that the importance of the power of "vested interests," to paraphrase economist John Maynard Keynes, is vastly exaggerated compared with the gradual encroachment of ideas, and that in the long run, "it is ideas, not vested interests" which prove most significant for the common good.

Thus the research project furnishing the information upon which this study is based was designed to investigate the actual religious beliefs of the average American adult. It was assumed that such findings would reflect those elements of the official doctrines of the churches currently appearing in what legal philosopher Pound has termed the *taught tradition,* as opposed to the more speculative conceptions presumed to be the normal concern of religious experts or theologians. In other words, an attempt was made to discover the relevantly operative elements of the major faiths still cherished by average participants, on the assumption that only such elements constitute the specifically religious "ideas" that may realistically be regarded as having existential significance.

Owing to the nature and purpose of this study, I have presented the findings with a minimum of comment or comparative references. The latter are available in any modern text on the sociology of religion, while in most instances I felt that extended comment on specific items should be reserved for a final interpretive essay. Hence after outlining the dimensions of the problem and defining my conceptual framework in Chapter One; and describing the denominational, residential and social characteristics of the major religious groups in Chapter Two; I devote the following five chapters to a more or less straightforward presentation of the basic findings.

Since a recurring theme in current interpretations of the religious condition implies that the major faiths are so thoroughly secularized that they no longer stand outside of and above society but have become fused with and subordinated to the secular values of democracy as expressed in the American way of life, I discussed this hypothesis at some length, particularly in Chapters Three and Eight. Briefly, the present study casts serious doubt on the adequacy of this interpretation. It uncovered no evidence that the actively participating, substantial "core" group of traditional believers in the major denominations was not as proportionately large as in the past. Although one might be inclined to concede the charge that religious values are apparently exerting decreasing influence in contemporary society, an alternate interpretation of this situation seems more in keeping with the facts.

In the final chapter I suggest that the churches in America

have failed to produce a religious elite capable of making the doctrines of the traditional faiths relevant to our complex, rapidly changing social order or to the new insights into human nature furnished by modern science. The result has been a gradual withdrawal of religious influence from increasingly extensive sectors of human activity and endeavor. The majority even of the actively affiliated faithful often fail to discover the relevance of religion in such areas, for their understanding of religious doctrine tends to remain at the Sunday school or childhood level. Yet a religious system must remain interpretively creative if it is to avoid becoming a mere cultural residue or a subsidiary institution of society. Unless it can produce an informed elite capable of providing a relatively consistent, orderly, meaningful interpretation of the total, evolving human situation experienced by its faithful, they must turn to other sources in their attempts to "make sense" of their world. Meeting this need for a religiously interpretive creativity is undoubtedly the major challenge the churches face in America today.

The research reported here is primarily the work of the late Ben Gaffin. He drafted the original proposal, developed the questionnaire and sampling procedures to be used, and directed the project throughout its various stages. It is a pleasure not unmixed with sorrow to acknowledge my deep indebtedness to him as a cherished friend and dedicated co-worker. Grateful acknowledgement is also due to the distinguished editor of *The Catholic Digest*, Rev. Paul E. Bussard, who financed the original project and lent it his closest support from inception to completion. Although it is impossible to thank adequately all those who have given me advice and encouragement while preparing this report, a special note of appreciation goes to W. Lloyd Warner, University Professor of Social Research, Michigan State University, and to Barry Keating, Research Associate, Bureau of Research and Survey, National Council of the Churches of Christ, for their careful reading of the text and stimulating criticism.

John L. Thomas, S.J.

Contents

Religion and the
American People

CHAPTER **1** What This Study Is About

THIS is a report on interviews with 2,987 American adults concerning the role that religion plays in their lives. The interviews focused on such significant topics as early religious training, beliefs about God and the Bible, participation in religious services, the functions of the church, and attitudes toward people with different religious convictions. Although a man's religion is usually regarded as a strictly personal matter, the majority interviewed appeared eager to cooperate. They evidently felt the study was important and expressed their opinions freely.

The current revival of popular interest in religion raises some challenging questions concerning the nature of contemporary beliefs and practices. Americans have always considered themselves a religious people. Today, as in the past, the term *God-less* implies opprobrium in all but the most sophisticated circles. The pervasive influence of religion in American society drew admiration from the keen, nineteenth century French observer, Alexis De Tocqueville. A century later, his perceptive fellow-countryman, André Siegfried, found it worthy of considerable

1

comment, though his interpretation of its significance was somewhat different. Few observers of the American scene, foreign or native, have refrained from expressing their views on the state of religion in this country. Opinions vary widely, but the fact remains that in any thorough discussion of the American people, the subject of religion is bound to come in for lengthy treatment.

Of course there are numerous grounds for a wide diversity of opinions concerning religion in the United States. Many changes have occurred in the dominant Anglo-Saxon Protestantism of the country since the rigors of seventeenth-century Puritanism were repudiated by a growing, optimistic nation. Although the permanence of a vigorous religious tradition stemming from colonial times remains beyond question, the modifications that it has undergone in the process of its development have been so considerable that scholars differ widely in interpreting its present significance. At the same time, the steady influx of Roman Catholic, Lutheran, and Jewish immigrants, particularly during the past century and a half, while further accentuating the importance of religion in the culture, has rendered the over-all picture much more complex and confusing.[1]

On the surface, at least, religion in American history appears to be characterized by a rhythmic ebb and flow of vitality. Starting with Jonathan Edwards' appeal for a "Great Awakening" in the seventeenth century, the country has been swept periodically by waves of religious revivalism, generating widespread enthusiasm and representing an apparent reaction to the assumed religious indifference of the period. The last great wave, sometimes associated with the name of revivalist Billy Graham, appears to have crested in the late fifties, and comtemporary observers are still far from agreement concerning its real nature and significance.[2]

The more optimistic contend, apparently on the principle that half a loaf is better than none, that though the movement has failed to reach the large, secularized masses in our urban centers, it has stimulated a renewed awareness of religion even among the more apathetic in the ranks of our major denominations. Others maintain that the results are superficial, that the wave was a backwash, built up by a kind of post-war generalized interest in religion rather than by a genuine revival of traditional beliefs. Indeed, they tend to regard the entire contemporary "return to religion" not as a renewal or revival, but rather as the development of a new type of religion, specifically American in origin, non-denominational in dogmatic content, and highly secular or naturalistic in goals and aspirations.[3]

Inasmuch as the research findings we shall present in this study are based on data gathered just as the current religious upsurge was getting well under way, they should throw considerable light upon its essential qualities. At best, a religious revival, even when employing the most efficient of Fifth Avenue techniques, must rely on a substantial core of beliefs and sentiments already shared by the participants. An analysis of past revivals in America shows that although they were built on modifications rather than simple restatements of traditional dogmas, revivalist leaders were always aware that their messages would arouse popular response only if presented as necessary developments or reinterpretations of contemporary, commonly shared beliefs.

What do modern Americans believe? What does religion really mean to them? During the past decade we have witnessed an amazing renewal of religious interest and activity apparently indicative of considerable vitality. Do packed churches, flourishing parish organizations, Sunday schools and discussion groups signify a dynamic return to past beliefs or a peculiarly American search for secular security through the promotion of "togetherness," "community," and "Brotherhood"? Does the traditional cult now mask a new creed, as some insist, so that with the troubled Isaac we are tempted to exclaim, "The hands are the hands of Esau, but the voice is the voice of Jacob"? The present study was designed to gather the factual information needed to give an adequate answer to this significant question.

In strict logic, a study of religious beliefs, practices, and attitudes should begin with some definition of religion.[4] However, inasmuch as an adequate definition of religious phenomena must be inclusive enough to cover all the varied manifestations of man's activity related to the sacred, while what men have historically regarded as sacred perhaps can be defined only as that which is the opposite of the profane, it is not surprising that no wholly satisfactory definition of religion has yet been formulated. Fortunately, the purposes of the present study do not require that we attempt such an all-inclusive definition. Our investigation is concerned primarily with several, well-defined historical religious systems rather than with religious phenomena in general. To place our study in context, then, it will be sufficient to describe briefly the general form and functioning of such systems in relation to man and society as revealed in the past. This will offer us a broad frame of reference within which we can consider the special characteristics of our Western religious tradition.

As we use the term here, a religious system represents the complex of creed, cult, and code of conduct constituting a group's total conception of their relationships to the transcendent, and the practical consequences that they believe stem from these relationships. Manifestations of the sacred never appear as segmented, relatively isolated phenomena either among the so-called primitives or in the higher civilizations. They are always part of a more extensive system, including the various religious experiences of the group, together with a set of traditional theories frequently embodied in rituals, symbols, and myths, explaining the origin of man and the world, the major characteristics of the human situation, and the speculative basis of approved moral norms.

Hence the primary elements of an integrated religious system include a set of concepts or beliefs concerning the transcendent, viewed either as an entity or entities having a significant relationship of supremacy over man and the human condition. The content of this creed is expressed in dogmas, myths, and symbols; while religious festivals, ceremonies and rites guarantee its purity and continuity in the group. Moreover, in addition to the distinctively religious acts prescribed by creed and cult, a religious system tends to furnish the basic principles underlying the group's major value-orientations and moral codes of conduct.

This latter point is highly pertinent to the present discussion, for it indicates the relationship between a religious system and the ethical outlooks of its adherents. In considering the nature of this relationship, it is well to note that it may manifest many modalities. In archaic cultures, for example, religion furnishes the type solution for every existential crisis, since their religious myths determine the exemplar models not only of all ritual and cult, but of all significant human activities. Among the major religious systems of civilized societies, the relationship tends to become somewhat more complex. Perhaps we can describe it most clearly by stating that in addition to the formally prescribed and proscribed activities normally associated with creed and cult, each religious system affects the ethical orientation of its adherents by defining the conception of man that they cherish. In the final analysis, all human values imply some conception of the human agent. Hence to the extent that a given religion supplies the essential elements in the group's definition of the origin, nature, and destiny of man, it furnishes the indispensable ideological foundation or rationale for the system of ultimate goals and premises of values lying at the core of their normative structure. Although this function of religious systems should be obvious, it is sometimes overlooked, because moral judgments in the practical order are frequently expressed without explicit reference to the ultimate moral principles upon which they are necessarily premised.

In other words, a religious system tends to determine the individual's status or position in the cosmic order by defining his essential relationships to space and time, to nature, to his fellowmen, and to the transcendental. The degree and extent to which different religious systems define these relationships may vary considerably, yet it should be noted in this connection that explicit definitions of the sacred involve implicit definitions of the profane, so that a group's attitudes toward the secular are necessarily conditioned by their religious beliefs and practices. At the same time, since religious systems do not function in a social vacuum, they are bound to be affected by the historical situation and cultural forms within which they operate. This all adds up to saying that the relationships between the sacred and profane, or the religious and the secular, are reciprocal. Explicit beliefs and attitudes in one area necessarily condition beliefs and attitudes in the other, with the result that we cannot adequately understand one without some understanding of the other.

Because a religious system becomes socially concretized or crystalized in a distinctive creed, cult, and code of conduct, it may affect individual members of society in a variety of ways. New members usually identify with the system and become participating members through the normal process of indoctrination and training. From the viewpoint of the individual, this process may imply no more than the routine acquisition of the family's or community's religious beliefs, attitudes and practices, or it may be accompanied by those personal experiences of the holy that Rudolf Otto characterized as numinous, that is, experiences induced by the revelation of what is assumed to be an aspect of divine power.

Moreover, since a religious system tends to become institutionalized, that is, to involve not only an ingroup of the faithful, a moral community, but also a visible system of symbols, objects, acts, offices, functions, organizations, and so forth, all members of the society within which a given system operates are more or less aware of it and consequently are affected by it. The resulting interaction, often unconscious and unperceived, may produce the greater sensitivity of all to the moral values and norms promoted by the religious system; or conversely, a hostile reaction to them, leading to added emphasis on opposing goals and practices.

At the same time, to the extent that a religious system affects cultural institutions either by determining their structure, by defining institutional goals and the acceptable means to achieve them, or by supplying the value referents to the social symbols operative in society, it necessarily influences the ethical orientations of all the participants of the culture. This explains why some members of a society who have never been associated directly with a religious system nevertheless may cherish value-orientations and moral codes representing the finest ethical development of this system and having no rational foundation apart from it. Thus Brunetière could write that Marx, in his concern over the exploitation of the poor, grasped the spirit of the Gospels more thoroughly than many Christians of his time, while there are numerous examples of dedicated social reformers who apparently drew their inspiration not from a specific religious system but from the religiously based value-orientations of the culture within which they were trained. Such instances are sometimes assumed to prove that religion has no necessary relationship to the moral values espoused, or that these values are self-evident. The first assumption indicates lack of awareness of the manner in which a religion may affect a cultural system, and consequently all the members of society; while the second ignores the fact that products of the Western cultural stream, for example, are accustomed to view man in Judaic or Christian frames of reference and that their self-evident "truths" are not so evident to men raised outside these traditions. Hence once the beliefs and attitudes of a religious system have become institutionalized, they continue to influence the ethical practices of people long after the religious system itself has ceased to attract their active adherence.

If it is to endure, a religious system must remain creative. This implies that it continue to supply a relatively consistent, orderly, meaningful interpretation of the total, evolving human situation experienced by its adherents, thus enabling them to "make sense" of their world, and by offering them an explanation of the significance and purpose of life, providing them with an intelligible frame of reference within which their perennial pursuit of happiness can be defined. Although a religious system that fails to remain creative in this regard may survive either as a cultural residue, or because it still serves as a convenient vehicle for the promotion of cherished social customs and ingroup solidarity, it is, in reality, no longer significant as a religious system, and men must look elsewhere for their interpretations of life.

It follows that a religious system must depend upon an elite for its development and vitality. Many religious systems make explicit or implicit provision for special statuses and functions in this regard, while systems that avowedly make no such distinctions among their membership, nevertheless rely upon a dedicated, well-informed, and specially concerned minority to conserve and promote continuity of creed and cult. In the long run, the progress and development of a religious system will be closely related to the quality of this minority. At the same time, in any on-going religious group there will exist some differences in the beliefs, attitudes, and practices of the majority and those of the minority. Because they tend to be primarily preoccupied with the more secular demands of daily existence, the former take the system for granted, concentrating on custom, required ritual observance, and personally pertinent practical applications.

On the basis of these brief observations concerning some aspects of the form and functioning of religious systems we may conclude that men develop their definitions of what is right or wrong in the practical order within a broader framework of value referents, organized into fairly consistent schemes or general patterns, and related to their conception of the nature of man and of the world in which he lives. It follows that religious systems affect ethical judgments primarily to the extent that they influence men's conception of human nature and the world. Since every religion attempts to define more or less clearly the status or position of man in the cosmic order, it is clear that whenever a religious system is accepted, it will necessarily affect the ethical orientation of its followers.

Furthermore, because man is a creator, bearer, and to a limited extent, a product of his culture, that is, of the organized systems of artifacts and symbols by which he modifies his environment and lends it symbolic meaning, a religious system will affect the ethical judgments of a group to the extent that it influences their culture, particularly in its functions of supplying a set of beliefs answering man's questions about himself and his world, and a set of standards for evaluating moral conduct. This influence may persist unperceived, since, short of periods of crisis, the majority of men do not question the foundations of their culturally learned beliefs or the ultimate premises underlying their standards of conduct. At the same time, however, in a pluralist, rapidly changing, complex society, some members of a religious group may adopt behavioral patterns based on unrecognized premises of values that conflict with their own. As we have suggested, it is the function of the elite to assure the continuity and creativity of their system by clarifying the relationships between approved practices and accepted principles, as well as by making logical applications of pertinent premises of values to changing situations.

Finally, the social implications of a religious system will depend upon how it envisages the ethical process. It should be obvious that a general religious imperative, such as the command to love one's neighbor as oneself, acquires ethical significance in the practical order primarily when it is applied to a specific human relationship in a concrete situation. There are several possible methods of making the application of general principles to specific practices. In archaic cultures, for example, primitive religious man simply regulated his activities in accordance with the ideal images revealed to him in his myths, for he believed that his religious myths offered the exemplar models not only of ritual but of all significant human acts. In some religious systems, ethical solutions to new situations are sought not by selecting and applying pertinent principles but, following the method of casuistry, by seeking for precedents in traditional religious documents regarded either as revealed or as the inspired dicta of great leaders. Some modern religious systems, at least in theory, by-pass the whole problem by divorcing the practical moral life from religious salvation. Holding that salvation is a purely religious problem solved by faith, predestination, or a unique personal religious experience, and consequently not dependent on human conduct, they regard particular patterns of ethical ideals and practices as relative, culture-bound products having no essential relationship of origin to religion. On the other hand, some religious systems assign human reason a large role in the development of their ethical practices, both because it is held that the Creator's law is discovered by reason in the natures of things, and general moral principles can be logically applied to concrete situations only after all the elements in the situation have been analyzed. Thus the ethical process is considered dynamic and existential in the sense that human reason, supplemented by principles drawn from religion, formulates patterns of ethical conduct in terms of the changing exigencies of the situation.

This brief description of the characteristic forms and functions of known historical religious systems does not constitute a definition of religion, yet it may serve as a convenient framework lending perspective and limits to our research findings on the American religious experience. Our study investigates the religious beliefs, practices, and attitudes of people who are primarily products of the Judaic and Christian Western cultural traditions. As such, they tend to think of religion in terms of a more or less definite set of beliefs and practices. Religion in the Western cultural stream generally implied belief in the existence of a special relationship between God and man. The nature of this relationship tended to be fairly well defined in a set of dogmas or beliefs concerning the nature of God and the origin, nature, and destiny of man. The faithful, or those who held the same basic beliefs, formed a distinct social group or "church" and came together for purposes of instruction and corporate worship. In theory, at least, it was maintained that essential life-values were closely related to religious dogmas, while the pertinence of religion to everyday conduct, as well as to happiness in the hereafter, was widely accepted.

This traditional religious Gestalt has exerted a profound influence throughout the development of Western culture. In the past, organized religion supplied the social means through which popular worship and belief in a transcendental being were promoted and vitalized. This belief in God, at the same time, served as the focal point around which established religious beliefs and practices were developed and fostered. Traditionally, religion has been primarily a social phenomenon, a matter of group concern. Centered in the community of the faithful, the *ecclesia*, it represented a group participation in a common spiritual heritage and shared experience at corporate worship. The view that religion might consist in a set of private beliefs and attitudes that each individual develops for himself has little popular precedent in Western society.

More significant for the future, perhaps, religion has tended to supply the supernatural sanctions for the Western world's ethical orientation. Western man's ideas concerning what was morally right and wrong in the practical order were closely related to the belief that there was a divine order and purpose in the world. Individuals were personally accountable to God for the observance of this order in their daily conduct. Human activity was evaluated within a moral framework at the center of which stood God, conceived as Creator, Ruler, and Judge of all mankind. It follows that if Western man's beliefs concerning God and his relationship to Him undergo radical change, he must find other sanctions for his ethical codes and a new focal point around which to organize his essential life-values.

A thorough investigation of religion in America is so important, therefore, because religion has played such a significant role in shaping our history and the culture of the Western world. If the traditional religious Gestalt is being essentially modified; if, as is frequently asserted, the American people are becoming "secularized," it seems highly pertinent to note the nature and direction of change. Supernatural religion, though varied in form, has permeated American society from its origin. Whether it was everywhere pervasive without being anywhere profound is open to question; but it should be clear that its rejection or radical transformation would have far-reaching consequences. To be sure, in recent times a "religion of humanity," modeled on one of the varied positivistic patterns, has been proposed to fill the personal and social void left by the loss of supernatural religion in the Western world. Up to the present, however, all attempts to persuade man to worship man have ended in dismal failure.

The present study tries to clarify the current status of religion by investigating the religious beliefs, practices, and attitudes of adult Americans. Unfortunately, no adequate comparable information concerning the past is now available, so we cannot measure accurately the changes that may have occurred. On the basis of our findings the most that we can hope to do is to point out apparent indications of trends. Briefly, our approach in this regard will be as follows. Our data provide fairly complete information on the major aspects of religion in America today, and though it is impossible to make detailed comparisons with the actual religious situation of twenty-five, fifty, or a hundred years ago, we can indicate in what respects the present state of affairs appears to differ from the traditional ideal.

Moreover, we know enough about the major aspects of our Western religious tradition in the past to judge if the present situation offers indications of continuous development or marked departure. As we have pointed out, organized religion in the Western world was characterized by a fairly well-defined set of beliefs, practices, and value-orientations, fulfilling definite personal and social functions in society. If it should be discovered that essential aspects of this traditional Gestalt are being de-emphasized, radically modified, or rejected, we may conclude that contemporary religion represents, to this extent, a departure from the past ideal. Whether the present be considered an excellent new development or a cultural residue, is not pertinent here. The essential point is that to the extent that it represents a departure from the past, it can no longer fulfill the personal and social functions allotted to religion in the past. In other words, modern man and society would have to look to a different source for the fulfillment of these functions.

When we stated that adequate comparable religious data concerning previous periods were lacking, we did not wish to imply that religious historians have been remiss in their work. There are excellent accounts of the growth and development of religion in America.[5] We possess numerous descriptions of the country's basic religious traits. Conjectures and predictions concerning the future abound. What we lack is adequate information about the actual beliefs and activities of adult Americans. Books on theology may tell us what the theologians, the "experts," are thinking; they tell us little about what religion may mean to the average American. It is this information that our study was designed to obtain.

Before proceeding to discuss our findings in detail, it may be useful to describe briefly a few of the more general traits considered distinctive of contemporary religion. Three distinguishing marks are usually singled out as characteristic of religion in America. First, there is no established church. Organized religious bodies are treated as voluntary associations of private citizens before the law. Further, religion in America tends to be highly individualistic. This is in keeping with the national temperament which encourages self-reliance and independence. Particularly among the Protestant groups, believers hold that they have the right to organize themselves into a church, and they maintain that this church should be a law unto itself in matters of dogma and religious practices.

Finally, the American religious tradition is characterized by a pervading and, until recently, an unquestioned optimism. This quality coincides with the prevailing national spirit, yet it represents a curious contradiction, inasmuch as the theological premises of the historic faiths brought to this country by immigrant groups present basically a pessimistic attitude toward human nature. This speculative pessimism, coupled with practical optimism, is considered one of the most distinctive traits of contemporary American theology. According to the distinguished church historian, Willard L. Sperry, it constitutes an "unresolved contradiction" at the very core of American religion.

In addition to these generally accepted characteristics, many others of a more questionable nature have been depicted by various observers. For example, we read that contemporary religion represents little more than a residue from the past. It is out of touch with the realities of common life and has become subtly "secularized" or "this-worldly" in its interests, being shaped by other institutions more than it shapes them. Middle-class church-goers, we are told, are as complacent as they are comfortable. They take their religion as part of their cultural heritage, but seem quite unaware that momentous changes have taken place in society since that heritage was formed.[6]

These observers insist that widespread indifference rather than organized opposition has stifled the religious spirit in America. Religion itself has been resolved into a set of individual and private beliefs and attitudes commonly judged to have little relevance to the market place or contemporary centers of thought. Critics maintain that the spirit of indifference and the consequent divorce between religion and life are so profound in our society that it is difficult to distinguish the religious from the irreligious. It appears that a considerable number of Americans prefer their religion without benefit of clergy. Under these circumstances it is hard to decide whether they should be classified as "fellow-travelers" or, to use one writer's happy expression, as "imperfectly irreligious." We are told that even among the small minority who profess no belief in God, relatively few are militant. Indeed, Maritain has aptly characterized the majority of them as "non-practicing" atheists.

On the other hand, some contemporary observers find evidence of a genuine growing interest in religion. In their opinion, the atom bomb furthered a trend that the depression of the thirties had already started. It put an end to the uncritical and seldom criticized optimism that had long dominated the national mind. They point out the profound, partially pessimistic sobriety that has arisen in some intellectual quarters. The age-old search for final causes and ultimate life-purposes that the father of positivism, Auguste Comte, thought he had successfully persuaded men to call off over a century ago, has now been renewed. There are those who believe that this bodes well for religion.

It cannot be denied that some elements of religion have become popular again. As might be expected, contemporary leaders have not been slow to reveal their awareness of this popular renewal of religious interest through their statements and speeches. They are not alone in this respect. Writers, counselors, teachers, and others have caught the spirit. Tributes to the morally stabilizing function of religion are now frequently heard at national conventions and other smaller gatherings of the professions. Many colleges and universities owing their origin to some religious denomination have dusted off their constitutions and rediscovered that they were initially established to be the intellectual support of religion. Church statistics concerning the number of parishes, members, communicants, and adherents, indicate a steadily increasing popular interest in religion. Although religious statistics in this country are proverbially unreliable, the existence of an extensive religious renewal during the past fifteen years appears beyond question.

These observations are suggestive and perhaps, to a limited degree, enlightening. But they leave unanswered the basic questions concerning religion in America. Does this religious renewal represent more than a passing fad? Does the contemporary "return to religion" merely reflect a shallow, wholly emotional reaction to the threat of communism, the atom bomb, and the cold war? There are serious critics who answer in the affirmative. To be truthful, nobody knows. In this matter, as in so many others, we lack reliable data upon which to base our judgment.

It should be recalled that we are dealing here not so much with a question of prophecy or prediction as with fact. What do the American people think of religion? What are their beliefs concerning God, the supernatural, the hereafter, organized religion, and the conduct of life? How many of them pray, attend church services, or observe some religious practices? What are their attitudes toward the diverse religious beliefs and practices of their neighbors?

The survey which furnished the data to be presented here aimed at securing reliable answers to these questions. Conducted during June and July of 1952, it is based on 2,987 personal interviews with a representative cross-section of United States adults 18 years of age and over. To our knowledge, this represents the first large-scale attempt to measure quantitatively some of the religious beliefs, practices and attitudes of American adults.

The questionnaire used in the study was prepared by Ben Gaffin and Associates, a Chicago marketing and opinion research firm. It was developed through a number of informal interviews with people of various religious affiliations, and revised on the basis of extensive pre-tests. Care was exercised to avoid slant or bias in the wording of questions. Prior to the inception of the field work, the final questionnaire was reviewed by Dr. George Gallup, who pronounced it free from denominational bias in orientation and question-wording.

The sample was initially stratified proportionately to the distribution of the United States population by census region, and by city size within census region. The specific interviewing points were selected and the quota assignments were made in

Father Divine movement or the Jehovah's Witnesses, the roster of religious bodies in the country reveals over 250 denominations and cults. Many of these, to be sure, represent relatively small, even highly localized groups, yet their presence bears witness to the perennial vitality of our religious heritage.

As a general rule, the traditional denominations still retain their dominant position and continue to attract the majority of church members throughout the nation. Around this central core clusters an interesting series of fringe groups, seemingly differing less in doctrine than decorum. Indeed, ever since the Great Awakening in the seventeeenth century when stagnating New England Calvinism received a vitalizing shot in the arm through the introduction of revivalism, American Protestantism in particular has displayed an amazing religious fertility. Nevertheless, despite this extensive multiplication of religious groups, up to the end of the nineteenth century at least, two forms of original Protestantism, the Calvinist and the Anabaptist, or radical sectarianism, appear to have been the major forces shaping American Protestant theological thought. By comparison, Anglicanism and Lutheranism exerted relatively little influence.[1]

Yet we would miss what is most typically American in the nation's religious history if we were to view it from the perspective of the major denominations alone. Running through this history almost from the beginning, and most clearly from the Founding Fathers, through Lincoln and down to the present, is an American version of the Enlightenment, characteristically latitudinarian, denominationally non-specific, and predominantly though not exclusively deistic. One might make out a strong argument to the effect that this peculiar religious orientation, prevalent among so many of the nation's political and literary elite, was more effective in molding the national religious temper and outlook than were the creeds of the major denominations.

On the other hand, among the mass of ordinary Americans, whether on the frontier, in rural areas, or among the urban working classes, there evidently persisted a basic deposit of traditional Christian beliefs and attitudes, handed down from generation to generation primarily through the family, and including rather simple conceptions of sin, redemption, duty, divine sovereignty, love, death, and the resurrection. Although the active membership of the major denominations is reported to have been relatively low throughout the nineteenth century, recurrent revivals continued to attract such widespread popular interest because they could rely on this fundamental deposit of faith among the common masses.[2] Without it, it would be difficult to explain the success not only of the frontier evangelists but of later great revivalist leaders like Beecher, Taylor, Finney, Moody, and a multitude of lesser talent. The people to whom they appealed felt a need for "getting right with God," because what Moody called, "the good old doctrines of our fathers: Man is fallen; Christ comes to seek, redeem, and save him," were still deeply embedded in those aspects of the culture to which they had been exposed.

It is more difficult to separate out the various currents in the American religious tradition during the past fifty years. At the turn of the century William James had pointed out what he considered the triumph of the "healthy-mindedness" of liberal Christianity over the "morbidness" traditionally associated with the "old hell-fire theology," and he predicted the continued growth of a "new sort of religion of Nature," based on the contemporary idea of universal evolution which lent itself so well to a theory of general meliorism and progress that it seemed tailored to the religious needs of the healthy-minded.[3] James' analysis of contemporary religious trends seems well substantiated, yet the success of liberal Christianity, with its enthusiasm for the social gospel, proved to be short-lived and apparently did not affect large fundamentalist segments of American Protestantism. A few years ago, it was customary to apply a kind of cultural lag theory in explaining such isolated segments. Because the members of these pietistic sects tended to be poor, as well as somewhat lacking in education and social prestige, most observers assumed they would join the mainstream of liberal Protestantism as they mounted the socio-economic ladder. Today, it is recognized that the grounds for the cleavage between these two wings of American Protestant-ism are much more substantial than was formerly assumed, though the eventual shape of the current realignment is not entirely clear.[4]

Some contemporary observers apparently feel that discus-sions of doctrinal differences not only among various denom-inations but also among the major historical faiths can have merely an academic interest since religion in practice has be-come the handmaiden to democracy and the major faiths represent "parallel shoots on a common stock." This somewhat startling contention merits more than passing consideration. We have already called attention to the far-reaching influence of Enlightenment thinking, as well as to William James' ob-servation concerning the triumph of "healthy-mindedness," while the charge that religion has has become "secularized" is a commonplace in modern religious writing.

Have American Protestantism, Catholicism, and Judaism be-come so closely identified with democracy or the "American way" that their primary function is to serve as convenient social vehicles for its promotion and conservation? Does the current religious revival merely reflect the coming of age of this "religion of democracy?" In other words, are the very real doctrinal differences existing among the major faiths and denominations now regarded as trivial because they are no longer emphasized by a clergy anxious to remain in step with the trends of the time?[5] In practice, this would add up to saying that the traditional creeds no longer furnished the faithful with transcendental criteria for evaluating their world, that the standards of value promoted by the churches are no longer derived from religious dogma but from secular society itself. As we have indicated, a religious system runs the risk of becoming nothing more than a cultural residue or a convenient instrument for promoting group solidarity if it ceases to be creative, that is, if it no longer furnishes the transcendental principles and derivative practical applications that enable the faithful to "make sense" of the complex, changing world in which they live.

Because "secularism," "democracy," "democratic values," and "faith in democracy" are such vague terms, seldom defined positively, it will not be easy to measure the extent to which our religious tradition has succumbed to their influence. Obviously, if the churches have become subservient to the democratic way and consequently serve as purveyors of a religion of democracy, this state of affairs would represent an implicit trend rather than a clear-cut position, so that our evidence for it would have to be based on tendencies and emphases rather than official statements. We feel that the present study is well designed to get at this evidence, for by investigating the beliefs, attitudes, and practices of average Americans, it gives us a picture of the general climate of opinion actually produced by the churches in the modern mind.

Nevertheless, inasmuch as the traditional religious divisions

of the population have remained fairly constant, it will be useful to know the relative numbers, distribution, and socio-
economic backgrounds of the people who now identify themselves as members of the various faiths and denominations.
The religious scene differs in New England from that in the
South, the Southwest, the Middlewest, and the West. In this
respect, as in so many others, historical circumstances and
regional differences have shaped and channeled religious endeavor in diverse ways. Religion in America, like Jacob's garment, is many-hued, but unlike that garment, it is made up of
a patch-work of many sectional patterns.

Thus we did not have to conduct this study to learn that the
American people express a wide variety of religious preferences.[6] Until the present research was completed, however,
we lacked adequate knowledge of what their preferences might
be. Do the majority of adult Americans identify themselves
with one of the major religious faiths? How many remain "unchurched"? What are the chief religious groupings, judged in
terms of expressed preference?

Question 28-a in the survey aimed to get at this knowledge.
After probing their basic religious beliefs and practices, people
were asked: "By the way, what is your religious preference—
Protestant, Catholic, Jewish or what?" Table 1 shows how
adult Americans identify themselves in this regard. Only about
one out of twenty stated that they had no preference, or indicated that they had some other preference. For all practical
purposes this relatively small group may be considered the
hard core of the presently "uncommitted," since the vast majority of them expressed a preference for no organized cult.

Viewed against the background of the nation's religious past,
the finding that the majority of adult Americans express a
preference for one of the three traditional faiths should occasion

TABLE 1. *Religious Preference, Active Membership, and Church Attendance*

MAJOR FAITHS AND DENOMINATIONS	Religious Preference (per cent)	Active Members (per cent)	ATTEND RELIGIOUS SERVICE				Millions of adults this represents
			Don't attend (per cent)	Once a month or less (per cent)	2 or 3 times a month (per cent)	Every week (per cent)	
Total U. S.	100	73	32	11	25	32	104.0
Roman Catholic	22.8	87	18	6	14	62	23.7
Protestant total	68.3	75	32	14	29	25	71.1
Baptist	17.3	78	26	13	33	28	18.0
Methodist	16.0	77	37	13	30	20	16.6
Lutheran	7.6	77	36	12	35	17	7.9
Presbyterian	6.9	80	31	14	37	18	7.2
Episcopal	2.9	76	30	25	25	20	3.0
Congregational	1.5	65	42	30	18	10	1.6
Other	16.1	70	34	13	22	31	16.8
Jewish	3.4	50	56	11	21	12	3.5
Other or no preference	5.5	4	81	9	5	5	5.7

little surprise. Of more interest is the relative proportion of preferences. The combined Protestant bodies still dominate the religious scene today as they have in the past, though Roman Catholics now constitute the largest single group among the formally organized religious communities. When commenting on the significance of this triple division in religious preferences, some contemporary observers seem to lose sight of the relative proportions involved. Protestants outnumber Roman Catholics three to one, while the Jewish group constitutes a relatively small minority. On the basis of our findings we must conclude that the United States is an essentially Protestant-oriented nation within which several religious minorities have developed and currently enjoy considerable acceptance.

As we have indicated, American Protestantism embraces a great diversity of subgroups. Table 1 reveals only the major divisions, but in the category termed *other Protestants* are included a vast array of minor bodies maintaining distinct organizations and religious activities. This diversity of subgroups has characterized American Protestantism from colonial times, though it would be an error to emphasize its practical significance today. There exists among most of these Protestant bodies an underlying "consciousness of kind" that unites them in a common religious ethos and clearly differentiates them from the Roman Catholic and Jewish minorities.

What does the term *religious preference* signify in this context? We can learn from this study, if we are not well aware of it already, that religious preference may mean many different things. A glance at the third column in Table 1 indicates that preference bears some relationship to active church membership, for almost three out of four Americans who stated a definite religious preference reported that they considered themselves to be active members of a church or religious group.

But what does active membership mean in this context? Perhaps we can gain some insight into the practical implications of the term if we check the responses to question 9-b of our questionnaire. People were asked: "About how many times would you say you attended Sunday or Sabbath church services during the last 12 weeks?" The remaining columns in Table 1 report some highly interesting findings.

It appears that nearly one third of the adult population attend some religious service every week; roughly another one third are not church-goers at all; one out of four attend two or three times a month; and the remaining eleven per cent put in an appearance only about once a month or less. The figures for the major faiths are also quite revealing. Although Roman Catholics have a serious obligation to attend at least once a week, somewhat less than two thirds reported that they fulfill this basic requirement. Members of the Protestant and Jewish faiths have traditionally regarded weekly attendance as a praiseworthy ideal rather than a seriously sanctioned obligation; nevertheless, it is somewhat surprising to find that only one out of every four Protestants and one out of every eight Jews gather each week for worship in common.

We might be tempted to question the "active" membership of people who admitted that they had not attended Sunday or Sabbath religious services in the previous three months. However, since they considered themselves to be active members, they apparently had not definitely separated themselves from active membership, at least in their own minds. On the other hand, the more than one fourth who expressed definite religious preferences but reported that they were not active members may at best be characterized as "fellow-travelers," and at worst as "imperfectly irreligious." In the latter case, their preferences would signify no more than hypothetical choices probably having little bearing on their general value-orientations or life-conduct.

Before we turn from Table 1, let us make one final observation concerning what it can tell us. Our findings show that although the majority of adult Americans express a definite religious preference when interviewed on this subject, such information has limited value in helping us estimate active membership and actual participation in the denomination of their choice. This fact should be kept clearly in mind when trying to interpret the findings of surveys like the United States Census Bureau's sample of religious preferences taken in March, 1957. In most cases, estimates for the various denominations based on such surveys will be considerably higher than official church figures.

For example, the Census Bureau estimated that approximately nine million more Americans classified themselves as Catholics than were listed by the 1957 *Official Catholic Directory*. Granting that the *Directory's* figures are not complete, for it simply compiles the more or less adequate reports submitted by the various United States dioceses, much of the assumed discrepancy can probably be accounted for by the fact that the *Directory*, by the very nature of its sources of information, tends to list only members who identify themselves with the church, at least to the extent of taking some part in church services. As we learn from Table 1, eighteen per cent of the people who stated a preference for the Catholic faith admitted that they had attended no religious church service in the previous four months, so that the discrepancy between the two estimates can be explained to a large extent by the fact that the Census Bureau and the *Directory* reported findings on two different categories of the population. The same observation applies to membership estimates of Protestant and Jewish groups based on expressed preferences rather than active participation.

It takes all kinds of people to fill our centers of worship, and though we have just indicated the wide diversity of faiths and denominations to which Americans adhere, even this presents something of an over-simplification of the national picture. As we travel from East to West, or North to South, we encounter varied "climates" of religious beliefs and activities. Indeed, even within each of our large metropolitan centers, we discover characteristic denominational concentrations, clearly signalized in the range from "storefront" churches to more elegant suburban structures.

To appreciate the significance of religion in America, we need to know something of the regional distribution of the major denominations, together with the social characteristics of their members. Conquest, immigration, and patterns of social control have combined to endow certain regions with distinctive religious traits, while social stratification and social class lines based on education, source of income, occupation, and ethnic background tend to be associated with specific denominational membership in our cities. Although details of the pattern are subject to constant change in our complex, open-class, highly mobile society, the overall scene remains fairly stable, so that the findings of the present study represent a relatively adequate portrait of the current situation.

Strangely enough, one of the most obvious facts about our country that some observers tend to overlook is its size and the consequent significance of regional or sectional differences for understanding the American people. It seems almost trite to point out that the industrial areas, or more specifically, the industrial areas of the East and Great Lakes regions are not America. Although modern means of communication are doing much to break down traditional regional barriers, it is still relevant to recall that America is a large, relatively young nation with the marks of its growth not wholly obliterated.

The steady westward march of settlers from the Eastern Seaboard, completed by the end of the nineteenth century with what Turner called the "closing of the frontier," added the Middlewest and Far West to the historical colonial divisions of North, Middle, and South. At the same time, the Louisiana Purchase and other acquisitions brought considerable numbers of Spanish- and French-speaking people into the national body, while successive waves of immigrants, totaling some thirty or forty millions, continued to modify the original regional pattern of religious groupings. As a result, we find the major denominations far from uniformly distributed throughout the country, a fact that is of considerable importance in understanding religion in mid-twentieth century America.

The first section of Table 2 shows the distribution of religious groups according to region. We have used the nine regional divisions employed by the United States Census Bureau, and though we are aware that students of regionalism have proposed various other divisions, there appears so little agreement concerning what constitutes a natural region that the Census Bureau's ninefold division seems as useful as any for our present purposes.

Table 2 shows that the South Atlantic, East South Central and West South Central regions remain heavily Protestant, with 86, 90, and 82 per cent respectively of their population expressing this preference. Yet even these figures do not adequately express the heavy concentration of Protestants in this area, for we know from other sources that approximately 75 per cent of the Roman Catholic population of the South is con-

TABLE 2. *Regional Distribution of Major Faiths*

REGION	MAJOR FAITHS				U.S. TOTAL (all groups)
	Protestant	Roman Catholic	Jewish	None or Other	
Per cent in each region					
U.S. Total	68	23	3	6	100
New England	38	55	4	3	100
Middle Atlantic	47	39	9	5	100
South Atlantic	86	7	3	4	100
East South Central	90	6	0a	4	100
West South Central	82	13	0	5	100
East North Central	71	21	2	6	100
West North Central	73	16	1	10	100
Mountain	76	17	0	7	100
Pacific	68	23	3	6	100
Per cent of each major faith					
New England	3	15	7	3	6
M.A.	14	35	55	19	21
S.A.	18	5	12	10	14
E.S.C.	10	2	1	5	7
W.S.C.	12	6	1	9	10
E.N.C.	21	19	13	21	20
W.N.C.	9	6	2	17	9
M.	3	2	0	4	3
P.	10	10	10	12	10

a Less than one-half of one per cent.

centrated in New Orleans and the southern parishes (counties) of Louisiana, while the 13 per cent of Roman Catholics found in the West South Central region is composed in large part of a fairly segregated group of Mexican descent.

On the other hand, there is a relatively heavy concentration of the Roman Catholic and Jewish groups in the New England and Middle Atlantic regions. Roman Catholics account for 55 per cent of the adult population in the New England region and 39 per cent in the Middle Atlantic, while the Jewish group accounts for 4 and 9 per cent respectively in the same regions. This section of the country was originally predominantly Protestant, but our findings show that the steady influx of Roman Catholic and Jewish immigrants has radically modified the religious preferences of the population.

The East North Central, West North Central, and Mountain regions, although they are predominantly Protestant, include a good percentage of Roman Catholics (21, 16, and 17 per cent respectively). Particularly in the East North Central region, the Roman Catholic population is located primarily in the large industrial centers, though this is somewhat less true in the West North Central. Finally, it is interesting to note that the distribution of religious groups in the Pacific region is roughly that of the national average.

Because the major denominations differ so considerably in size, it will be useful to know what proportion of each group is found in the various regions of the country. Let us turn to the second section of Table 2 for this information. The percentages presented here serve to emphasize the relatively heavy concentration of Protestants in the three southern regions, and of Roman Catholics and Jews in the New England and Middle Atlantic. In fact, roughly three fourths of the Jewish group, and well over one half of the Roman Catholic, live in the regions bordering on the Eastern Seaboard.

While taking a final glance at Table 2, it will be well to reflect that if distinctive religious preferences involve political, economic, or social consequences, we should expect these to become most apparent in regions of heaviest group concentration. At the same time, this uneven distribution of the major denominations should have wider implications in terms of mixed marriages, inter-group tensions, and comparative social prestige. Although regional distribution and relative size are not the only factors affecting inter-denominational relationships, they are clearly among the most important.

It is rather generally known that members of the Roman Catholic and Jewish groups in this country tend to be urban. As we can learn from Table 3, Roman Catholics and Jews constitute half the population of our major cities, though this proportion drops to roughly one third in cities ranging between 25,000 and one million. On the other hand, the Protestant groups are predominant in rural areas, small cities and towns. In other words, over four out of every five farmers, and about three out of every four small city or town dwellers you meet will be Protestants. There are almost no members of the Jewish group in rural areas, and they account for only one in fifty of the adult population living in cities numbering under 100,000.

Various factors have been advanced to explain this peculiar rural-urban distribution of our major religious groups. The following are perhaps the most significant. The poverty of many Roman Catholic immigrants prevented them from buying land. In particular, members of the New Immigration (those arriving after 1885 and composed largely of Roman

TABLE 3. *Residential Distribution of Major Faiths*

CITY SIZE	MAJOR FAITHS				U.S. TOTAL (all groups)
	Protestant	Roman Catholic	Jewish	None or Other	
Percent in each type					
U.S. Total	68	23	3	6	100
Over 1 million	43	37	13	7	100
100,000—1 million	61	27	4	8	100
25,000—100,000	60	33	2	5	100
10,000—25,000	76	19	2	3	100
Under 10,000	76	17	2	5	100
Rural	82	13	*[a]	5	100
Per cent of each in each type					
Over 1 million	9	22	52	18	14
100,000—1 million	16	21	20	26	18
25,000—100,000	9	14	5	9	10
10,000—25,000	8	6	4	4	7
Under 10,000	40	28	17	30	36
Rural	18	9	2	13	15

*[a] Less than one-half of one per cent.

Catholics), entered the country after much of the free land had been occupied. Moreover, as alien groups in a dominantly Anglo-Saxon Protestant culture, they tended to cluster together in close-knit national aggregates in our large industrial centers, thus guaranteeing adequate access to national churches and schools. The Jewish minority also grew primarily through immigration. Its members had little tendency to take up agricultural pursuits in their new country since they had a long tradition of urban residence in Europe and were trained for urban occupations.

The relative degrees of urbanization among the major denominations can be studied in the second section of Table 3. Over two out of every five Catholics and seven out of every ten Jews were found to reside in cities of 100,000 or over. Only one fourth of the Protestant membership was thus urbanized—in fact, well over half reside in rural areas or in cities numbering less than ten thousand. However, owing to farm mechanization and other factors, the farm population has been decreasing so steadily that the bulk of Protestants will soon be urban residents.

Modern social scientists are not fully agreed concerning the over-all, long range effects of urbanization on the attitudes and practices of religious groups, though significant differences between urban and rural populations in such matters as age at marriage, birth rates, family disorganization, standards of living, and so forth, have been clearly indicated in the past. It is rather generally assumed that urbanism produces secularizing tendencies hostile to religious vitality. This assumption may be substantially correct, though it obviously requires some qualification. The concentration of a religious group in urban centers also makes possible the establishment of a more adequate church and school system. One might question, for example, how well the Roman Catholic or Jewish minorities would have survived had their members been distributed equally throughout the country. On the other hand, evangelical Christianity in particular seems to have flourished under rural conditions, so that rapid urbanization may pose a serious challenge to some Protestant denominations.

Although it may be difficult to measure with any degree of precision the full effects of formal education upon religious beliefs and practices, there can be no doubt that educational achievement plays a major role in determining the prestige and socio-economic position of modern Americans. As a nation, we have traditionally placed great faith in the possibilities of human betterment through education, while the typically American belief in equal opportunities for all has led to the establishment of a remarkable public and private school system making at least a high school education readily available to the majority. At the same time, in a rapidly expanding, technically advanced society with an open class system, formal education becomes an easily accessible "ladder" for social mobility, so that a study of the relative educational achievements of various religious groups throws considerable light on their cultural vitality.

According to the United States Census Bureau estimates for 1950, more than three out of every four persons (76 per cent) eighteen years and older had some schooling beyond eighth grade, and nearly one out of five (19 per cent) had been exposed to some college education. As we can learn from Table 4, the findings of the present study differ somewhat from the Bureau's estimates. Only 69 per cent of the people interviewed stated that they had received some education beyond eighth grade, although the proportion that reported some college attendance was roughly similar to the Bureau's estimate. We do not have any satisfactory explanation for this variance, but judging from the findings of several national opinion-poll studies conducted in the forties, the Bureau's estimate of the percentage that had received more than a grade school education appears too high.[7]

When evaluating the present findings, it should be kept in mind that Table 4 indicates the educational attainment of the major faiths considered as inclusive groups. It is well known that there are marked differences among the various Protestant denominations in this regard, inasmuch as members of the Episcopalian, Congregational, and Presbyterian bodies traditionally outrank others, while members of the large "pietistic" fundamentalist segments, to which we have previously alluded, are usually found at the bottom of the scale. A somewhat analogous situation exists among Roman Catholics, though the differences are associated with ethnic background rather than religious commitment.

The percentages in Table 4 tell an interesting story. Roughly three out of every four Americans who had attended college were Protestant, while only about one in every seven was Roman Catholic, and one in every twenty-five was Jewish. To the extent that some education beyond high school is helpful for gaining wealth, social prestige and influence, these relative percentages are quite revealing. More significant, however, are the findings related to educational achievement within each of the major faiths. Twenty-three per cent of the Jewish group, 20 per cent of the Protestant, but only 11 per cent of the Roman Catholic had received some college training. We can underline the differences among the major divisions in other terms as follows: only 40 per cent of the Jewish group, and 48 per cent of the Protestant, but 55 per cent of the Roman Catholic had not completed high school.

TABLE 4. *Educational Achievement of Major Faiths*

EDUCATION	MAJOR FAITHS				
	Protestant	Roman Catholic	Jewish	None or Other	U.S. TOTAL (all groups)
Per cent in each class					
U.S. Total	68	23	3	6	100
0-8th grade	67	23	3	7	100
1-3 yrs. high school	65	28	2	5	100
High school graduate	69	24	4	3	100
1-3 yrs. college	75	15	4	6	100
College graduate	76	13	4	7	100
Per cent of each in each class					
0-8th grade	30	31	26	41	31
1-3 yrs. high school	18	24	14	19	19
High school graduate	32	34	37	19	32
1-3 yrs. college	10	6	12	9	9
College graduate	10	5	11	12	9

An important factor in the lower educational attainment of Roman Catholics is the immigrant background of a considerable number of their group. A large portion of the New Immigration was composed of Catholics from Central and Southern Europe who came primarily from small rural communities or from the working classes in the cities. Raised as peasants or industrial workers in societies that provided them with little opportunity for higher education and social mobility, many of them were slow to recognize the need for more than a grade school education. In contrast to members of the Jewish minority, for example, the first generation descendants of Catholic immigrants were inclined to encourage their children to seek employment almost as soon as they could get a job. Although this situation is changing rapidly, it will be some time before the proportion of Catholic college graduates will match that among the Protestant and Jewish groups.

The distribution of members of the major faiths according to occupation is, of course, closely related to their educational status and regional location. In a highly mobile, technically advanced society like our own, means of employment, or the ways men make a living, tend to be multiplied, sub-divided, and modified so rapidly that it becomes difficult to ascertain the social significance of many occupations. At present, the majority of the American work force are employees living off of their pay checks rather than proceeds from the ownership of private productive property under their direct control. Most occupations are no longer regarded as quasi-vocations, conferring distinctive status or social position in the community. As the economic system becomes more completely mechanized, fewer workers are required in agriculture and heavy industry, while increasing numbers enter the service trades.

We do not know how these broad occupational changes affect religious beliefs and practices. Clearly, there has been an increase in leisure time, but this may only mean that the churches must now compete with various forms of commercialized diversion. On the other hand, some observers maintain that as modern man's relationship to his work becomes more impersonal, he tries to escape the resultant sense of impotent isolation by identifying with a specific religious community.

Although we are not prepared to advance any hypotheses concerning the nature of the relationship between occupation and religion, in Table 5 we present our findings on the occupational distribution of the members of the major faiths. As might be expected, this distribution is closely related to the educational status and regional location of the groups that we have already noted. For example, we find that the Protestant bodies are over-represented in the professions and in farming; Roman Catholics are under-represented in these two categories but over-represented among manual workers, while members of the Jewish group are over-represented among proprietors or managers and among white-collar workers but unrepresented among farmers.

The occupational distribution within each group, presented in the lower half of Table 5, brings out these differences clearly. Thus we find 43 per cent of the Jewish group, 22 per cent of the Protestant, and only 16 per cent of the Roman Catholic in the two top categories classified as professional and proprietor or manager. On the other hand, 51 per cent of the Roman Catholic, 39 per cent of the Protestant, and only 21 per cent of the Jewish group are manual workers. Table 5 also shows the amazing effects of farm mechanization on the distribution of the national work force. Although 88 per cent of all farmers are Protestants, the occupation of farming accounts for only one

Table 5. Occupational Distribution of Major Faiths

OCCUPATION	Protestant	Roman Catholic	Jews	Others and none	U.S. TOTAL (all groups)
Per cent in each class					100
U.S. Totals	68	23	3	6	100
Professional	75	17	2	6	100
Proprietor or manager	66	18	10	6	100
White-collar worker	67	24	5	4	100
Service worker	68	24	2	6	100
Manual worker	63	29	2	6	100
Farmer	88	8	0	4	100
Other	72	19	5	4	100
Per cent of each in each class					
Professional	9	6	4	8	9
Proprietor or manager	13	10	39	15	13
White-collar worker	16	17	23	13	16
Service worker	8	8	5	8	8
Manual worker	39	52	22	45	41
Farmer	10	3	0	7	8
Other	5	4	7	4	5

tenth of the Protestant group; and we could safely conclude on the basis of these figures, if we did not already know it from other sources, that the nature of this occupation has undergone correspondingly radical changes.

Inasmuch as occupational status in a mobile, technically advanced society tends to be closely associated with educational achievement, it seems safe to predict that some of the relative differences among the various religious groups that we have noted will tend to be equalized as the descendants of rural migrants and of the New Immigration continue their drive for higher education. Of course there are also significant differences among various sub-groups within the major divisions; for example, between some of the Baptist and Episcopal bodies. It is generally assumed that owing to regional distribution and economic factors these differences are likely to be modified only gradually. At the same time, although we are making some progress in eliminating discrimination against such traditionally exploited minorities as the Negroes, Mexicans, and Puerto Ricans, there appears little likelihood that they will enjoy equality of opportunity in many sections of the country for some time to come.

To recapitulate briefly, our findings show that the vast majority of Americans express their religious preference in terms of one of the three major religious groupings—Protestant, Roman Catholic, or Jewish. Religious preference, however, does not necessarily indicate active church membership. Approximately 27 per cent reported that they were not active church members; while 32 per cent admitted that they had not attended any Sunday or Sabbath church service in the previous three months and an additional 11 per cent stated that they seldom attended. In other words, less than three out of five could be classified as active participants in common worship.

The distribution of the major religious groups throughout the nation was found to be far from uniform. The Roman Catholic and Jewish groups tended to be concentrated in the New England and Middle Atlantic regions as well as in cities of 100,000 population and over. More than four out of every five rural inhabitants were Protestants.

Finally, significant differences in the educational and occupational status of the various groups were discovered. The Protestant and Jewish groups included a relatively high percentage of those who had attended college. Three out of every four engaged in the professions, and over seven out of every eight engaged in farming were Protestants. Although members of the Jewish group represented less than 4 per cent of the population, they accounted for one out of ten in the proprietor and manager class. Somewhat over 50 per cent of the Roman Catholic group were found in the manual worker class.

Notes

1. See *Protestant Thought in the Twentieth Century: Whence & Whither*, ed. Arnold S. Nash (New York: The Macmillan Company, 1951); *Religious Thought in the last Quarter-Century*, ed. by Gerald Birney Smith (Chicago: The University of Chicago Press, 1927); *The Shaping of American Religion*, eds., James Ward Smith and A. Leland Jamison (Princeton: Princeton University Press, 1961), pp. 232–401.

2. See William C. McLoughlin, Jr., *Modern Revivalism: Charles Grandison Finney to Billy Graham* (New York: The Ronald Press, 1959); Bernard A. Weisberger, *They Gathered at the River: The Story of the Great Revivalists and their Impact Upon Religion in America* (Boston: Little, Brown and Company, 1958).

3. See William James, *The Varieties of Religious Experience* (New York: Longmans, Green, 1902).

4. See McLoughlin, *op. cit.*, pp. 465–66.

5. See Herberg, *op. cit.*, and Marty, *op. cit.*, for full development of this position.

6. See *Yearbook of American Churches*, National Council of the Churches of Christ in the U.S.A. (published annually).

7. See Liston Pope, "Religion and the Class Structure," *Annals of the American Academy of Political and Social Science*, 256 (March 1948), 84–91.

CHAPTER 3 What They Believe

THIS study was designed to learn what Americans think about religion. The findings discussed in the last chapter confirm the widespread assumption that we have remained a religious nation, broadly tolerant of great diversity in creed and cult yet firm in the conviction that some identification with one of the three major faiths is a social asset. Although not all adult Americans are active church members, nearly three out of every five feel that religion is sufficiently important to merit regular participation in organized church services. Granted this climate of opinion, one might ask why some observers are so critical of the current situation.

As we have indicated, the burden of their concern involves the qualitative rather than the quantitative aspects of contemporary developments in our religious tradition, for they maintain that though our places of worship are filled and interest in religion is widespread, the process of secularization has proceeded so far in our churches that it has become impossible to distinguish active members from non-participants on the basis of religious beliefs and attitudes. Secularization is given a specific meaning in this context. It implies that during the process of their development in this country the major faiths have become so closely identified with the "American way of life" that they have become "culture religions," that is, religions representing the coalescence or syncretistic fusion of traditional religious ideologies and American secular value-orientations. Increasing numbers of Protestants, Catholics and Jews attend church services not because they regard religious experience as a unique, ultimate value in itself but because religion is considered a useful instrument for the maintenance and promotion of other values—the "American way of life."[1]

Expressed in one form or other, this evaluation of contemporary religion has become part of the accepted folklore for many commentators and observers who apparently fail to note that it rests on several unexamined assumptions concerning not only the relationships between religious systems and the cultures within which they operate, but also the actual functions that religion has fulfilled and continues to fulfill in American society. We shall discuss the theoretical implications of this interesting hypothesis after we have presented our findings on current religious beliefs and attitudes as revealed in our interviews. This approach is based on the assumption that what the faithful believe reflects what the churches teach, or at least that portion of their teaching absorbed by the people. If the three major faiths have become "culture religions," we should discover some indications of this doctrinal modification by studying what people believe.

When we analyzed the form and functioning of religious systems in an earlier chapter, we pointed out that every organized religion offers its adherents a more or less clear definition of man's position or status in the cosmic order, and further, that such a definition necessarily involves a set of beliefs concerning man's relationships to time, space, nature, his fellow-man, and the transcendental. According to the system of beliefs furnishing the broad framework within which Western culture developed, man and the entire cosmos owed their origin to a personal God, conceived as a father-figure who was concerned with the welfare of his children. There was order in this cosmos, and somehow, Divine Providence guided the destinies of nations and of men. Man, the human agent, was a composite of two co-principles, physical and spiritual, or in common terms, body and soul. Created out of divine love and endowed with the capacity for divine friendship, man was originally destined to dwell in Heaven with God throughout eternity.

But it was also held that at the very beginning of its history, the human race was deprived of divine friendship by a disorder of the will that sacrificed God to self and spirit to impulse. The effects of this original alienation from God were perpetuated down through human history, affecting every facet of man's nature. Hence the human situation, as the Christian West conceived it, was man's separation from God by sin. As a sinner, man stood, as it were, in opposition to God. To solve this human dilemma, Christianity offered Christ—as mediator between the Father and man, as victim for sin, and as model for virtuous living. Life was a pilgrimage rendered painful by the effects of the Fall, and death was both a day of reckoning for the sinner and a doorway to a new kind of existence for the faithful.

How did men know that all this was true? Because these were the answers formulated in the traditional creeds, or to give the fundamentalist Protestant version as expressed in the modern song, "Because the Bible tells me so." Historically, these answers were embodied in diverse institutional forms and associated in the average person's mind with various common practices, rituals and symbols, so that he normally tended to absorb them as part of the culture. The major Christian bodies may have differed in the clarity with which they expressed these beliefs, the explanations they offered for them and the emphasis they placed on some of them, yet the central core of doctrine remained substantially similar.

What do modern Americans think of these traditional "eternal verities"? The summary of our findings presented in Chart 1 indicates a surprising continuity of basic beliefs particularly among the Christian bodies. The information relating to members of the Jewish group calls for some explanation. In the first place, two of the items, belief in the Trinity and in the divinity of Christ, obviously do not pertain to their traditional doctrine, and the small number who did express affirmative responses in these items apparently identify with the Jewish group on the basis of nationality or culture rather than religion. Further, although the members of the Jewish group were asked whether they were "Orthodox, Reformed, Conservative, or other," and it was assumed that there would be considerable differences in belief among these various categories, the total number interviewed within each category was relatively limited, so it was not judged feasible to present our findings for each of the sub-groups considered separately.

Using Chart 1 as a general point of reference, let us consider our findings for each item in some detail. In regard to the first, one point stands out clearly—few Americans are willing to admit that they are atheists. Only one per cent stated that they did not believe in God, and even among the group who reported no religious preferences, non-believers amounted to no more than 12 per cent.

How firm was this conviction that God exists? Among all

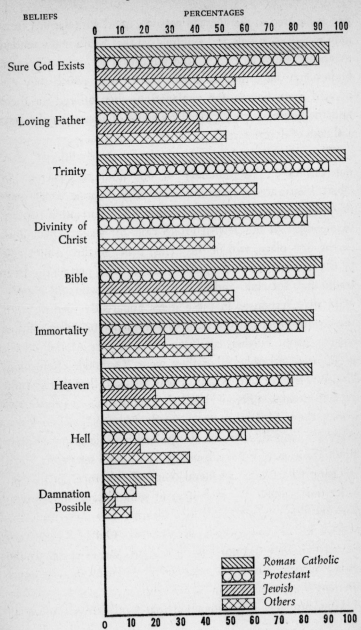

FIGURE 1. *Religious Beliefs of Major Divisions*

the people interviewed, 2 per cent were not quite sure, one out of ten was fairly sure, and 87 per cent were absolutely certain. The major religious groups differed considerably on this point. Whereas 92 per cent of the Roman Catholic and 87 per cent of the Protestant group were absolutely certain, only 70 per cent of the Jewish and 55 per cent of the group expressing no religious preference shared this firm conviction. Most of the people who were not absolutely certain were fairly sure that God exists. We do not know what significance people attach to the difference between being absolutely certain and fairly sure in their beliefs. It would seem safe to assume that the latter position implies some doubt, or at least grants the possibility that the existence of God can be questioned. Considering the central position that belief in God has traditionally held in Western culture, the fact that roughly one out of every eight adults harbors some doubt about it cannot be regarded as insignificant. Belief in God has long been associated with important personal and social consequences, so that lack of certitude concerning His existence is bound to diminish whatever influence such belief might have on daily conduct or basic value-orientations.

Most Americans believe in God and the majority express absolute conviction that He exists, but the term *God* may have many different meanings. During the interviews, people were asked: "How do you think of God—as a loving Father who looks after you; as some kind of supernatural power but don't know what; or how?" The idea of God as a loving Father implies belief in a personal relationship between God and the individual that has been characteristic of Western religion from the beginning. We may conclude that persons whose belief in God does not include this viewpoint have probably moved far from traditional doctrines and should be classified broadly as deists. They tend to regard God as some kind of impersonal power or force, necessary to explain "how things got started," perhaps, but not as a divine person with a fatherly interest in each individual and to whom all owe love, worship, and service.

Roughly four out of five of all the people interviewed looked upon God as a loving Father, while 17 per cent regard Him as some kind of supernatural power, and 5 per cent offered various other descriptions of their attitudes. The percentages add up to more than 100 per cent because some people gave more than one answer to the question. As we see from Chart 1, the major religious groupings displayed some differences in their conceptions of God. Eighty-two per cent of the Protestant and 81 per cent of the Roman Catholic, but only 40 per cent of the Jewish and 50 per cent of the non-preference groups thought of God as a loving Father. Belief in God as a loving Father appears closely related to active participation in religious services among Roman Catholics, though somewhat less so among Protestants and Jews.

The third item in Chart 1, belief in the Trinity, has always been one of the distinguishing marks of the Christian. The Scriptural formula for the religious rite by means of which the individual is formally affiliated with the body of the faithful clearly states this belief, for it is performed "in the Name of the Father, and of the Son, and of the Holy Spirit." Inasmuch as the Trinity is a strict mystery, that is, it involves a truth that by definition is beyond the reach of human reason, Christians do not attempt to explain it in itself, though they offer various descriptions of what it implies in the economy of redemption. Christian groups may also differ widely in the emphasis they place upon the role of one divine person rather than another, as we can see, for example, in the predominant place given to the Holy Spirit among the "holiness" sects.

Although this essential Christian mystery has apparently been called in question by some Protestant leaders, our findings show that the adult American public holds firmly to the belief. Almost nine out of ten stated that they believed in the Trinity, only 6 per cent clearly expressed non-belief, and the remaining 5 per cent reported that they were either uncertain or did not believe in God. Chart 1 shows the differences among the major groups. Ninety-eight per cent of the Roman Catholic, 91 per cent of the Protestant, and 62 per cent of the non-preference groups told interviewers that they held this belief.

When discussing religious beliefs among people raised in Western cultural traditions, a basic question, of course, is what they think of Christ. Belief in the divinity of Christ is by definition an essential attribute of the Christian, for the term *Christian*, used in a religious sense and not as an all-inclusive adjective standing for a vague cultural precipitate, can logically have no other meaning. Historically, all followers of Christ, the Christians, have believed that He was capable of redeeming them, that is, of restoring them to the lost friendship and son-ship of the Father, precisely because He was divine. The early Christians, the men of the Middle Ages, the fathers of the Council of Trent, and all the leaders of the Reformation never doubted this doctrine, so that we must conclude that people who deny the divinity of Christ, however "religious" they may be, cannot be characterized as Christians in the traditional meaning of the term.

During the interview, the question was asked: "Do you believe that Jesus Christ ever actually lived?" Only 1 per cent stated that they did not believe that He had ever lived, and another 3 per cent admitted that they were not certain about it. What do the American people think of Christ? Seventy-four per cent think that He was God, 6 per cent that He was the

Son of God, 12 per cent that He was another religious leader like Mohammed or Buddha, 1 per cent gave some other explanation, and 3 per cent expressed no opinion. Granted the widespread belief in the mystery of the Trinity, the distinction between thinking of Christ as God or as the Son of God seems minor, for the latter title merely stresses His attribute of sonship. Hence we can say, on the basis of our findings, that four out of five adult Americans believe in the divinity of Christ. Differences among the major religious groups as shown in Chart 1 indicate that 92 per cent of the Roman Catholic, 82 per cent of the Protestant, and 45 per cent of the non-preference groups believe in His divinity.

Religion among the major faiths in the Western world has been closely associated with belief in the fact of divine revelation. Revelation is usually defined as the act whereby God speaks to men either directly through Himself or through His messengers. Revelation, in this sense, should not be confused with an interior, emotional religious experience of an individual. Briefly, it implies that a personal God who is outside of and distinct from the recipient, at a definite time and in a definite place, makes a statement of truth to man. Because God has made this statement, it is accepted as true. When an individual assents to this truth, he makes an act of faith—he believes because of the authority of God "who neither deceives nor can He be deceived."

The Bible, containing the books of both the Old and New Testament, is regarded as the primary deposit of revelation in the Western world. The Jewish groups, of course, do not include the books of the New Testament among their sacred writings. The other major faiths have historically accepted most of the books in both the Old and New Testaments as revealed, although there are wide differences among them concerning interpretations of texts, emphasis on certain books, and the recognition of the function of other sources such as tradition and authority in furnishing the basis for religious beliefs and practices. In general, however, belief in the Bible as the revealed word of God may be regarded as a significant characteristic of traditional religion in the Western world.

How do the American people regard the Bible? The question was asked: "Do you believe the Bible is really the revealed word of God; or do you think it is only a great piece of literature?" Eighty-three per cent stated that they believed it was the word of God; one out of ten thought it was only a piece of great literature; 2 per cent expressed some other views; and 5 per cent said that they had no opinion. Chart 1 shows that the major groups differed somewhat in their views on this point. Eighty-eight per cent of the Roman Catholic, 85 per cent of the Protestant, 45 per cent of the Jewish, and 52 per cent of the non-preference groups believed that the Bible was the word of God. Hence our study shows that the traditional belief in the Bible is still maintained by the majority of adult Americans, but we shall be able to judge whether this belief is really operative or merely a cultural residue only when we evaluate our findings on Bible reading to be presented later.

The last four items in Chart 1 are related to various conceptions of a future life. Mankind in all ages has speculated about the meaning of death, for death is one of the inevitable facts that even the most perfectly organized social system can neither prevent nor fully explain. Societies have developed various rites and ceremonies usually to cushion the shock of death for the survivors and to provide them with acceptable means for expressing their grief, but whether the circumstances of death are faced with the stark realism of the Spanish peasant or disguised with sentiment, soft music, and flowers as in America, the fact that man is mortal lurks as an inescapable, frustrating conviction in the minds of all. Is there a future life? Does the soul live after death? Is there a relationship between our conduct in this life and our lot in the hereafter? Universally, it has been one of the functions of religion to supply the answers to these insistent human questions for the faithful, and though the answers were often vague, they usually held out some hope of survival and reward for the just.

The historical Christian view is clear. Man has an immortal soul. Sickness and death came into the world as punishment for sin. Life is a brief pilgrimage, a period of testing in the service of God. After death comes the judgment, following which the "just" shall dwell in happiness with God, and the doers of evil who have died without repentance shall be banished from the Divine Presence into a place of punishment called Hell. Although the major faiths differed considerably in their interpretations of various elements in this doctrine, they uniformly explained the future life within this general framework. Indeed, it is impossible to understand the history of religion in the West if one leaves out these basic assumptions on the immortality of the soul, the inevitability of the judgment after death, and the existence of Heaven and Hell.

What do the American people think of these answers today? The question was asked: "Do you think your soul will live on after death?" Considering the responses given to our questions relating to the existence of God, the Trinity, and the Bible, our findings on belief in immortality appear a little surprising. Only 77 per cent thought that their soul would live on after death, while the remaining 23 per cent either denied such survival or stated that they did not know what would happen after death. In other words, nearly one out of every four adult Americans no longer believe in a key conception taught by the traditional faiths. Members of the major religious groups differed widely in their responses to this question. Eighty-five per cent of the Roman Catholics and 80 per cent of the Protestants expressed belief in immortality, but only 35 per cent of the Jewish, and 43 per cent of the non-preference groups shared this conviction.

Following a commonly held opinion, we suggested above that the thought of the inevitability of death would cause most people to wonder about the future life. That this is not a necessary consequence is revealed in our study. People were asked: "Do you ever think about what may happen to you after you die?" Two out of every five replied that they did not. The negative responses of the major groups reflected the expected differences as follows: Roman Catholic, 36 per cent; Protestant, 40; Jewish, 65; and others, 63. In the light of these findings, it would be interesting to speculate whether, contrary to what is sometimes asserted, the much discussed insecurity of modern man is not related primarily to fear or frustration in the attainment of secular goals rather than to confusion concerning ultimate purposes. At any rate, it seems safe to conclude that a good proportion of the American people are not haunted by "intimations of immortality."

When the question is put to them, what do people think about the future life? Our interviewers asked: "Do you think there is a Heaven where people who have led good lives are eternally rewarded?" Seventy-two per cent, or all but 5 per cent of the respondents who had reported that they believed in immortality, expressed belief in Heaven. Chart 1 shows the wide differences existing among the major groups on this point as follows: Roman Catholic, 83 per cent; Protestant, 75; Jewish, 21; and others, 40.

Inasmuch as a correlative of belief in Heaven has been belief in Hell, particularly among the major Christian faiths, the further question was asked: "Do you think there is a Hell to which people who have led bad lives and die without being sorry are eternally damned?" Although 72 per cent of the people thought there was a Heaven where the just would be rewarded, only 58 per cent believed there was a Hell where unrepentant evildoers would be punished. As we can see in Chart 1, the major religious groups reveal characteristic differences on this point, with 74 per cent of the Roman Catholic, 56 per cent of the Protestant, 15 per cent of the Jewish, and 33 per cent of the non-preference groups expressing belief in the existence of Hell.

It is easy to miss the profound implications of these findings because the term *Hell* has come to be regarded as nothing more than a byword in vulgar speech. Considered in the perspective of Christian realism, however, Hell is the alternative to justification and salvation. The essential human dilemma as viewed by the Christian is man separated from God by sin—fallen man in need of redemption through Christ. The alternative is Hell. Only in terms of this stark realism can the Christian "make sense" of the redeeming death of Christ. To deny the existence of Hell is implicitly to deny the need for redemption. In the traditional Christian definition of the situation, to redeem implies a freeing from sin, and consequently from eternal alienation in Hell, as well as a freeing for divine friendship and its culmination in Heaven. If there is no need for redemption, the major symbol of Christianity, the Cross, loses its primary significance. Christian groups may emphasize one aspect of the economy of redemption rather than another, but each element can be fully understood only in relationship to the whole, and the whole is summarized in the redeeming death of Christ symbolized by the Cross. Viewed in the light of these considerations, the fact that over one out of every four Roman Catholics and almost half of the Protestants no longer believe in the existence of Hell may be judged highly significant.

It would be interesting to speculate on the possible practical consequences of this loss of belief in Hell. Reflections on eternal damnation and hell-fire may produce sobering thoughts. If we can judge from the religious literature and art of the past, it has frequently had this effect. The accusation has even been made that religious leaders used to hold the threat of Hell over their wavering flocks in order to frighten them into being good. We do not know to what extent this may have been true, or, if true, whether it alone was ever very effective. In this connection, someone has remarked of the fierce Calvinism of the Puritan Fathers that it did not keep them from sinning, it merely kept them from enjoying it.

At any rate, our study suggests that religion in mid-century America is not characterized by fear. In addition to the 42 per cent who did not believe in Hell, we found another 46 per cent who felt that there was not any real possibility that they might go there. In other words, only a little more than one out of eight adults regarded Hell as a possible future alternative, and it could be only among this relatively small group that fear of damnation could be operative. Obviously, Hell is a place reserved for the "other fellow," the criminals like Hitler, Mussolini, and Stalin. The vast majority of Americans feel quite secure and complacent about it, apparently as confident as the Calvinist "elect" whom Lorenzo Dow once cynically described as "safe as a codfish, pickled, packed and in port."

Yet this judgment may be too severe. When discussing religious beliefs and attitudes, we must never dismiss the possibility that the average adult participant is currently conscious only of the specific elements of his faith that are most frequently or graphically stressed. The remaining elements may become active, motivating forces if an occasion revealing their relevancy should arise. With the exception of the elite, the members of a religious community tend to be so preoccupied with the routine demands of living that they are little inclined to speculate about the total system and remain content to gauge their participation in accord with their felt needs. This pragmatic approach makes it difficult to define either the dimensions or the quality of their religious commitments. Hence our findings on the core religious concepts presented above do not tell the whole story, and we shall turn now to a series of items that may throw additional light on the problem.

Regardless of their basic beliefs, we found that the majority of adult Americans hold religion in high esteem. The question was asked: "How important would you say religion is in your own life—very important, fairly important, or not very important?" Only one out of twenty said that it was not very important, one out of five felt that it was fairly important, and three out of four maintained that it was very important. If we consider the distinction between "fairly important" and "very important" to be significant, there were marked differences in evaluation among the major religious groups as follows: Roman Catholics, very important, 83 per cent, fairly important, 14, not very important, 3; Protestants, very important, 76, fairly important, 20, not very important, 4; Jews, very important, 47, fairly important, 37, not very important, 15, undecided, 1; and among the non-preference group, very important, 37, fairly important, 30, not very important, 30, and undecided, 7.

Does this high esteem have any significance, or are people merely assenting to what they consider to be a highly respected—and respectable—American tradition? Some observers are of the opinion that this evaluation implies nothing more than an optimistic faith in the social usefulness of religion. People have "faith in faith," that is, they maintain religion is important regardless of its doctrinal content. In this view, it is religion regarded as an instrument of social solidarity and "peace of mind" rather than as a system embodying a set of definite beliefs concerning God and man's relationship to Him that counts. Although this critical observation may have some foundation in fact and probably accounts for a good deal of the renewed popular interest in religion, a fair proportion of the American people, as we have indicated, still profess belief in the essential tenets of their faith. If we judge that religion in America has become secularized or superficial, we must seek additional explanations for its condition.

One hypothesis that gains some confirmation from our study is that there has been a withdrawal of attention and affect from religion and the objects of its concern. A good percentage of people frankly admitted that there was considerable discrepancy between religious beliefs and practices in their lives, since they felt that they were not as serious about the future life as they should be. The question was asked: "Which do you think you yourself are most serious about—trying to live comfortably, or preparing for a life after death?" Forty-six per cent replied that it was "trying to live comfortably"; 21 per cent that it was "preparing for life after death"; 30 per cent that it was both; and 3 per cent that they were not sure. Among the major religious divisions, 39 per cent of the Roman Catholic, 45 per cent of the Protestent, 84 per cent of the Jewish, and 69 per cent of the non-preference groups admitted that they were "trying to live comfortably"; while the percentages among the same groups who stated they were serious about "preparing for life after death," were 23, 22, 1, and 6, respectively. However, in reply to the question: "Which do you think you should be most serious about—trying to live comfortably, or preparing for a life after death?" only 22 per cent of the total answered that it should be "trying to live comfortably"; 51 per cent that it should be "preparing for life after death"; 23 per cent that it should be both; and 4 per cent were not sure. The percentages for the major groups were: "trying to live comfortably," 19, 19, 68, and 42, respectively; "preparing for life after death," 53, 54, 8, and 32, respectively.

This all adds up to saying that approximately one out of every four adult Americans sensed the contradiction between his "this-worldly," secular aspirations and the life-goals implicit in his religious beliefs. Such admissions seem to involve more than the typical humble avowal that one's conduct is not all that it should be. Rather, it implies the recognition of an orientation, an habitual stress or emphasis on immediate values that the individual feels does not fully square with the theological premises he professes to hold. When the statement is made that religiosity has replaced religion in America, it is this practical divorce between theology and life that is probably indicated. Evidently, some people still acknowledge the validity of traditional beliefs, but the many concerns generated by our affluent society tend to focus their primary attentions on the achievement of more immediate goals.

We uncovered some indications that a society of abundance may not furnish the most propitious environment for the growth of religious sentiments. People were asked: "When are your religious feelings strongest—when everything is going well, or when the going gets rough?" The responses revealed an interesting pattern. Nearly half (47 per cent) associated strong religious feelings with difficult situations, while only about one out of ten (11 per cent) experienced them when everything was going well, and the remainder (42 per cent) felt that the situation made no difference. The pattern was roughly similar for all the major groups. Although one may not conclude on the basis of our findings here that one of the major functions of religion is to help people to deal with the critical situations that must inevitably arise in their lives, there is some indication that they tend to turn to the sacred when the secular fails to meet their needs.

Up to this point we have been discussing the more or less general attitudes of people toward a vaguely defined phenomenon called religion. Perhaps we can get clearer insight into the meaning of religion today by finding out what people think the churches should do. What is the function of the church? Religious commentators and others have frequently pointed out that the American people are more interested in practices than principles. If true, this orientation would obviously indicate a lack of religious maturity, for rational programs of action always represent the logical application of pertinent principles or premises of values to a specific set of relevant social facts. Whether the premises of values are stated explicitly or merely assumed, they are necessarily involved whenever judgments in the practical order are rational.

As we have indicated, the various Christian groups originally placed great stress on dogma and doctrine because they conceived the essential human dilemma in terms of fallen man's separation from God through sin. The reconciliation of man to the Father through Jesus Christ furnished the central core of doctrinal principles around which they constructed their religious approach. Thus it was one of the chief functions of the churches to keep these doctrines before men's minds through preaching, Bible reading, art, symbols, liturgy, ritual and ceremony. As a result, the accepted definitions of the human situation always involved transcendental dimensions. Past, present, and future, natural and supernatural, present life and future existence were all interrelated, though the nature and implications of the relationships were defined differently among the various groups.

The universally observed neglect of doctrinal principles in America, apparently already underway at the time of the first Great Awakening, suggests a profound shift in the entire climate of opinion relating to religion. Emphasis on practice rather than dogma carries the implication that the human situation is conceived primarily in terms of man's conflict with nature and society. In this view, the essential function of the churches gradually comes to be defined as social service, to teach people the need to subdue nature, both outside and within themselves, and how to get along with their fellowmen. Christ comes to be looked upon as a great leader and innovator in the field of human relations, while his role as sacrificial victim for sin and as mediator between fallen man and the Father is pushed into the background.

To what extent has the climate of opinion concerning the function of the churches really shifted in this country? In order to get at this problem, we asked the following question: "Which do you think is most important for the church to do— to convert people to a spiritual belief so that they can earn a happy life after death; or to teach people how to live better every day with all other people?" Our findings indicate clearly the shift to a human relations approach. Only 17 per cent of our respondents felt that the most important function of the church was to convert people to a spiritual belief; nearly one half (49 per cent) thought that it should teach people how to live better with all others; one third believed that it was both; and 1 per cent stated that they were not sure. Members of the major religious divisions expressed some differences of opinion as follows: convert to spiritual life, Protestants, 19 per cent; Roman Catholics, 16; Jewish, 2; and non-preference group, 6; teach people how to live better, Protestants, 47; Roman Catholics, 44; Jewish, 79; non-preference group, 67; should teach both, Protestants, 33; Roman Catholics, 39; Jewish, 17; and non-preference group, 20.

This strong emphasis on the promotion of human relations as the primary function of the churches, expressed by all the major groups, lends considerable support to the contention that the frame of reference within which modern man defines the essential human dilemma has lost its transcendental referents. The fact that almost half the American people believe that the most important function of the churches is to teach people how to live better every day with all others reflects an amazing disregard of dogma and doctrine in much contemporary religious thinking, as well as a profound misconception of the teaching role of the churches in organized religious systems. Were the churches to abandon their role of converting people to a spiritual belief, they might become excellent social service centers, but they would cease to be churches in the traditional Western definition of that term and would become promoters of "culture religion." Although some observers insist that this situation has already arrived, our findings suggest that a substantial proportion of the American people, including roughly half the adult population, still regard the churches as representatives of a transcendental point of view. On the other hand, our findings may indicate a trend. Only about one in every six regarded the spiritual function of the churches as paramount, and it might be argued that the additional one third, who thought the churches should promote both human relations and spiritual belief, were well along the path leading to a wholly secular view.

A further indication of what people think about religion should be found by studying their attitudes toward inter-faith marriages. Outgroup marriages pose a considerable threat to the survival of a religious minority, for marriage establishes an intimate bond of union readily transcending religious beliefs; and as a procreative partnership, a mixed union endangers the normal growth and continuity of the group by limiting the acquisition of new members. Hence, to the extent that a religious minority is determined to maintain its distinctiveness and survive, it uses various means to prevent the dissipation of its forces and the dissolution of its traditions through outgroup marriage.

Despite the prohibitions of religious leaders, however, attitudes toward mixed or outgroup marriages in practice are determined by current evaluations of outgroup members in terms of social prestige, class, nationality, *and* religion. Hostile attitudes may range from mere ridicule and scorn to absolute prohibition, but they are seldom based on religious factors alone. Among the major faiths, members of the Jewish group are least inclined to enter outgroup marriages, though there is evidence that the rate has increased since World War II. Somewhere between one fourth and one half of all marriages involving Roman Catholics are mixed. Rates vary according to the number of Catholics in the total population of the region, socioeconomic class, and the persistence of ethnic solidarity among various national subgroups. With the exception of some of the minor sects, members of the various Protestant denominations currently tend to intermarry with few reservations based on religious grounds, since they apparently feel that what doctrinal distinctions still persist among them can be reconciled within the broader framework of uniformly accepted beliefs. This tendency, however, does not rule out definite affinities or preferences between some denominations, for example, between Baptists and Methodists.

What do adult Americans think about mixed marriages? The question was asked: "All other things being equal, do you think that people who marry will be happier if they both have the same religion, or don't you think it makes any difference?" Considering the actual rate of mixed marriage in this country, the responses were surprisingly conservative. Three out of four thought that couples would be happier if they shared the same faith. Differences among the major faiths were not as great as expected and did not run in the expected direction. Thus, 76 per cent of the Protestant, 73 per cent of the Roman Catholic, 80 per cent of the Jewish, and 61 per cent of the non-preference groups favored sameness of religion in marriage. Because of the clear-cut stand of their religious leaders on mixed marriages, we should have expected higher percentages of the Roman Catholic and Jewish groups to have replied in the affirmative. Roman Catholics are free to enter a mixed marriage only after receiving special permission from their bishop, while even non-practicing members of the Jewish group tend to stress fidelity to their distinctive cultural past. At the same time, the relatively high affirmative response of the Protestant denominations indicates that they clearly recognize the marital implications of religious differences and may even reflect their reaction to the concessions they are expected to make particularly in marrying a Roman Catholic. Although our findings may lend themselves to various interpretations, it seems clear that they give little support to the contention that modern Americans no longer recognize the practical consequences of religious convictions. The fact that actual mixed marriage rates are higher than we might expect from the attitudes expressed in our study may only be one further proof that Cupid is blind.

We turn now to two final items, divorce and birth control, both of which have considerable general interest, inasmuch as they indicate marked differences in attitudes among the major faiths and offer additional insights into the nature of modern religious beliefs. Divorce is one of the important moral issues on which the Roman Catholic Church has consistently differed from other major Western faiths. We use the term *divorce* here to signify complete dissolution of the marital bond and not mere cessation of cohabitation, or separation "from bed and board." Roman Catholic teaching maintains that a valid, consummated marital union is indissoluble by its very nature and can be dissolved only by the death of one of the partners. Jewish teaching places strong emphasis on family stability and obligations, though it has traditionally recognized divorce for a limited number of reasons.

The definitive break with traditional Roman Catholic marriage doctrine among Christian groups took place during the Reformation. Both Luther and Calvin rejected the Roman Catholic belief that marriage was a sacrament under the jurisdiction of the Church, and their teaching has dominated Protestant thinking in subsequent centuries. According to their views, marriage is a quasi-necessary, honorable state of life involving mutual fidelity and serious commitment. It is a natural though *sui generis* contract, not directly under the jurisdiction of the church, and can be dissolved, like any other civil contract, for serious reasons. Other Protestant leaders developed their marriage doctrine in the tradition of Luther and Calvin, contributing little that was original.

Despite their differences regarding the sacramental nature of marriage, all the major religious groups in America attempted to instill profound respect for the sacredness of the marriage bond, and apparently with great initial success. De Tocqueville wrote that there was no country in the world where the tie of marriage was so much respected or conjugal happiness more highly appreciated. It is doubtful that he would have written in a similar strain a half century later, for particularly in the post-Civil War period, the literature is filled with worried comments on the liberal marriage laws enacted in some of the new states, the increase of separations, divorce, and general family instability, and the growing power of the feminist movement. In line with their traditions, religious leaders continued to work for family stability, but as the rate of social change rapidly accelerated under the impact of industrialization and urbanization, the churches appeared powerless to exert any great influence on the new climate of opinion that gradually crystalized after the turn of the century. At present, marriage is regarded as a private affair, and for all practical purposes, divorce is granted on the consent of the partners. Marriage and divorce laws differ from state to state, and are not uniformly enforced where they do exist. Statistical information on marriages and divorces is so patently inadequate that it suggests widespread public indifference. Paradoxically, modern Americans hold marriage in high esteem, assigning it an essential role in their definition of the good life, yet they seem incapable of mustering sufficient agreement to develop the economic, juridical, and social supports normally required to secure family stability.

We must evaluate our findings on divorce against this general backdrop of religious tradition, social change, apparent public indifference, and confused thinking. What do the American people think about divorce? During the interview, the following question was proposed: "Some religions hold that divorced people who remarry are living in sin. Do you agree or disagree with this stand?" The wording of the question was designed to discover whether people believed that civil divorce really dissolved the marriage bond, that is, if it were thought to grant the right merely to legal separation, remarriage would obviously be considered wrong. Only about one out of four (26 per cent) felt that remarriage would be sinful under these circumstances.

Granting the changes we have described above, this over-all response should occasion no surprise, yet a breakdown of the answers according to the major religious groups yields some startling information. In spite of the clearly stated and uniformly well-known position of their church, only 51 per cent of the Roman Catholic group thought that people who remarried after obtaining a divorce were living in sin. Even when we allow for the 13 per cent of this group who stated that they were not active members, and the additional 11 per cent who admitted that they never or seldom attended church services, it is difficult to account for this response. A charitable interpretation might be that some Catholics mistakenly believed that their church's condemnation of remarriage after divorce applied only to Roman Catholics, but considering the wording of the question, this interpretation seems somewhat farfetched.

It may also come as a surprise to some that one out of five of the Protestant, 4 per cent of the Jewish, and 11 per cent of the non-preference groups felt that remarriage following divorce was wrong. Some of the strongly fundamentalist sub-groups usually classified as Baptists, and many of the "holiness" sects remain strongly opposed to divorce for any reason, while several of the major Protestant denominations used to concede the right to remarriage in the church only to the "innocent" partner in a divorce. Our findings apparently reflect a lack of doctrinal agreement among the various Protestant denominations and sub-groups on this question, rather than failure to accept a clearly defined doctrine of their church as among members of the Roman Catholic group.

Although the historical relationship is frequently forgotten or goes unrecognized today, the issue of contraceptive birth control has been closely associated with the problem of divorce throughout the last century. Because the success of medical science in achieving the postponement of death has dramatically upset a balance that mankind has hitherto taken generally for granted, and what Malthus termed "the prevalence of people" is becoming one of the major challenges modern man must face, there is a tendency to speak of the contraceptive birth control movement as if it were initiated primarily to deal with problems of overpopulation. Such lack of historical perspective takes the issue completely out of context and renders it impossible to explain the rapid and widespread acceptance of contraceptive practices in spite of the initial silence or condemnation of the churches. Changed attitudes in regard to both divorce and birth control were the result of almost a century-long struggle for sexual reform conducted by a wide variety of groups frequently associated with the general woman's rights movement. The practical aims of this broad movement were varied—reform in marriage and divorce laws, the education of women, women's equal rights in the family and before the law, and so on—yet it should be obvious that none of these reforms could have proved very effective in the practical order unless accompanied by voluntary control over women's reproductive role in marriage. Although contraceptive birth control was frequently advocated as a remedy for the burdens of poverty, its initial rejection by the traditionally conservative lower socio-economic classes indicates that its widespread acceptance among the middle and upper classes had been preceded by a changed climate of opinion concerning sexual equality and the function of sex in marriage.

This view does not rule out the considerable influence of social and economic factors. The structure of the American family was undergoing rapid change throughout this period as the population moved from a rural to an industrialized urban environment. Emphasis shifted from an extended to a conjugal type of family unit, increasing numbers of women entered the workforce as industry supplied new opportunities for employment outside the home, and the implications of bearing and rearing children were drastically changed in the family's modern urban setting, inasmuch as children required more formal training, remained economically unproductive longer, and also prevented women from remaining in or entering the workforce. Such factors clearly focused attention on the problem of family limitation, but their interpretation by individual couples who, in the final analysis, must make the decision to limit offspring, depended on the value systems the couples embraced, and it was in this area that the really basic change had occurred. That traditional views had been profoundly modified became obvious during the depression years of the thirties. The 1940 Census Reports revealed such a drastic reduction of the birth rate that demographers predicted the stabilization of the population within the near future. Although the return of economic prosperity accompanying World War II and the post war period resulted in a sustained baby boom that has led sincere population experts to suspect that they still know very little about the laws of population growth, there is no reason to believe that attitudes concerning the morality of contraceptive practices have been modified. Americans now marry younger, give serious thought to family size, and tend to "bunch" pregnancies in the early years of marriage. Implicit in this type of family planning is some form of conception control either for spacing, limitation, or avoidance during the later years of the reproductive span.

It is interesting to note that this changed attitude toward family size and the various methods used to control it occurred with little official direction from the churches. Indeed, one might almost say that society presented the churches with a *fait accompli* toward which they reacted in various ways only when they could no longer ignore it. The Anglican Communion appears to have been the first major Protestant body to give the problem systematic attention. In 1930, the 260 Anglican bishops of the Lambeth Conference reversed the stand of the 1908 and 1920 Conferences condemning birth control and adopted, by a vote of roughly three to one a somewhat cautious resolution stating that "where there is a clearly felt moral obligation to limit or avoid parenthood" although complete abstinence is the "primary and obvious method," if there are morally sound reasons for avoiding abstinence, "the Conference agrees that other methods may be used, provided that this is done in the light of . . . Christian principles." Many of the major American Protestant bodies eventually followed with various statements embodying similar views. At present it appears that the overwhelming weight of Protestant opinion favors some form of family limitation, as well as the use of contraceptive birth control at least to some degree, though no clear-cut, over-all Protestant position has yet emerged.[2]

The official Roman Catholic position was repeated in the early thirties by Pius XI in his carefully prepared encyclical on marriage, *Casti Connubii*, as follows: "Any use whatsoever of matrimony exercised in such a way that the act is deliberately frustrated in its natural power to generate life is an offense against the law of God and of nature, and those who indulge in such are branded with the guilt of grave sin." However, this position is not opposed to the prudent regulation of family size through the use of periodic continence, as Pius XII states clearly in his well-known address, "Apostolate of the Midwife," in 1951.

There is no official Jewish position on this issue. Nevertheless, with the exception of some of the Orthodox, Jewish religious leaders uniformly maintain that there are no doctrinal grounds for the rejection of prudent family planning and the use of contraceptives to achieve this purpose.

What does the average American adult think about the morality of contraceptive practices? The question was asked: "Some religions forbid married couples to use mechanical birth control methods. Do you agree or disagree with this stand?" A little over one out of five (22 per cent) agreed, almost two thirds (63 per cent) disagreed, and the remaining 15 per cent expressed no definite opinion. Judging on the basis of our previous discussion of this issue, these responses reflect attitudes similar, for the most part, to what we should have expected. Our findings on the differences among the major groups will probably occasion more surprise. Fifty-one per cent of the Roman Catholic, 14 per cent of the Protestant, 10 per cent of the Jewish, and 11 per cent of the non-preference groups agreed.

It is interesting to note that these responses parallel rather closely the answers given to the question on divorce and remarriage, though it should be remarked that more Protestants accepted birth control (86 per cent) than divorce (80 per cent), while more of the Jewish group accepted divorce (96 per cent) than birth control (90 per cent). The fact that approximately half the Roman Catholic group do not accept their church's teaching on the morality of contraceptive practices indicates a startling degree of secularization. Even when we allow for the 24 per cent who stated that they are not active church members or seldom attend religious services, we find one out of four who reject the moral guidance of their church in this area. In evaluating the significance of our findings here, we must be mindful of the fact that we are dealing with attitudes not practices. It is quite understandable that faced with acute problems of finance, health, frequent pregnancies, and so on, some Catholic couples should deviate, at least for a time, from approved religious norms, but this failure to conform fully to their church's moral standards has far different significance from the open rejection of the church's teaching. The Roman Catholic faith includes belief in a divinely established teaching authority concerning matters of faith and morals; for a Catholic to reject an explicit, clearly stated, serious moral directive of the church is tantamount to rejecting the faith, though a considerable number of Roman Catholics are apparently not aware of this obvious implication.

Up to this point we have been discussing the major religious attitudes and beliefs of the American people from the viewpoint of the three major faiths, Protestant, Roman Catholic, and Jewish. This approach, of course, ignores significant intra-faith differences in beliefs, for the major faiths, with the exception of the Roman Catholics, include a considerable number of important subgroups. We have already mentioned the three chief divisions among the Jewish group, Reform, Conservative, Orthodox, and the more than 250 Protestant bodies currently reporting statistics on membership. However, among the latter there are only 82 reporting memberships of 50,000 or more, and among these, we find a half dozen traditional denominational families or bodies that account for roughly three fourths of the Protestant total. These major divisions reveal some differences in organizational structure, historical development in this country, and doctrinal approaches, though it is rather generally assumed that they are moving closer toward each other in teaching and practice. It will be of no little interest, therefore, to present our findings on the beliefs they currently profess.

When studying the responses recorded in Table 6, we must keep in mind that the major divisions are denominational families including numerous subgroups that may cherish somewhat dissimilar doctrinal emphases and approaches. For example, there were 26 Baptist, 21 Methodist, 18 Lutheran denominations, and so on, in 1956. The process of merging or dividing within the larger denominational families appears endemic, though not significantly related to long term, over-all growth of a given denomination.[3] In the last column of Table 6 we have been forced to lump together an amazingly disparate range of churches such as Mennonites, Latter-Day Saints, Unitarians, Jehovah's Witnesses, and various pentecostal and holiness sects. The collective findings are probably not very useful, yet a glance at the column indicates that the responses were highly tradition-oriented.

The chief impression that emerges from studying Table 6 is that the major Protestant divisions still include memberships differing significantly in many basic religious beliefs. If the questions we asked denoted traditional beliefs, then affirmative responses indicated tradition-oriented or conservative participants. Judging on the basis of this criterion, it becomes evident at once that the Baptist bodies are by far the most conservative of the Protestant groups. On every item of belief recorded in the table, the percentages of their affirmative responses were consistently higher than for any other group. With the exception of one or two items, particularly in regard

TABLE 6. Religious Beliefs of Major Protestant Divisions

BELIEFS	MAJOR PROTESTANT DIVISIONS							
	Baptist	Methodist	Lutheran	Presbyterian	Episcopalian	Congregational	Others
Existence of God:							
Absolutely certain	93	86	80	90	77	72	89
(Fairly sure)	(6)	(11)	(17)	(8)	(17)	(20)	(9)
Trinity	95	90	93	89	89	83	89
God—Loving Father	88	82	77	77	76	61	82
Divinity of Christ	90	83	79	81	74	62	81
Bible revealed	93	85	86	84	72	76	85
Immortality	87	77	78	80	67	63	78
Heaven	83	72	74	71	58	59	71
Hell	75	51	59	45	26	35	52
Divorce is wrong	29	14	12	12	7	4	25
Birth control is wrong	18	13	15	8	11	9	14

to belief in the existence of Hell and absolute certainty that God exists, the Methodist, Lutheran, and Presbyterian bodies appeared to be roughly similar in basic beliefs. The Episcopal and Congregational bodies were the least conservative of all the Protestant denominations, revealing a marked pattern of differences, with the exception of the responses relating to belief in the Trinity and God as loving Father by the Episcopal bodies.

Although it would be hazardous to attempt to explain the differences recorded in Table 6 on the basis of our findings alone, one might offer the hypothesis that the Baptist and Congregational bodies represent the two extremes of the (pietistic) fundamentalist-liberal Protestant continuum we have previously mentioned. The firm belief in the Bible as the revealed word of God, in the divinity of Christ, immortality, Heaven, Hell, and the indissolubility of the marriage bond shown by the Baptist bodies suggests that we are dealing with what is generally described as pietistic fundamentalism, while the views of a fair percentage of the Congregational group on these same items offer some indications of liberalism.

Our discovery that the members of the major faiths and denominations vary considerably in the degree of religious conservatism that they display raises several interesting questions. Does the degree of conservatism vary with age? Is there a relationship between beliefs and formal education achieved? Are urban residents less conservative than people living in small towns or in the country? We shall present a summary of our findings in the three following tables.

As we can see from a rapid reading of Table 7, there appears to be no consistent relationship between age and religious conservatism. This finding appears to contradict some rather commonly held opinions, for it is generally assumed that older

TABLE 7. *Religious Beliefs According to Age of Participants*

BELIEFS		AGE CATEGORIES					
		18–24	25–34	35–44	45–54	55–64	65+
Existence of God:							
Absolutely certain		87	85	85	87	88	91
(Fairly sure)		9	11	11	10	9	7
Trinity		90	87	88	86	92	90
God—Loving Father		80	80	77	76	77	81
Divinity of Christ		82	81	80	77	78	81
Bible revealed		83	86	83	81	82	88
Immortality		75	76	77	76	80	81
Heaven		70	71	72	71	74	76
Hell		59	58	59	54	58	56
Divorce is wrong		32	26	24	25	25	28
Birth control is wrong		27	21	21	21	21	26

people tend to be more conservative, either because increasing age raises inevitable questions about the hereafter or increasing secularism renders modern youth more sceptical. If the religious outlook of the American people is becoming more secularized, the data presented in Table 7 do not show it. Either the older generation received a religious indoctrination quite similar to the present or they lost some of their conservatism with age, and there is no basis in our findings for this latter conclusion. On the other hand, there is little evidence to support the contention that people become more religiously conservative with age. Although religious practice may differ with age, it seems that basic beliefs are acquired in youth and retained throughout life relatively unchanged.

Is formal education related to religious conservatism? The majority of the American people are educated in religiously neutral schools, and one might contend that this lack of integration between religion and learning would lead to a weakening of basic religious beliefs. Although it appears to be something of a paradox, the hypothesis has been advanced that the public school system, precisely because it is religiously neutral, has led to the preservation of basic religious beliefs because separation of religion and education prevents the open confrontation of religion and science, at least up through high school. In other words, students are not forced to reconcile their acquired beliefs with the findings of modern science, but tend to preserve religious beliefs and secular learning in separate compartments of their minds.[4]

The data presented in Table 8 appear to substantiate this hypothesis in some respects. College graduates gave consistently less conservative responses on all items, and the major breaking point on most items appeared between high school graduates and people with some college training. It is interest-

TABLE 8. *Religious Beliefs and Educational Attainment*

BELIEFS		EDUCATION			
	8th grade	*1–3 years high school*	*High school graduate*	*1–3 years College*	*College Graduate*
Existence of God:					
Absolutely certain	87	87	87	85	78
(Fairly sure)	9	10	10	8	13
Trinity	90	90	91	86	76
God—Loving Father	79	84	80	75	63
Divinity of Christ	82	81	82	79	65
Bible revealed	86	85	87	79	68
Immortality	76	75	81	78	72
Heaven	73	70	77	69	60
Hell	62	58	58	50	41
Divorce is wrong	31	25	26	21	14
Birth control is wrong	25	23	23	17	14

ing to note that roughly one third of the college graduates did not believe in the divinity of Christ, in God as a loving Father, and in the Bible as the revealed word of God. They were also considerably more sceptical about the existence of Heaven and Hell, while their attitudes toward divorce and birth control differed markedly from others. Of course, one may not conclude on the basis of our data that a college education is inimical to religious belief. As we indicated, the various faiths were not equally represented in this category, and one would also have to make allowances for the type of college or university in which the student was trained. It would seem reasonable to maintain that colleges conducted by the various churches would lend considerable support to the religious beliefs of their students, provided the churches had come to grips with the modern world and offered students an integrated interpretation of life. Making a purely *a priori* judgment, one would surmise that fundamentalist church members would be least likely to keep their beliefs intact during college, though a great deal would depend upon the course of studies pursued and the climate of opinion around the school. It appears that some students are capable of leading quite segmented intellectual lives, feeling no need to relate what they learn in one discipline to what they believe in another.

It has long been part of the folklore of religious sociology that people living on the land or in small towns are more religiously conservative than urban dwellers. American Protestantism, in particular, has never fared well in the large industrial centers; a fact clearly recognized by modern Protestant leaders, who regard the current extensive urbanization or suburbanization of the population as a major challenge.[5] The majority of American Roman Catholics and Jews have been urban residents from the beginning and because of their minority status have probably survived better under urban conditions than if they had been dispersed throughout the rural hinterlands.

In discussing contemporary urban and rural differences in beliefs, as well as in speculating about the prospects of religious survival in modern cities, we must be well aware that with the exception of the rural areas in the South and Southwest, current means of transportation and communications have so modified living conditions that past precedents have little predictive value. Few isolated rural regions remain, while modern suburbs are quite different from cities of the past. Furthermore, inasmuch as the movement from the land to the large metropolitan centers has been relatively rapid in this country, many city dwellers obviously retain the religious beliefs acquired in their small town or rural background during youth. It consequently becomes difficult to ascertain whether the religious beliefs expressed by urban residents reflects the influence of the city or their rural past. There is some evidence to suggest that in some cases, at least, the assumed "loss of faith" in the cities was a convenient myth—one cannot lose what one never possessed.[6]

The findings presented in Table 9 suggest that there is some relationship between residence and religious conservatism. The affirmative responses of people living in rural areas were consistently higher than all others on every item of belief except the morality of divorce and contraceptive practices, while the similar responses of large city dwellers were consistently lower except in these last two categories. Since Roman Catholics constitute 37 per cent of the population in cities of one million or over, and we have seen that they are far more conservative in their views on divorce and birth control than others, the relatively high percentage of affirmative responses to these

TABLE 9. Religious Beliefs and Size of Community

BELIEFS	Over Million	100,000 to 1 million	CITY SIZE 25,000 to 100,000	10,000 to 25,000	under 10,000	Rural
Existence of God:						
Absolutely certain	81	84	86	81	89	92
(Fairly sure)	14	11	10	14	9	6
Trinity	78	84	91	90	91	93
God—Loving Father	69	73	79	82	81	85
Divinity of Christ	72	74	82	78	82	87
Bible revealed	76	80	82	86	86	90
Immortality	70	75	76	72	81	82
Heaven	61	68	71	68	77	79
Hell	49	52	62	50	58	72
Divorce is wrong	32	22	29	29	22	32
Birth control is wrong	29	23	27	27	16	23

items in the first column of Table 9, in contrast to all other items, undoubtedly reflects Catholic opinion. How account for the religious conservatism of the rural group? One factor, of course, is education, since it includes few college graduates. Further, the rural group is chiefly Protestant and of the more conservative persuasion, that is, Baptists, Methodists, and Lutherans. One might speculate on the relationship between ruralism and conservatism. Are these Protestant bodies conservative because rural, or rural because conservative? A generation ago, most observers would have chosen the former explanation, since they felt that fundamentalism, which is really what we are discussing here, was closely related to lack of education and lower socio-economic status. Subsequent events have shown that fundamentalism or neo-fundamentalism is thriving very well under middle class conditions; indeed, the most conservative Protestant bodies continue to register the largest gains in membership, though whether this is owing to the widespread rejection of the social gospel approach of the liberals, the failure of neo-orthodox leaders to develop more than a system of ethics based on Christian naturalism and consequently to miss their appeal to the mass of believers, or the perennial search of Christians for religious absolutes anchored in Christ and the Bible, remains open to question.

This concludes our presentation of what American adults believe. We have shown that the majority hold religion in high esteem, believe in God, the Trinity, the divinity of Christ, and the Bible as the revealed word of God. Somewhat fewer believe in the immortality of the soul and the existence of Heaven, and considerably fewer in the existence of Hell, while only a small proportion believe that eternal damnation presents a real possibility. With the exception of Roman Catholics, the majority felt that remarriage after divorce and the use of contraceptive methods of birth control were not wrong. Even among Roman Catholics, only about half agreed with the explicit, formal teaching of their church on these moral issues. The average adult does not appear overly concerned with his ultimate destiny. Two out of five reported that they never think about what may happen to them after death, and nearly half admitted that their most serious present concern was trying to live comfortably. Their attitudes regarding the most important function of the church reflected similar secular value-orientations, for roughly half stressed the promotion of human relations rather than conversion to spiritual belief.

At the beginning of this chapter we noted the hypothesis that religion in America had become so secularized that the major faiths represented no more than three types of "culture religions." A summary appraisal of our findings might well lead one to conclude that they lend considerable support to this hypothesis. A substantial number of participants in each of the major faiths apparently esteem religion as a valuable element of the culture, as a useful instrument for the promotion of social solidarity, peace of mind, and the preservation of significant secular values, but not as the source of a unique experience relating them to a personal God and relevant transcendental values. This fact is beyond question, but is it new? What did religion mean to the Founding Fathers, to Lincoln, and to many of the socially prominent supporters of the churches throughout the history of this country? There seems little doubt that the present revival of interest in religion has swelled the ranks of the secular-minded within the various denominations, but today, as in the past, the strength of our religious tradition must be sought in the substantial, solid core of the faithful who still cherish the essential tenets of their faith. The basic issue, therefore, involves the nature and quality of their beliefs. Do our findings throw any light on this issue?

If we might hazard a generalization, it seems that the faithful have firmly retained those traditional religious beliefs that are most consonant with an optimistic, activistic view of life. Thus they believe in God, the Trinity, the divinity of Christ, and the Bible, but the concept of Hell is far less popular than that of Heaven, while the awareness of sin, with the prospect of possible eternal alienation from God, obviously haunts relatively few. Fifty years ago, William James had pointed out what he called the victory of "healthy-mindedness" over the "morbidness" of the old hell-fire theology within the Protestant churches. Our survey suggests that he was discussing no passing phase but a permanent shift in emphasis affecting all the major faiths in America.

One does not have to be a theologian to sense the obvious contradictions implicit in this shift. Religious thought in the past operated within a framework of beliefs that assumed the existence of Heaven and Hell, personal responsibility, final judgment after death, human frailty and the consequent need for self-restraint and penance. The sobering realization that this earthly pilgrimage was a time for working out one's salvation by fidelity in God's service was never far from the faithfuls' thoughts, however conveniently they may have rationalized the practical implications of this belief for their daily lives. With the shift toward "healthy-mindedness," obvious inconsistencies developed within our religious tradition. Ancient symbols of divine redemption are still retained, traditional theological formulae covering sin and the supernatural continue to be repeated in prayers and rituals, but they no longer appear inherently relevant to the formulation of personal value-orientations or practical norms of conduct. Some observers believe that this situation reflects merely the immature optimism characteristic of youth; others might be inclined to maintain on equally solid grounds that it betrays the sterile apathy typical of senescence.

Both judgments seem quite premature. If our study points up any one single truth, it is that the American religious tradition has become a highly complex phenomenon, embracing a wide variety of unintegrated, often contradictory or inconsistent beliefs, attitudes, and practices. As we pore over our findings, the impression grows that the churches have attempted to adjust to their rapidly changing American environment on an *ad hoc*, segmented, more or less pragmatic basis; that is, they have not used their essential beliefs either as the frame of reference or the point of departure for interpreting new situations and formulating realistic designs for living. As a result of their failure to grasp and integrate the practical implications of what they profess to believe, many of the faithful appear only vaguely aware of the many inconsistencies in their attitudes and activities.

Assuming that the religious beliefs of the practicing faithful reflect the *de facto* teaching, that is, the "taught tradition," to borrow a legal phrase from Pound, of the churches, we must conclude that what some observers have identified as secularism, or syncretistic fusion of religious and secular ideologies, is rather segmentation, or lack of integration, owing to the failure of religious leaders to remain creative under conditions of rapid and extensive change in a pluralist society. As we have pointed out, a religious system must remain creative if it is to endure, that is, it must continue to supply a relatively consistent, orderly, integrated, personally meaningful interpretation of the total, evolving human situation experienced by its adherents, thus enabling them to "make sense" of their world, and by offering them an explanation of the significance and purpose of life, providing them with an intelligible frame of reference within which their perennial pursuit of happiness can be defined. When a religious system fails to remain creative in this sense, the faithful find increasingly extensive sectors of their activities outside the pale of religion, and they consequently turn to other sources in search of relevant interpretations. The resulting segmentation of value-orientations among the faithful presents the appearance of the secularization of religion itself, though it really reflects the lack of creative vitality among the religious elite.

We have mentioned the failure of religious leaders or religious elite, because the maintenance and continued elaboration of the practical moral implications of a religious system involve clear understanding of essential dogmas, an abiding awareness of the assumed relationship between religious doctrine and general moral principles, and an ability not only to apply general moral principles to specific categories of action but also to recognize what principles are pertinent to the changing situation. Obviously, this creative task must be the concern of only a minority in any given religious system, for with the exception of brief, often critical interludes, the majority do not reflect on the moral standards and norms they observe or the logical coherence of their various programs of action with more general moral principles. Preoccupation with the immediate tasks at hand, together with the unquestioning acceptance of the prevailing normative structure of their society, tends to preponderate in their conduct.

The elite, on the other hand, are persons who display unusual sensitivity and reflectiveness concerning religious dogmas and their moral implications. Appearing not only as innovators, they also function as conservatives, preserving continuity with doctrinal positions of the past. Contrary to the majority who take their values and norms for granted, the elite scrutinize, refine, and seek to improve them in the light of new experience. In this sense, they are bearers of what students of comparative culture have variously named the great tradition as opposed to the little tradition, of high culture versus low, of classic versus folk culture, of hierarchic versus lay culture, of the learned versus the popular tradition. As Redfield puts it: "In a civilization there is a great tradition of the reflective few, and there is a little tradition of the largely unreflective many." Apparently in religious systems as in cultures, these two traditions are interdependent, but continuity and integrated development in both depend primarily on the efforts of a creative, reflective minority.

The American religious tradition appears to have been deficient in producing such a reflective minority. Obviously, religious leaders who boast that they preach a "practical theology," one that scoffs at "dogmatic subleties and philosophical abstractions" but "gets things done," are not to be numbered among the members of the needed creative elite. It is becoming increasingly evident that "healthy-mindedness" leaders with their "undogmatic heartiness" tend to reduce organized religion to fulfilling the socially useful function of promoting the spirit of brotherhood and interpreting man's persistent efforts at the more efficient exploitation of nature as the essence of the Christian ideal. As our findings indicate, their followers have not found it too difficult to reconcile interest in religion with the optimistic pragmatism characteristic of American culture.

Yet the tension inherent in traditional religion's definition of the human situation is still recognized by a substantial proportion of the faithful, as we may conclude from the recent success of revivalism, the unexpected vitality of neo-fundamentalism, and the present findings. The beliefs the faithful still profess can constitute an adequate frame of reference within which the churches may serve both as instruments of salvation and strong unifying forces, integrating theory and practice in men's lives. The American people have not forgotten the God of their forefathers, but they have worked out a fairly comfortable relationship with Him, because the churches have tended either to emphasize only the more optimistic aspects of their traditional beliefs, or failed to spell out in currently understandable terms their practical implications.

Notes

1. See Will Herberg, "There is a Religious Revival!", *Review of Religious Research* 1 (Fall 1959), 45–50; and Marty, *op. cit.*

2. For an excellent review of Protestant thought on this subject, see Richard M. Fagley, *The Population Explosion and Christian Responsibility* (New York: Oxford University Press, Inc., 1961).

3. See Richard C. Wolf, "Religious Trends in the United States," *Christianity Today* (April 27, 1959).

4. See Timothy Smith, *op. cit.*, p. 18.

5. See Marty, *op. cit.*, pp. 90–105.

6. For a revealing study of a similar situation in France, see Paul Schmitt-Eglin, *Le Mecanisme de la Dechristianisation* (Paris: Editions Alsatia, 1952).

THE majority of adult Americans evidently hold religion in high esteem and profess firm belief in most of the essential tenets promoted by the traditional faiths. We may logically assume that if these beliefs are vital, that is, are regarded as something more than respectable cultural residues, they will be associated with various forms of religious activity, such as worship, prayer, instruction, and study. An organized religious system can survive only if the faithful understand the basic elements of its creed, participate in its cult, and maintain reasonable observance of its prescribed code of conduct. Particularly in a pluralist society where there is no established church and the major social institutions lend support to no specific value systems, each denomination must provide for its own survival by promoting adequate means for religious instruction and shared activity among its followers. Organized religious groups may differ considerably in the means they propose and the sanctions they impose upon group members for nonfulfillment, but certain minimal requisites, like the recruitment and indoctrination of new members, as well as the maintenance of some sense of solidarity, must be met if there is to be any assurance of vital continuity.[1]

This chapter is concerned with the religious activities in which the American people habitually engage. We proceed on the assumption that the study of such activities will tell us a good deal about the nature and quality of the beliefs discussed in the last chapter, for religious beliefs that are not associated with observable activities may be regarded as latent or inoperative, and probably as no more than verbalizations. Of course not all activities sponsored by the churches are directly related to religious beliefs—bingo and parish socials may promote solidarity and lend financial support to the religious enterprise, but in spite of the enthusiasm they tend to generate or the aura of active participation they create around a given parish, they offer little insight into the beliefs of the participants. On the other hand, the activities we are about to discuss, such as group worship, prayer, religious training, and so on, represent the formal exigencies of specific religious beliefs as traditionally developed by the major faiths. If such professed beliefs are unaccompanied by appropriate activities, we may at least suspect the marked withdrawal of affect and attention predictive of possible eventual rejection.

One of the major difficulties related to forming an adequate estimate of the quality of religious commitment in a given population stems from the very nature and function of religious beliefs. People may esteem religion highly because they believe it is essential for the maintenance of social order and control; thus, taking men as they appear in the mass, it is assumed that transcendental sanctions fulfill an indispensable function in bolstering up a society's normative structure and generating sufficient consensus to render coercion of deviants feasible. On the other hand, men may value religion because it responds to their personal need to find order and meaning in their lives, since they feel that the pursuit of happiness can be defined only in terms of some definition of man and his position in the universe. Both viewpoints imply certain assumptions about the nature of man and society. Are the majority of men law-abiding and cooperative, or religious and self-seeking? Do they seek integration and significance in their lives, or do they readily settle for the satisfaction of immediate needs? Both viewpoints will be associated with different approaches to religious activities, since the first will tend to promote religion as a social good, while the second will stress personal participation in religious activities.

Furthermore, we may assume that there exists some relationship between active religious participation and what people think of the current state of morals in their society. It would seem reasonable to conclude that the disparity between religious ideals and general conduct in a secular society would be most keenly felt by people actively engaged in the pursuit of religious perfection. Granting that irrespective of religious beliefs, some people in every age seem disposed to believe that the world is "going to the dogs," there can be little doubt that people's outlook on the moral condition of their times is colored by their active religious commitments, for every religious system teaches a more or less clearly defined moral code and we would expect that people who are trying to live according to this code would be most inclined to notice deviations from it and pass judgment accordingly. Failure to do so would suggest either that they are not actively committed or that they regard their code as a personal value judgment not necessarily applicable to others.

It must be admitted, of course, that the climate of opinion

prevalent in the dominant culture can gradually modify attitudes and opinions based on religious beliefs. We have called attention to the contention that the spirit of optimism characteristic of our rapidly expanding nation gradually transformed the gloomy outlook of the Puritan into a healthymindedness having little in common with the pessimistic view of human nature inherent in early Calvinist theology. When such inconsistencies between theological premises and practical outlooks develop, we have an indication that religious beliefs no longer serve as the basis for the normative structure in terms of which men guide their actions or judge society. Considering the apparent increase of crime, juvenile delinquency, family disorganization, payola, and so on, in our society, it would seem that adults who take an optimistic view of the current state of morals are basing their judgments not on the traditional standards of the major faiths but on the secular premises of an affluent society. This point may be significant because people who feel all is going well with society may feel less inclined to engage in religious practices.

Hence before discussing our findings on religious activities, it may prove helpful to consider what people think of the present situation. During the interviews people were asked: "Do you think people in general today lead as good lives—as honest and as moral—as they used to?" Forty-seven per cent of the adult population thought that they did; 46 per cent answered in the negative, and 7 per cent were not sure. Considerable differences of outlook appeared among the major religious groups. Members of the Protestant bodies were least optimistic, since only 44 per cent felt that people were as honest and moral as in the past, and 49 per cent disagreed; while among Roman Catholics, 54 per cent agreed and 37 per cent disagreed; and among the Jewish group 58 per cent agreed, as opposed to only 34 per cent who felt people were less honest and moral today.

We find these differences highly interesting. Nearly half the Protestant membership felt that morals had deteriorated, and a glance at the findings for the various Protestant denominations indicated that the groups usually thought to be most fundamentalist were the least optimistic. For example, 60 per cent of the Baptists and 49 per cent of the Methodists, as opposed to 40 per cent of the Lutherans, 39 per cent of the Presbyterians, 38 per cent of the Episcopalians, and 33 per cent of the Congregationalists felt that people were less honest and moral today. On the other hand, there was some indication that people's outlook in this regard was colored by their socio-economic status. Using education, occupation, and income as an index, the upper socio-economic classes appear to be more optimistic than the others. For example, only 41 per cent of the college graduates as opposed to 51 per cent of people with a grade school education or less; 39 per cent of the professional class and 36 per cent of the proprietor or manager class as opposed to 51 per cent of the service workers and 48 per cent of the manual workers; and 37 per cent of the upper income class as opposed to 54 per cent of the lower, felt that morals had deteriorated.

Evidently, both fundamentalist religious background and socio-economic position affect Protestant views on the current moral situation. The nature of our data does not permit further causal specification, but the indicated relationships are suggestive. The relative optimism of the Roman Catholic and Jewish groups may be consonant with their traditional theological viewpoints, which assume a rather uniform degree of human failure in each generation. At any rate, considering the population as a whole, our findings indicate that the American people are about equally divided in their views on the present state of morals. Although both religious and social reformers may still attract an audience, their message will have little appeal to at least half the American public.[2]

Perhaps we can gain some further insight into the prevailing climate of opinion concerning morals if we examine our findings on the judgments expressed in regard to modern youth. The rising tide of juvenile delinquency has brought the problem of youth into such prominence that few adult Americans can fail to have given it some thought. Many studies dealing with delinquency place primary emphasis on the environmental and situational factors contributing to delinquency, while the possible weakening of moral controls is seldom investigated. In line with this general approach, when remedies for the situation are proposed, the need to promote the development of internalized moral controls associated with religious beliefs receives little attention. Juvenile delinquency is not viewed primarily as a moral problem. Rather, it is assumed to develop out of a specific social situation and is to be remedied by manipulating various factors in that situation. If young people get into trouble, it is not that they lack proper attitudes and adequate habits of self-control. Their environment is not conducive to good behavior—society is the patient.

How widespread are these more or less sophisticated views of juvenile delinquency? To get at the answer, we asked: "Do you think that young people today have as strong a sense of right and wrong as they did, say, fifty years ago?" Our findings suggest that the American people are inclined to take a very favorable attitude toward modern youth. Fifty-seven per cent felt that they had as strong a sense of right and wrong as formerly, 34 per cent disagreed, and 9 per cent offered no opinion. Among the major religious groups, Protestants and Roman Catholics held almost similar views (57, 35, 8 per cent, and 56, 34, and 10 per cent respectively). Members of the Jewish group, noted, of course, for their low rate of juvenile delinquency, expressed an even more favorable attitude (73, 20, and 7 per cent). On the other hand, the non-preference group were more severe in their judgment. Fifty-one per cent felt that young people were as moral as formerly, 37 per cent disagreed, and 12 per cent expressed no opinion.

The attitudes of the various Protestant denominations and socioeconomic classes followed a pattern somewhat similar to their views on the general state of morals. Favorable responses were expressed as follows: Baptists, 51 per cent; Lutheran, 55 per cent; Episcopal, 57 per cent; Methodist and Presbyterian, 62 per cent; and Congregational, 68 per cent. Only 50 per cent of the people having a grade school education or less expressed favorable attitudes, whereas 60 per cent of the high school graduates, 67 per cent of the people with 1–3 years of college, and 56 per cent of the college graduates were favorable. People in the upper income bracket tended to judge youth rather favorably (64 per cent), while members of the lower income group were more severe (50 per cent favorable).

Although we have been told frequently that juvenile delinquency is one of our major national problems, it is interesting to note that only one third of the American people feel that young people do not have as strong a sense of right and wrong today as formerly, and well over one half believe they are just as morally sensitive as in the past. Granting that the average adult is in no position to form a valid judgment on the subject, nevertheless, when considered against the background of the known public concern over juvenile delinquency, the optimistic attitudes expressed by so many suggest that they regard delinquency as basically a social problem. In other words, they do not see it within the wider context of morals, or within the framework of a stable value system. This finding is significant for our present purposes because it indicates a secular orientation or "mind set" that does not habitually relate behavior to moral values and religious ideals. Norms of conduct, values, and religious ideals seem to be confined in separate compartments.

With these observations in mind, let us consider some of the major religious activities in which people tend to participate. One of the first questions that comes to mind in this regard is what religious training did our respondents receive in their youth. Of course the immediate family circle or the home has been and remains the most important single influence shaping the religious beliefs, practices, and attitudes of youth in Western society. This conclusion is based on the very nature of the parent-child relationship in our family system, and it may be noted that parental influence can produce negative or indifferent, as well as positive religious attitudes. In general, the immediate family circle gives the child a basic religious orientation or outlook that extra-familial agencies such as church, school, and peer group may modify and complete but can seldom effectively obliterate.

Church historians tell us that organized religious bodies in the past placed strong emphasis on the religious instruction and training of youth. Because children were thought to be rebellious by nature owing to original sin, parents were frequently reminded of their obligations to be firm in discipline and to set a good example through family prayer, Bible reading, and attendance at religious services. One of the chief functions of formal education was to promote religion, either through general indoctrination or the preparation of future ministers.

Many of our famous institutions of higher learning were founded for this latter purpose, and the amazing number of church-supported small colleges that sprang up throughout the country after the Civil War offer ample proof of widespread religion-centered thinking and zeal.[3]

For the most part, adult instruction in the faith was promoted by lengthy sermons, revivals or missions, and church-sponsored discussion groups or study clubs. Private prayer and pious reading were universally encouraged, of course, though it was generally held that some form of corporate worship or group service constituted an essential element of active religious participation. Opinions may differ as to how well these ideals were put into practice. We have far from adequate information on the extent or degree of religious observance in the past, yet one fact seems clear: the American people have been comparatively generous in their support of religious schools, missions, church buildings, and the ministry.[4] No established church exists, but as the famous English historian and diplomat, Lord Bryce, remarked a half century ago, far from suffering from want of state support, religion in the United States appears more firmly grounded without it.

Organized religious groups today generally try to supplement the home training of youth by special religion classes on Sunday, by religious or parochial schools, or by other means such as "released time" on school days, summer schools, and periods of intensive training before the admission to certain rites such as First Holy Communion and Confirmation.[5] Our survey reveals that all but 6 per cent of the adult American people had received some religious training in youth. Seventy-two per cent had attended Sunday school; 21 per cent, religious or parochial school; 4 per cent, some other type of training; and 37 per cent had received instruction at home.

These percentages add up to more than one hundred because some respondents named more than one source.

As we would expect, there were marked differences in the type of training received by members of the various religious groups. The Roman Catholic (62 per cent) and Jewish (36 per cent) groups included the highest proportions of those who had received their training in religious or parochial schools, while among the Protestant bodies (total, 7 per cent) the Lutheran group (24 per cent) were most likely to have received this form of training. Sunday school was the common source of religious training among Protestant bodies. Eighty-six per cent of their members had received such training, as compared to 35 per cent of the Roman Catholic, and 34 per cent of the Jewish groups.

What do people think of the religious training they received? In line with their general optimism, 78 per cent thought that it was quite satisfactory. Of the 22 per cent who were not satisfied, the majority stated that they should have received more or better training. They felt they should have attended more often, been given better training in the Bible, received their training at a religious or parochial school, and so on. Only about 5 per cent of the dissatisfied maintained that they should have received less religious training and another 5 per cent felt that their training should have been more tolerant.

It seems logical to conclude that we can gain some understanding of what people think about their own religious training by finding out what type of training they desire for their children. In a sense, this is similar to the question: If you had your life to live over again, what religious training would you prefer? Intelligent parents obviously guide their children in terms of their own experience. If they value the training they received in youth, they will want their children to enjoy similar privileges. Only 2 per cent of the adult population reported that they would not want a child of theirs to receive religious instruction. The remaining 98 per cent named the following choices: 75 per cent, Sunday school; 25 per cent, religious or parochial school; 39 per cent, instruction in the home; and 5 per cent, some other religious training. Evidently the average American holds the traditional forms of religious instruction for youth in high esteem.

There were the expected differences in choice of training among the various religious groups. Seventy-four per cent of the Roman Catholic and 40 per cent of the Jewish groups desired religious or parochial school training for their children. Among the Protestant bodies (total 9 per cent) the Lutheran (21 per cent) and Episcopal (11 per cent) groups were prominent in choosing this form of religious training. It is interesting to note that among respondents who stated that they had some other or no religious preference, 69 per cent desired Sunday school, and 11 per cent, religious or parochial school training for their children. Only 17 per cent of this group felt that their children needed no religious training. To the extent that the attitudes recorded here are put into action, the present generation of young Americans will receive about the same type of religious training as their parents.

However, a curious inconsistency in the thinking of some of our respondents appeared at this point, since they stated that they wanted their children to be free of formal religion until they were old enough to make up their own minds. As this view is sometimes expressed, religion should not be imposed upon children; they should be left free to make their own choice. Such an attitude obviously relegates religion to a very minor role in the development of personality, and what is more significant, it is patently unrealistic. It implies, in the first place, that children are not profoundly affected by the religious beliefs of their parents; and second, that children be provided with the opportunity to study the credentials of the various faiths and denominations in order to make up their minds with some degree of rationality. Since the proponents of this approach make no provisions for such comparative studies of religion, we may conclude that they place formal religion in the same category as various other voluntary associations in which people may choose to participate.

How widespread is this view? During the interviews people were asked: "Do you think children should be raised as church members or do you think they should be free of formal religion until they are old enough to make up their own minds?" Almost one out of four (24 per cent) thought they should be free to make up their own minds; 4 per cent were undecided; and 72 per cent stated that they should be raised as church members. This is a curious finding, for it will be recalled that when people were asked whether they wanted their children to receive any religious instruction, only 1 per cent replied that they did not, and it was clear that they were thinking of religious instruction along denominational lines, inasmuch as 75 per cent wanted them to attend Sunday School and 25 per cent desired religious or parochial school training.

What do these inconsistent responses indicate? Either the one fourth who felt that children should be free to make up their own minds were merely expressing what they thought was the most sophisticated answer or they were serious. In the latter case, a considerable proportion of people who stated that they wanted their children to receive religious instruction did not really mean it. It is impossible to conclude that they did not understand the implications of their answer, since they clearly specified the type of training they desired. Perhaps there was some tendency to give the "expected answer" in both instances, for, on the one hand, it is thought to be a mark of broad-mindedness and sophistication to maintain that children should make up their own minds about religious membership; on the other hand, since religion is held in such high repute, few would wish to admit that they did not desire a specific type of religious training for their children.

There were some differences of opinion among the major religious divisions in this regard. Whereas only 7 per cent of the Roman Catholic group felt children should be free to make up their own minds, 28 per cent of the Protestant, 23 per cent of the Jewish, and 46 per cent of the others felt that they should. There were marked differences among the various Protestant bodies. Only 14 per cent of the Episcopal and 16 per cent of the Lutheran group felt that children should be free to make up their own minds in this respect, whereas 38 per cent of the Baptist bodies, 26 per cent of the "other" denominations, 25 per cent of the Methodist, 24 per cent of the Presbyterian, and 22 per cent of the Congregational groups held that they should.

As we have suggested, people who think that their children should not be raised as church members but should be free of formal religion until they are old enough to make up their own minds, lack both a sense of realism and firm religious convictions. To the extent that their attitudes in this matter form the basis for a practical program of child rearing, we must conclude that almost one fourth of the nation's children will be raised without benefit of definite religious formation and with slight appreciation for the significance of religious experience in their lives.

Although we touched on participation in religious services briefly in Chapter Two when discussing religious preferences, this important activity merits more detailed treatment here. As we learn from Table 1, 73 per cent of the adult population consider themselves to be active church members. In the Western world, active church membership is normally associated with more or less regular attendance at Sunday or Sabbath religious services by the faithful who are able. The major faiths differ in their insistence on weekly attendance at such services but it is rather universally assumed that a faithful church member will obey the ancient command to "keep holy the Sabbath day" by joining with group members in some form of corporate worship or "service." The fact that the churches must now compete with many forms of entertainment and recreation in attracting members to religious services is in itself indicative of a significant change in the position of religion in society. At the same time, since organized religion in the past has uniformly implied some type of corporate experience represented by church services, the extent to which church members no longer attend such services can be taken as a fair gauge of their departure from traditional religious ideals.

How faithful are the American people in attending Sunday or Sabbath church services? Nearly one-third (32 per cent) said that they never attend such services, and an additional 11 per cent stated that they attend once a month or less. On the other hand, almost one out of three (32 per cent) attend every Sunday; 13 per cent, about three times a month; and the remaining 12 per cent, about twice a month. In other words, only about 57 per cent could be classified as "churchgoing" people, for people who admit that they attend only once a month or less cannot reasonably be numbered among the "churchgoers."

Table 1 presented our findings on church attendance for the major religious groups. Since the members of the Roman Catholic Church have a serious obligation to participate in offering the Sacrifice of the Mass on Sunday unless they are legitimately excused, it is not surprising to find that this group has the best record for church attendance. Roughly three out of five stated they attend every Sunday, and an additional 14 per cent, about two or three times a month. One out of every four Protestants said they attended church services every Sunday, and an additional 29 per cent, about two or three times a month. Somewhat less than one out of every eight of the Jewish group attended services every week, and a further 21 per cent, about two or three times a month. As was to be expected, few of our respondents who had some other or no religious preference, could be characterized as "churchgoers." One out of twenty attended services every Sunday and a further 5 per cent, two or three times a month.

These findings on attendance at religious services might tempt us to conclude that modern churches are finding it increasingly difficult to compete with outside attractions in their services. However, before we could safely draw such a conclusion, we would have to know much more about church attendance in the past. In the present state of knowledge, it is hazardous to conclude that the contemporary churches are worse off in this respect than they were, for example, a century ago. Indeed, it is claimed that church membership is considerably higher.[6] Hence prudence suggests that we refrain from making comparisons with the past and attempt to evaluate the present situation on its own merits.

One fact stands out clearly. Religion, as it has been organized in the Western world, implies shared activity and some type of corporate religious experience traditionally expressed in various forms of church services. Consequently, people who do not participate in such services can scarcely be characterized as "religious" in the traditional meaning of that term. Our findings show that 43 per cent of the adult American population seldom or never participate in Sunday or Sabbath church services. Whatever religion they have is confined to a set of private beliefs and opinions which they have developed to meet their personal needs. It has been stated that because of the multiplication of denominations, sects and cults, the American people have never developed the idea of a universal church. It might well be added, in this connection, that nearly half of them apparently have never discovered a personal need for any form of organized religion.

Why do people break off contact with the church? In the first place, it should be noted that some of them never had been active church members. Of the 27 per cent who stated they were not church members, 41 per cent declared that they were never active members. Among the remaining 59 per cent, roughly one half had not maintained active church membership within the previous 15 years. To what religious groups had they formerly belonged? Approximately 78 per cent had been members of one of the Protestant bodies, 15 per cent had been Roman Catholic, somewhat over 2 per cent had held membership in the Jewish group, and the remainder belonged to various other groups.

Why had they ceased active membership? They offered various reasons. Somewhat over one third said that they had moved and simply did not get around to take up membership in another church. One out of four said they had lost interest and "just quit going." One out of eight stated that they were too busy to attend. A small percentage said that they had quit because of a disagreeable experience with a clergyman, or had lost their faith and felt it was hypocritical to continue going, or had married outside the church, or had married a divorced person, and so on. If these reasons do not represent rationalizations, we must conclude that indifference rather than serious disagreement led the majority to cease active church membership.

Of course attendance at religious services is not the only index of religious vitality. The practice of prayer either in private or together with one's family has always marked the true believer. In the Bible, which played such a fundamental role in the development of the religious thought of the West, we find frequent exhortations to pray. Through public acts or private devotion it has been customary to praise and thank God for His blessings, as well as to ask His protection and assistance in time of need. The act of prayer implies an acknowledgment of God's power and love and, of course, the recognition of one's dependence on Him. Although some forms of public prayer may represent little more than a shallow formality tolerated through custom rather than conviction, the fact that such customs are still observed is not without significance. The least that can be said is that they are a tribute to the traditional beliefs and religious convictions upon which our institutions were founded. Their careful preservation suggests that there are many for whom the practice of prayer has retained some meaning.

Do the American people pray? Our findings reveal that only 8 per cent admit that they never pray. In other words, less than one out of every ten adult Americans feel so indifferent about God that they never acknowledge His existence and their relationship to Him through prayer. Perhaps what is more important as a criterion of religious vitality is how frequently people pray. The question was asked: "About how many times would you say you prayed during the last seven days?" Forty-three per cent stated about once a day; 17 per cent, about twice a day; 21 per cent, three times a day or more; 5 per cent, infrequently; and 6 per cent gave no answer. In short, four out of five adults reported prayer as a daily experience. Differences in this regard among the major religious groups appeared as follows: Roman Catholic, 92 per cent; Protestant, 82 per cent; Jewish, 65 per cent; and the remainder, 38 per cent.

When do people pray? In addition to the organized Sunday or Sabbath services, certain circumstances of the daily cycle have long been recognized as appropriate for prayer. Thus, there are morning prayers, night prayers, grace before and after meals, and occasional prayers in an emergency or during the day. Night prayers are the most common. Sixty-one per cent stated they usually say night prayers; 23 per cent, morning prayers; 33 per cent, grace before meals; 39 per cent, short prayers during the day; 31 per cent, occasional prayers in emergencies; and 5 per cent specified some other form of prayer. These figures throw some light on certain religious practices traditionally related to the family. Only one out of three adults offered grace before meals, less than one out of four said morning prayers and less than two out of three said evening prayers. It is usually assumed that at least the practice of grace at meals and night prayers are taught to all children in families that like to think of themselves as religious. We must conclude that either this is not the custom or else a good percentage of the children drop these practices when they reach adulthood.

The pattern of prayer among the major religious groups revealed expected differences. Night prayers, morning prayers, and grace before meals were reported as follows: Protestants, 60, 16, and 36 per cent, respectively; Roman Catholics, 77, 47, and 33 per cent, respectively; Jews, 33, 17, and 15 per cent, respectively; and the remainder, 25, 5, and 7 per cent, respectively.

Why do people pray? The 92 per cent who said they prayed

gave various reasons. Approximately 39 per cent stated that they pray to ask God for favors, help, guidance, and strength. Twenty-three per cent said that they experienced a feeling of comfort or confidence while praying. Faith and belief in God led 16 per cent to pray. Another 15 per cent prayed to give thanks, about 10 per cent prayed as a matter of habit or training, somewhat over 3 per cent prayed to ask for forgiveness, and 13 per cent offered other reasons. These percentages total to more than 100 because some gave more than one reason for praying.

Even on the basis of our findings, it is difficult to assess the significance of prayer in the religious life of the American people. The fact that only 8 per cent of the adult population stated they never pray to God indicates that the practice of prayer is still acceptable. In other words, whether he prays very frequently or not, the average American apparently recognizes the personal relationship between man and God that the practice of prayer implies. On the other hand, the part that prayer plays in the daily life of the average person is not very great. Only 38 per cent stated that they prayed oftener than once a day. At the same time, since certain types of prayer such as grace before meals and evening prayers are sanctioned by longstanding custom, it is impossible to judge whether they represent residues of family tradition or religiously meaningful practices in the individual's daily life.

Another practice closely associated with prayer, particularly among Protestants, was Bible reading. The sombre portrait of the psalm-singing, Bible-reading Puritan colonist remains deeply etched in the imagination of every American school child. Recent historians may raise serious doubts concerning the applicability of this picture to any but the northern colonists, but the stereotype has become too firmly embedded in the religious folklore of the country to be easily obliterated. At any rate, it can safely be assumed that the reading of the Bible represented an essential religious ideal for the majority of practicing Protestants in the past. It is difficult to see how this could have been otherwise. Religion in the Western world was founded on revelation. According to the teaching of the major Protestant bodies, the Bible not only constitutes the sole source of revelation, but it is written so clearly that every Christian is capable of understanding (interpreting) it. Hence, since it is maintained that God speaks directly to the faithful through His written word, it behooves Christians to read and meditate frequently upon His message in the Bible. Logically, therefore, Bible reading became a major religious practice among the Protestant groups, so that none of the various denominations and sects that eventually developed have ever questioned it though their founders obviously differed concerning the contents of the message they discovered in the process.

The practice of Bible reading has never been one of the major religious preoccupations of the average Roman Catholic. Like the Protestant bodies, they hold the Bible in high esteem as a basic source of revelation, but they maintain that Christ founded an authoritative teaching church to interpret and promulgate His redemptive message throughout the world. The religious life of the Roman Catholic is closely associated with the Sacrifice of the Mass and the sacramental system through which it is held that the merits of Christ's passion are channeled down to the individual believer. To be sure, Roman Catholic liturgy is largely composed of passages from the Bible, the faithful read portions of the Gospels and Epistles at Mass, "Bible history" is one of the basic courses in the training of Catholic youth, and the faithful are encouraged to read and study the Bible, yet by the very logic of their doctrinal position, Bible reading among Roman Catholics has never assumed the essential role it must necessarily play among the religious practices of Protestants.

The Books of the Old Testament were always held in high esteem among the faithful of the Jewish group. Considerable portions are frequently committed to memory, and most established Jewish communities include scholars learned in the Scriptures. Jewish prayers and religious services draw heavily upon the Sacred Books although it appears that Bible reading in the Protestant form has not received major emphasis from the average member of the group in recent times.

As we have shown in Chapter Three, 83 per cent of the American people professed belief in the Bible as the revealed word of God. In other words, the Bible is still held in high esteem by over four out of every five adult Americans. Do people ever read the Bible? This question is particularly significant in judging the vitality and continuity of the Protestant tradition, for Bible reading is rightly assumed to have played such an important role among the religious practices of these bodies in the past. If a large proportion of Protestants no longer read the Bible frequently, we may safely conclude that a major change in their traditional religious practices has occurred, while the stereotype of the Bible reading Protestant would cease to check with reality.

Only 12 per cent of the American people stated that they never read the Bible. This relatively low percentage, however, should not lead us to conclude that the average American can be classified as a Bible reader. The question was asked: "About how many times would you say you read the Bible during the last 12 weeks?" Four per cent did not reply, 28 per cent said practically never, and another 22 per cent answered that they read it only "every few weeks." The remaining 34 per cent reported that they read it once a week or oftener. This latter group constitute what is left of the "Bible readers" in the country, inasmuch as it does not seem meaningful to classify as Bible readers people who say they read it practically never or only every few weeks. As we would be led to expect from their tradition, Protestants include the largest proportion of Bible readers (40 per cent), while only 22 per cent of the Roman Catholic, 14 per cent of the Jewish and 15 per cent of the non-preference groups would qualify for this title.

Are there any special reasons why people no longer read the Bible? Unfortunately, this question was posed only to the 12 per cent who stated that they never read the Bible. Of this group, one-third offered no explanation, one-fourth reported that they were too busy and did not have time enough to do so, one out of six stated that they did not own a Bible or could not understand it, and the remainder gave various answers such as: can't read, the Catholic Church discourages it, read prayer book or other book instead, and so on. The pertinent question remains unanswered. If 83 per cent of the American people believe that the Bible is the word of God, and if, particularly among members of the Protestant bodies, the reading of the Bible formerly constituted an essential religious practice, why do we find such a relatively low percentage of Bible readers in America today? Our findings suggest a change of emphasis. It appears that the Protestant denominations, with the possible exception of the fundamentalist bodies, are moving toward an institutionalized type of formal religion in which individual religious initiative, particularly in the home, is being replaced by emphasis on sharing or participation in group services.

The religious activities we have been discussing thus far constitute the traditional religious practices uniformly associated with participation in the major faiths. However, modern means of communication now make it possible for the faithful to read, hear, and view a great variety of material related to religion, and though such activity may only loosely be termed *religious practice*, it merits study as an indication of religious interest and concern. For example, the modern press is one of the most powerful and efficient instruments for the mass dissemination of ideas now in existence. Through magazines, journals, and newspapers of various types, information, indoctrination and propaganda covering all areas of human interest and endeavor are made constantly available to the reading public. Organized religious bodies have not been slow in recognizing the possibilities of the press. A whole series of highly varied religious publications, appealing to every type of reader, has appeared in recent years. Although these publications differ greatly in content, purpose and quality, they represent a sizeable portion of the total output of the press in America. In other words, readers interested in religious subjects are offered a fairly wide choice of current printed matter. If they choose to read, the material is available. Of course, religious magazines and newspapers find it difficult to compete with secular publications, inasmuch as they tend to be slanted toward one specific religious group and the number of their potential subscribers is consequently limited, with the result that they can rely much less on paid advertisements than can their secular competitors. Furthermore, the religious press will find it more difficult to appear sensational—accounts of murder and adultery, to say nothing of "cheesecake," whether presented under the sophisticated subterfuge of art and advertising or the thinly disguised pretext of realistic reporting, apparently have strong reader appeal.

Do adult Americans read religious publications regularly?

Approximately 55 per cent of the people who identified them-selves with one of the three major religious groups replied that they did not. The percentage for each group was as follows: Protestant, 58 per cent; Roman Catholic, 44 per cent; and Jewish, 81 per cent.

To be sure, there are several factors that must be con-sidered in evaluating the religious reading habits of the Ameri-can public. The well-nigh universal use of radio and television obviously limits the amount of time to be spent in reading. Foreign observers insist that Americans tend to read less than their European cousins. From studies of American communities we learn that the members of the lower socio-economic classes spend little money for the purchase of reading material, while members of the middle class tend to purchase certain prestige publications for display rather than use. On the other hand, the fact that well over half of the adult American public ad-mitted that they were not regular readers of any religious pub-lication is significant. At best, it suggests a lack of serious, mature interest in religious issues. Religious commentators, particularly among the Protestant bodies, have frequently de-scribed what they call the "youthfulness" or "immaturity" of religion in America. Their observations receive considerable support in our findings.

What religious publications do Americans read? The reli-gious reading pattern of the Protestant bodies was as follows: 58 per cent did not read any religious publication regularly; 3 per cent, *The Christian Advocate*; 3 per cent, *The Upper Room*; 3 per cent, *The Christian Herald*; 2 per cent, *Presby-terian Life*; 2 per cent, *Home Life*; 1 per cent, *Methodist Women*; and 34 per cent read various others. The percentages add up to more than 100 because some read more than one magazine.

Among the Roman Catholic group, the reading pattern was as follows: 44 per cent read no religious publication regularly; 9 per cent, *The Catholic Digest*; 8 per cent, *St. Anthony's Messenger*; 8 per cent, *The Sunday Visitor*; 6 per cent, *Extension Magazine*; 3 per cent, *The Sign*; 2 per cent, the *Maryknoll Mission Magazine*; 1 per cent, *The Catholic Courier*; 1 per cent, *The Rosary*; and 43 per cent read various other publications. Again the percentages total more than 100 because some people read more than one magazine.

Members of the Jewish group presented the following reading pattern: 81 per cent read no religious publication regularly; 4 per cent, *The Jewish National Monthly* (a B'nai B'rith publication); 2 per cent, *Forward*; 2 per cent, Hadassah publications; 1 per cent, *Jewish Congress*; 1 per cent Zionist publications; 1 per cent, *The Anti-Defamation League Bulletin*; and 18 per cent read various others. Again the percentages add up to more than 100 because some members read more than one publication.

Although many Americans spend little time reading religious literature, perhaps they follow other channels of information. Radio and television have opened up potent new avenues of mass entertainment and instruction in the modern world. They penetrate the intimacy of the family circle even in the most isolated regions. Though one may question the quality of some of these programs, there can be no doubt that they are received by an eager and ever increasing audience. The use of television, in particular, has spread with startling rapidity. Television apparently appeals to all age groups and social classes alike. Young and old, rich and poor seem similarly addicted to its use. It is too soon to predict what effect its use will have upon American society, but it seems safe to conclude that, like the automobile, it will affect more than the family budget.

The educational and religious possibilities of these new instruments have not been fully investigated or exploited. The potentialities of television in particular remain relatively untapped in this regard. However, educational programs are being initiated and encouraged in many sections, and a few religious programs have achieved national prominence on both radio and television. In other words, an increasing number of religious programs are now available, although at the time that our study was made, the majority of them were on radio. Whether or not people listen to them is a matter of free choice. In a sense, the size of audience they attract may be considered a better criterion of popular religious interest and concern than the reading of religious publications, for no added expenditure is involved. If people do not follow the programs, they indicate that they simply are not interested, or are not interested enough to pass up some other program which may be available at the same time.

How many Americans regularly listened to any religious programs on radio or television? Fifty per cent of the Protestant group, 51 per cent of the Roman Catholic, and 72 per cent of the Jewish, replied that they did not. These percentages indicate that religious programs can rely on attracting relatively large audiences, although approximately fifty per cent of the Protestant and Roman Catholic, and almost three fourths of the Jewish groups had not found any religious program that appealed to them. We do not know whether this lack of appeal was due to religious indifference on their part or to the quality of the available programs. It remains to be seen how successfully well-directed religious programs can compete with those in the entertainment and educational fields. Few can deny that up to the present, the primary emphasis in program development has been on entertainment. Educational and religious leaders are beginning to suspect that the American public is ready for a somewhat more substantial diet.

What programs did people follow regularly? Bishop (at that time, Monsignor) Fulton J. Sheen enjoyed great popularity. Seventeen per cent of the Roman Catholic group, 2 per cent of the Protestant, and 4 per cent of the Jewish followed his program regularly. Other programs that came in for frequent mention: Fr. Justine's Rosary Hour, 8 per cent of the Roman Catholics; the Catholic Hour, 7 per cent of the Roman Catholic and 2 per cent of the Protestant groups; Fuller's Old Fashioned Revival Hour, 5 per cent of the Protestant group; Billy Graham's Hour of Decision, 3 per cent of the Protestant group; Eternal Light, 3 per cent of the Jewish group; Lamp Unto My Feet, 2 per cent of the Jewish group; The Greatest Story Ever Told, and Mormon Tabernacle, 1 per cent each of the Protestant group; and all other programs, 43 per cent of the Roman Catholic, 39 per cent of the Protestant, and 21 per cent of the Jewish groups. The percentages total more than 100 because some people followed more than one program regularly.

Before attempting to draw some general conclusions from this broad overview of religious activities, it may be helpful to consider briefly whether religious practices are related to denominational differences, age, education and residential backgrounds. In the following tables we have selected several traditional practices from among others to serve as indicators of comparative religious vitality, on the assumption that if people attended church services regularly, prayed, and read the Bible frequently, they were taking their religious beliefs seriously.

Table 10 presents the religious activities of the major Protestant denominations. It may be recalled from Table 6 that we discovered several significant differences in religious beliefs

TABLE 10. *Religious Practices of Major Protestant Denominations*

| DENOMINATIONS | Church-goers per cent | PRAYERS | | | | | Bible Readers |
		Night Prayers	Grace before Meals	Morning Prayers	Twice a day or more	
Baptist	61	60	43	15	39	48
Methodist	50	58	33	14	35	34
Lutheran	52	67	39	16	37	29
Presbyterian	55	58	33	14	41	38
Episcopal	45	58	33	19	34	34
Congregational	38	57	22	13	20	19
Other	53	61	35	20	41	46

among these groups, and Table 10 reveals a similar pattern. For example, the Baptists are most assiduous in attending church services and in Bible reading, while Congregationalists are least inclined to engage in such activities. Night prayers remain relatively popular among all groups, and since this seems to be the only time during the day that a good proportion of our respondents prayed, as we can gather from the relatively lower percentages who stated they prayed twice a day or more, it is regrettable that we obtained no information on the specific forms of prayer that were used for this purpose.

On the other hand, morning prayers are apparently not very popular among modern Protestants, though lack of adequate information on previous periods makes it impossible to judge whether this represents a significant change. Finally, considering the usual insistence on grace before meals at public gatherings involving religious groups, it is surprising to discover that the practice is not more widely observed in the privacy of the home. Significantly more Baptists and Lutherans offer grace before meals than do members of other denominations or faiths, yet the total picture suggests that the stereotype of the religious family piously bowed in prayer before partaking of their daily bread is ceasing to be applicable in our affluent society.

Table 11, which presents the religious activities of various age categories, is of interest on two scores. First, it is generally assumed that the pattern of religious practices shifts with the age of the participant, yet a rapid survey of the data presented in Table 11 lends minor support to this hypothesis. The proportion of churchgoers is roughly similar throughout all the categories, while participation in night prayers and grace before meals reveals no uniform patterns. On the other hand, people

TABLE 11. *Religious Practices and Age of Participants*

| AGE GROUP | Church-goers per cent | PRAYERS | | | | Bible Readers |
		Night Prayers	Grace before Meals	Morning Prayers	Twice a day or more	
18–24 years	56	67	34	21	37	29
25–34	57	62	34	16	35	33
35–44	54	59	35	20	34	32
45–54	57	58	31	26	39	37
55–64	57	61	35	29	42	35
65 and over	53	64	32	34	49	47

65 years old and over are more likely to say morning prayers, pray oftener during the day, and read the Bible regularly.

Second, since our table covers several generations, it should give some indication of the changes that may have occurred in religious training and practice during this time. As the table shows, with the exception of Bible reading, morning prayers, and frequent prayer during the day, the youngest age category appears as active in religious activities as the oldest. Since the majority of people 65 years old and over have probably retired and consequently have more time on their hands, it is possible that additional leisure time rather than differences in training accounts for the discrepancies we noted. At any rate, on the basis of our findings we would suggest that assumptions concerning marked differences in religious activities during various age periods or between different generations be carefully checked.

To what degree is formal education related to participation in religious activities? The findings presented in Table 12 do not follow the pattern we were led to expect from our study of religious beliefs. It may be recalled from Table 8 that college graduates were more inclined than others to reject the traditional beliefs of the major faiths, yet with the exception of night prayers, Table 12 shows that they lead all others in religious participation. There are several possible explanations for this unexpected finding. One might assume, for example, that inasmuch as religion is held in high esteem, college graduates would be active participants for the sake of the social prestige involved, particularly if they were in the professional classes where such prestige may not be ignored. This explanation would account for the relatively high incidence of churchgoers but not for greater participation in Bible reading and frequent prayer.

TABLE 12. *Religious Practices and Educational Attainment*

EDUCATION	Church-goers per cent	Night Prayers	Grace before Meals	Morning Prayers	Twice a day or more	Bible Readers
				PRAYERS		
0-8th grade	52	60	30	25	38	33
1-3 years of high school	56	63	32	22	36	32
High school graduate	58	63	34	21	38	33
1-3 years of college	55	62	38	19	42	41
College graduate	60	54	41	28	44	44

Our own explanation would be that a college education may lead to a clarification of religious commitments. Hence some graduates would cease even to pay lip service to traditional beliefs because they had definitely rejected them, while a college training would enable others to think through the implications of their childhood beliefs and accept them as adults. Furthermore, it should be noted in this connection that the term *college graduate* does not specify the type of college at which the training took place or the course of studies followed. It seems probable that different areas of specialization would affect the faith of students differently.

It has been customary to classify certain regions of the United States as "Bible Belt" areas. This term implies that the inhabitants of these regions emphasize the Bible as the sole rule of faith and take a fundamentalist approach in their interpretation of it, that is, they tend to interpret the Scriptures literally. The term Bible Belt also has connotations of religious obscurantism or anti-intellectualism and is usually applied to the rural or small town rather than urban areas even of the "Bible Belt" regions. The responses presented in Table 13 tend to support the assumption that residents of rural areas are more likely to attend religious services and read the Bible frequently than others. If there is a "Bible Belt," it will include chiefly rural areas.

We can test this hypothesis by checking the relative distribution of Bible readers in the various national regions. According to our findings, the primarily rural West South Central (51 per cent), the East South Central (49 per cent), and the South Atlantic (42 per cent) are the regions that include the highest percentages of Bible readers and stand in sharp contrast to the New England (18 per cent), Middle Atlantic (27 per cent), East North Central (28 per cent), and Pacific (30 per

TABLE 13. *Religious Practices and Size of Community*

SIZE OF COMMUNITY	Church-goers per cent	Night Prayers	Grace before Meals	Morning Prayers	Twice a day or more	Bible Readers
			PRAYERS			
Over 1 million	54	58	31	28	37	33
100,000–1 million	47	58	28	23	35	35
25,000–100,000	57	64	31	27	32	30
10,000–25,000	55	62	27	22	36	34
Under 10,000	59	62	37	21	42	37
Rural	62	63	38	21	40	46

cent) regions in this respect. To the extent that the term "Bible Belt" implies Bible readers, it should be applied only to the first three regions mentioned above.

Finally, because all surveys of religious beliefs and practices indicate that women are more religiously inclined than men, we shall offer a brief review of our findings in this regard. To save space, the percentages for only the major items will be presented, and the first figure after each item will apply to women. Relative beliefs were as follows: absolutely sure that God exists (89–84), regard God as loving Father (84–73), believe in the Trinity (91–86), believe in the divinity of Christ (83–76), Bible as the word of God (87–81), immortality (80–75), Heaven (75–70), Hell (59–57), possibility of going to Hell (11–14), mixed marriage less desirable (77–73), divorce is wrong (28–24), contraceptive birth control is wrong (23–21). Relative practices were as follows: churchgoers (60–52), Bible readers (41–27), night prayers (68–54), grace before meals (37–30), morning prayers (26–18), pray twice a day or oftener (52–37). It is interesting to note that the only item in which men surpassed women dealt with the belief that there was a real possibility that one might be eternally damned. Evidently women enjoy greater peace of mind on this score, though the total proportion of the seriously concerned (among both sexes) was very small, as we have had occasion to remark when dealing with this item.

Viewed from the perspective of our findings on basic beliefs and practices, how does the American religious tradition appear to be shaping up? Figure 2 offers a comparative summary of our findings on basic practices. Prescinding from the manifold differences apparent among the major faiths and denominations, the over-all process appears somewhat as follows. Religion continues to exert a pervasive influence in the lives of the

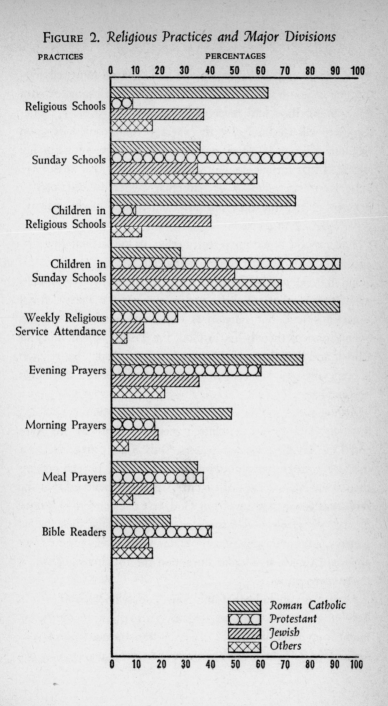

FIGURE 2. *Religious Practices and Major Divisions*

American people. All but 6 per cent had received some religious training in youth and for the most part were well satisfied with the training they had received. This process of early indoctrination will continue, for the average American looks upon religious training in youth as an excellent preparation for life and feels that formal training should be given either at Sunday School or in a religious or parochial school. Indeed, only 2 per cent stated that they did not want a child of theirs to receive religious instruction.

This process of extensive early religious indoctrination probably goes far toward explaining the high esteem in which religion is held and undoubtedly accounts for the widespread persistence of basic beliefs among the great majority. Most Americans feel that religion is important in their lives and openly profess their belief in God, the Trinity, the divinity of Christ, and the Bible as the inspired word of God. That religion is everywhere pervasive is beyond question, but is it anywhere profound?

Although 73 per cent of the adult population considered themselves to be active church members, only 57 per cent could be classified as churchgoers. Only 8 per cent stated that they never pray, yet less than two out of five prayed oftener than about once a day. Although 83 per cent believed that the Bible was the inspired word of God, just one third read it once a week or oftener. A variety of religious magazines, newspapers, radio and television programs were available, but they apparently held no regular attraction for roughly one half of the modern public.

Must we conclude that the American religious tradition is becoming a mere cultural residue, carried on, perhaps, by momentum built up in the past, or transformed into a convenient social vehicle for the promotion of valued secular objectives? Does the prestige it currently enjoys have its roots so deeply buried in the nation's past that modern Americans feel they must regard it, to borrow a classic phrase from Burke, as something they ought to venerate where they are unable presently to comprehend? Many contemporary observers have advanced such judgments, echoing, in this regard, a familiar ring in religious literature from the first century on.

We feel their dire verdicts are somewhat premature in the present instance. To be sure, one may compare the current religious situation as revealed in our study with some mythical past "age of faith" and come up with distressing conclusions about present trends. What do we really know about the extent and depth of the religious commitments of past generations? Some writers seem to confuse the relative social conservatism and traditionalism characteristic of much of our rural past with religious vitality, thus identifying respect for what we might call the socially or secularly "sacred" (the traditional) with reverence for the religiously "holy." Is it not possible that much of what passed for religious involvement in a simpler, less complex rural environment was secular involvement under the guise of religion; or, stated in other terms, is it possible that the churches formerly fulfilled a series of social and secular functions in the community that have been gradually lost or taken over by other institutions in our complex, rapidly changing, technically advanced urban environment?

At any rate, our findings reveal the persistence of a substantial core of actively participating faithful who apparently still cherish the essential beliefs of the Western religious tradition. Whether this core group is as proportionately large as in the past, or whether its religious commitment is as profound and all-inclusive, we are in no position to judge. Surrounding this vital nucleus in every faith and denomination cluster relatively large numbers of adherents whose knowledge and understanding of religion obviously remain at the childhood or grade school level since they recognize neither the transcendental dimensions nor practical implications of the beliefs they profess. Renewed popular interest in religion has probably considerably increased the proportion of such "fellow travelers," but they are not to be confused with the substantial nucleus of active believers representing what is vital in our organized traditional religions. We would suggest that it is not the obvious secularism of the "fellow travelers" but the need for creative leadership of the central core of the faithful that must constitute the present major concern of the churches.

Notes

1. See John L. Thomas, *The American Catholic Family* (Englewood Cliffs, N.J.: Prentice-Hall-Inc., 1956), pp. 327–373.

2. It is possible that the relative prosperity of the country is related to this optimism in some degree.

3. See *Religious Perspectives in American Culture*, ed. by James Ward Smith and A. Leland Jamison (Princeton: Princeton University Press, 1961), pp. 11–52.

4. Expenditures for new religious buildings during 1961 are estimated to run about 1 billion according to the United States Department of Commerce.

5. See Rolfe L. Hunt, "Religion and Education," *Annals* (Nov. 1960), Vol. 332, 89–100.

6. See Benson Y. Landis, "Trends in Church Membership in the United States," *Annals*, Ibid., 1–8.

CHAPTER 5 Organized Religion in
Action

THE three major traditional faiths we are studying represent well institutionalized religious systems, that is, they
involve not only a moral community, an ingroup of the faithful,
but also a visible system of symbols, objects, activities, offices,
functions, and organizations of which most adult Americans
are more or less aware. No organized religion, of course,
operates in a social vacuum, yet for historical reasons or out
of set policy the churches differ greatly in the related institutions they support and the activities they promote. Since there
is no established church in America, each organized religious
group must develop its own programs for survival, and the
minimal requisites in this regard would appear to be a meeting
place and some organized means for assuring indoctrination,
solidarity, and identity. Under these circumstances, the faithful
take it for granted that they will be called upon to make considerable sacrifice for the support of church structures, schools,
religious officials, teachers, and related charitable programs,
though the amount of their expected contributions will necessarily vary in relation to the nature and quality of the services

they feel their church should offer. At the same time, external factors such as competition, prestige, and the desire to preserve ethnic or denominational differences play no minor role in determining the activities which engage the churches, so that to some extent organized religion becomes necessarily involved in the wider social, economic, and political sectors of our entire social system.

How do people view such relationships between the secular and the sacred? What is their attitude toward concessions that have been made in favor of organized religion? To what extent are they satisfied with the manner in which religious institutions operate in our society? The answers to these questions should give us some helpful insights into what religion means to the American people, for, as we have discovered, it is not easy to measure the pervasiveness of religious influence in a pluralist, complex, rapidly changing society. Surely the popularity of religion at any given period is no necessary indication that it either profoundly affects men's thinking or shapes the normative structures of their social systems. On the other hand, the places they assign to various religious institutions and functions within the total system should throw some light on the importance they attach to religion in their own lives and as a means of promoting the welfare of the community.

We have seen in Chapter Four that most Americans received some formal religious instruction in their youth and wish their children to enjoy similar privileges. In spite of this widespread, and apparently perennial demand, the proper relationship between religious and secular education has never been worked out to the satisfaction of all groups and is currently one of the most controversial domestic issues with which Americans must deal. At present, the elementary and secondary schools are overwhelmingly public rather than private, though there has been a trend toward more nonpublic schools during the last decade.[1] Modern Americans have come to take for granted the principle of governmental responsibility for education, and since government-controlled schools may not in theory offer "sectarian" instruction, it is generally assumed that public schools are secular or neutral. Hence if public school children are to receive religious instruction, this must be added on to the hard core of neutral or secular education constituting their basic training, either by teaching religion on some type of released time basis, through Sunday or vacation schools, or by some other means. Church-related schools, of course, offer special religious instruction and at the same time attempt to infuse religion throughout the entire course of studies.

The primary right of parents to educate their children in schools of their choosing has been clearly defined by the Supreme Court, yet the practical implementation of that right under conditions of religious pluralism in a society that assumes governmental responsibility for education is bound to generate some highly controversial problems. Some people profess to discover a note of divisiveness in religious schools or in any relationship between religion and public education, either because they regard all differences as divisive or because they feel their own rejection of Christianity will become less obvious if religion is completely ignored. Others are opposed to religious schools because they contend that the family and the churches should handle the religious instruction of youth, while in supplying secular training, the public school system would serve as one of the major social means for promoting the unity and solidarity requisite for the smooth functioning of a democratic society. Still others see no real need for a separate school system inasmuch as the public school teachers in their areas tend to profess the same religious beliefs as the parents of the children they teach and consequently the public school is not regarded as wholly secular or neutral.[2]

There can be little doubt, however, that the basic issues involved in the current controversy over tax support for private schools stem from two sources. First, who shall pay the bill? Many people contend that if members of a religious minority wish to maintain a separate school system for their children, they should support it through voluntary contributions. Second, and perhaps of most significance, there is the fear that some religious groups will gain a greater advantage from tax support than others in the perennial interdenominational competition for membership. Some religious groups are neither prepared nor seemingly disposed to maintain separate schools and are consequently little inclined to grant this advantage to others.[3]

Because the relationship between religion and education has aroused so much controversy and such a variety of solutions have been proposed or adopted, we attempted to investigate people's attitudes concerning all significant aspects of the problem. Does the average adult American regard religious schools as divisive? The question was asked: "Some religious denominations support their own schools, to which members prefer to send their children rather than to public schools. Do you think these religious schools are good or bad for the country, or don't you think it makes any difference?" The majority did not appear greatly perturbed about the existence of such schools. Only 16 per cent felt that religious schools were bad for the country, while 42 per cent thought they were good, 31 per cent believed they made no difference, and 11 per cent offered no opinion.

As we may learn from studying Table 14, members of the major religious groups revealed considerably different attitudes

TABLE 14. *Attitudes of Major Religious Groups Toward Religious Schools*

MAJOR GROUPS	NATIONAL SIGNIFICANCE				QUALITY OF EDUCATION			
	Good	Makes no Difference	Bad	Undecided	Better	About Same	Not as Good	Undecided
Roman Catholic	73	22	2	3	48	43	6	3
Protestant total	34	33	20	13	18	35	21	26
Baptist	36	29	18	17	16	36	17	31
Methodist	35	33	21	11	18	37	22	23
Lutheran	46	35	13	6	22	43	18	17
Presbyterian	23	34	27	16	20	29	30	21
Episcopal	34	29	25	12	17	35	27	21
Congregational	22	45	24	9	22	26	30	22
Others	33	33	21	13	16	35	20	29
Jewish	29	32	28	11	21	32	19	28
Other and none	26	40	21	13	20	34	14	32

toward religious schools. Almost three out of four Roman Catholics thought such schools were good, over one out of five, that they made no difference, and only 2 per cent that they were bad. Roughly one third of the Protestants thought that they were either good or made no difference, and one out of five that they were bad. Members of the Jewish group expressed a less favorable opinion, for only 29 per cent felt that they were good, 32 per cent that they made no difference, and 28 per cent that they were bad.

Among the major Protestant denominations, the Lutheran bodies were most favorable in their judgments of such schools, as we would expect from the fact that they tend to support a considerable number of their own private schools. Over four out of five Lutherans felt that they were either good or made no difference, while only 13 per cent thought they were bad for the country. The Presbyterian bodies took the least favorable view, since only 57 per cent believed they were good or made no difference, and 27 per cent felt they were bad. It should be noted that with the exception of Roman Catholics, a considerable number of respondents expressed no opinion on this question or on similar issues related to religious schools.

Formal education was inversely correlated with favorable attitudes toward such schools. For example, among people with a grade school education or less, 46 per cent thought they were good, and only 13 per cent felt they were bad, while among college graduates, only 33 per cent believed they were good, and 25 per cent regarded them as bad for the country. A similar pattern was revealed by the occupational classes, since among the professional and managerial classes, 35 and 37 per cent respectively felt they were good, and 23 and 21 per cent respectively believed they were bad, while among service and manual workers, 48 and 46 per cent respectively felt they were good, and only 13 per cent thought that they were bad. As was to be expected, a survey of the different income categories showed a similar pattern. Only 37 per cent in the upper income bracket felt that they were good and 25 per cent thought they were bad. Among members of the lower income class, however, 46 per cent believed they were good and only 13 per cent felt they were bad.

The consistency of this pattern among the various educational, occupational, and income categories throws some light on the publicity that opposition to religious schools has received in recent years. As we have seen, only a relatively small minority (16 per cent) of the adult American population feel that religious schools are bad for the country, yet this minority tends to be heavily concentrated in the upper educational, occupational, and income brackets. Inasmuch as the members of these upper brackets enjoy considerable social prestige and have relatively easy access to the principal channels of communication, it is not surprising that they exercise an influence considerably out of proportion to their numbers in the total population.

The maintenance of religious schools calls for a considerable expenditure on the part of the faithful since such schools do not enjoy state support and must consequently be financed by private initiative. The question naturally arises whether the quality of education offered in such schools compares favorably with that given in the public school system. Of course, for all practical purposes, this question has been answered by the various state boards of education. Teachers in religious schools must meet the same qualifications as public school teachers, and the standard courses required by the various state boards must be taught. Whatever differences exist, therefore, must be incidental to these basic requirements.

There is some interest, however, in finding out what the general public thinks of the quality of education given in religious schools. Although popular attitudes will be based, in the most part, on unverified and perhaps, unverifiable data, there is considerable value in knowing what people think in regard to a matter so closely related to a highly controversial issue. Hence the question was asked: "How would you rate the quality of the general education given in religious grade schools as compared with the public grade schools—about the same, better, or not as good?" One out of four thought that it was better, 37 per cent felt it was about the same, 17 per cent believed it was not as good, and 21 per cent modestly admitted that they were undecided. In other words, nearly two thirds of the people believed that religious grade schools were about the same or better than public grade schools.

As Table 14 indicates, the major religious groups expressed different opinions on this subject. Members of the Roman Catholic group were most favorable in judging the quality of the general education given in religious schools. Ninety-one per cent thought it was better or about the same; 6 per cent felt it was not as good; and 3 per cent were undecided. The corresponding percentages for the total Protestant group were: 53, 21 and 26 per cent respectively; for the Jewish group: 53, 19, and 28 per cent respectively; for people with some other or no religious preference: 54, 14 and 32 per cent respectively.

Among the various Protestant divisions, members of the Lutheran group passed the most favorable judgment on the quality of education given in religious schools. Only 18 per cent thought that it was not as good, and 65 per cent felt it was better or about the same. Among the remaining Protestant denominations, it is interesting to note that the Presbyterian and Congregational groups included the highest percentages who believed the quality was not as good (30 per cent each), and also the highest percentages who thought that it was better (20 per cent and 22 per cent respectively). A little more than one fourth of the total Protestant membership stated that they were undecided. It is possible that there were no religious grade schools in their areas so that they probably had not thought very much about the comparison. This hypothesis receives considerable support from the data on regional differences. In sections of the country where religious schools were common, relatively few people were undecided, whereas the percentages of undecided increased significantly in regions where such schools were rare. For example, in the New England and Middle Atlantic regions, only 12 per cent and 14 per cent respectively were undecided. In the South Atlantic and East South Central regions, 28 per cent and 32 per cent respectively were undecided.

High esteem for the quality of general education given in religious schools was not closely correlated with the formal educational attainments of the respondents. Twenty-three per cent of the respondents with grade school education or less, 26 per cent of high school graduates, 29 per cent with 1–3 years of college, and 22 per cent of college graduates thought it was better. On the other hand, unfavorable attitudes were directly correlated with degree of formal education. Only 12 per cent with grade school training or less thought it was not as good, whereas 18 per cent of high school graduates and people with 1–3 years of college, and 28 per cent of college graduates expressed this opinion.

A similar pattern was revealed among the various occupational classes. This is to say, there was no direct correlation between occupational status and high esteem for the quality of education given in religious schools, but there was a marked inverse relationship for unfavorable attitudes. For example, 28 per cent of the professional, 24 per cent of the proprietor or manager and of the white-collar worker, 31 per cent of the service worker, and 25 per cent of the manual worker classes thought that the quality was better. However, the percentages of these same classes who thought it was not as good ran: 25, 20, 18, 16, and 14 per cent respectively. A similar pattern was revealed when respondents were divided according to income. Twenty-three per cent of the upper, 35 per cent of the middle, and 26 per cent of the lower income classes thought that the quality was better, whereas the percentages of those who thought the quality was not as good ran: 22, 17 and 14 per cent respectively. In other words, although those who thought the quality was not as good constituted a relatively small percentage (17 per cent) of the total population, they tended to be concentrated in the upper socio-economic class as measured by education, occupation, and income.

One of the issues that has aroused considerable controversy in many states is whether children in religious schools should share in some of the free services supplied out of public funds to pupils in the public schools.[4] Perhaps few issues indicate more clearly the profound opposition to the existence of religious schools on the part of some citizens. Implicit in this opposition, of course, is a denial of the constitutionally guaranteed right of parents to educate their children in a school of their choice. If parents have this right, it is not consistent with justice to penalize them or their children when they choose to make use of it; yet a curious lack of logic, associated with fear and prejudice wherever they are found, comes to the fore whenever this issue is discussed. For this reason, information concerning what people think about the use of public funds for this purpose will throw considerable light on the feelings resulting from religious pluralism in this country. Some observers maintain that the American people recognize three equal religious communities—Protestant, Catholic, and Jew. It appears more consonant with our findings to hold that a good percentage of the American people acknowledge one religious community, the Protestant, and tolerate the other two as minorities that have developed in their midst. Or as one writer has stated it in regard to social classes, "We are all equal, but some are more equal than others!"

To get at people's attitudes on this issue, we asked the following question: "Public funds are used in some states to give free bus service and free books to children in the public schools. Do you think public funds should also be used to give free bus service and free books to children in religious schools, or not?" Approximately half (51 per cent) of the people thought that they should; 40 per cent disagreed; and 9 per cent were undecided. Table 15 indicates that there were marked differences among the major religious groups. Nearly four out of five (79 per cent) of the Roman Catholic group thought that they should; 12 per cent disagreed; and 9 per cent were undecided. The percentages for the other groups were as follows: Protestant, 41, 50 and 9 per cent respectively; Jewish, 45, 44 and 11 per cent respectively; and those with some other or no religious preference, 42, 42, and 16 per cent respectively.

We can learn from Table 15 that the various Protestant divisions have different views on this issue. In general, the relatively large bodies comprising the Baptist, Methodist, and "other" denominations are most favorably inclined toward the use of public funds for services to pupils of religious schools

Table 15. *Attitudes of Major Religious Groups Toward Public Support for Religious Schools*

MAJOR GROUPS	FREE TRANSPORTATION AND BOOKS			TAX SUPPORT		
	Yes	*No*	*Undecided*	*Yes*	*No*	*Undecided*
Roman Catholic	79	12	9	63	25	12
Protestant Total	41	50	9	34	56	10
Baptist	47	42	11	40	47	14
Methodist	42	49	9	34	55	11
Lutheran	39	53	8	28	61	11
Presbyterian	32	59	9	23	73	4
Episcopal	25	66	9	24	70	6
Congregational	34	56	10	35	57	8
Other	42	49	9	37	54	9
Jewish	45	44	11	35	49	16
Other and none	42	42	16	31	57	12

(47, 42, and 42 per cent respectively). A much less favorable attitude was expressed by members of the Episcopal (25 per cent), Presbyterian (32 per cent) and Congregational (34 per cent) groups, and their opposition was clear: 66, 59, and 56 per cent respectively.

Attitudes on this issue were closely related to education, occupation, and income status. As measured by these three indexes, members of the upper socio-economic class were least favorably disposed to have pupils of religious schools share in public services. For example, 59 per cent of the people with a grade school education or less were in favor, and only 28 per cent were opposed, while among college graduates, only 28 per cent were in favor, and 64 per cent were opposed. Thirty-one per cent of the professional class were in favor, and 60 per cent were opposed, whereas 59 per cent of the manual worker class were in favor, and only 32 per cent were opposed. Following a similar pattern, 37 per cent of the upper income bracket were in favor, and 55 per cent were opposed, but 60 per cent of the lower income class were in favor, and only 28 per cent were opposed.

According to the present findings, if the issue were put to a vote, it would be decided affirmatively in cities of over one million population and in those ranging between 25,000 and 100,000. In rural areas and in all other communities, it would be decided by the position that people who were currently undecided would take. Further, in a vote according to regions, it would be decided affirmatively in the New England, Middle Atlantic, and South Atlantic regions. In all other regions it would be decided by the vote of the currently undecided, with the exception of the Mountain region, in which 54 per cent of the population stated that they were opposed. Of course, the above hypotheses presuppose that 100 per cent of the voters would go to the polls in case of a ballot on this issue.

The issue of tax support for religious schools has only recently come in for the same amount of discussion as the use of public funds to supply bus service and free books to pupils in religious schools. There are several schools of thought on this issue.[5] Some oppose tax support for religious schools on the same grounds that they oppose the sharing of public services by pupils of religious schools. Some are opposed because they feel that this would invite state interference in private and religious schools. Others maintain that because all pay taxes for the support of education, all children should benefit from such taxes.

What do the American people in general think about the problem? Our study posed the following question: "People who send their children to religious schools pay taxes for the support of the public schools, as well as paying for the support of the religious schools. Do you think public taxes should be used to support the religious schools also, or not?" Forty per cent of the people thought taxes should be so used; 49 per cent disagreed; and 11 per cent were undecided. As Table 15 indicates, members of the major religious divisions were fairly well divided on this issue. Sixty-three per cent of the Roman Catholic group were in favor; 25 per cent disagreed; and 12 per cent were undecided. Of the Protestant total, 34 per cent were in favor; 56 per cent disagreed; and 10 per cent were undecided. Among the Jewish group, 35 per cent were in favor; 49 per cent disagreed; and 16 per cent were undecided. Greatest opposition was expressed by those with some other or no religious preference. Thirty-one per cent were in favor; 57 per cent disagreed, and 12 per cent were undecided.

It is evident from Table 15 that there is considerable difference of opinion on this issue among the various Protestant bodies. Greatest opposition was expressed by the Presbyterian, Episcopal, and Lutheran groups (73, 70, and 61 per cent respectively). The relatively large membership of the various Baptist bodies registered considerably less opposition (47 per cent), and 40 per cent stated that they were in favor of tax support. Although over half the members of the Methodist and "other" denominations stated that they were not in favor of this move (55 and 54 per cent respectively), their opposition was much less marked than that of the first three groups mentioned.

Following the pattern of opinion revealed in all questions dealing with religious schools, there was a significant relationship between attitudes on tax support and education, occupation, and income status. The upper socio-economic class as measured by these three indexes registered a relatively high degree of opposition to such support for religious schools. For example, among respondents with a grade school education or less, 47 per cent were in favor, and 39 per cent were opposed; among college graduates, only 17 per cent were in favor, and 77 per cent were opposed. Of the professional and proprietor or manager classes, 20 per cent and 32 per cent respectively were in favor and 76 per cent and 57 per cent respectively were opposed. Forty-eight per cent of the service and manual worker classes were in favor, and only 39 per cent and 41 per cent respectively were opposed. In the upper income bracket, 26 per cent were in favor, and 66 per cent were opposed, whereas in the lower income group, 49 per cent were in favor and only 38 per cent were opposed.

If the issue were put to a vote in various sized communities throughout the country, in all but two types of community it would be decided by the way the currently undecided would vote. Only in cities with a population ranging between 10,000 and 25,000 and in cities with 10,000 or less, were half or more than half of the population opposed. In these two types of communities, the percentages opposed were 53 and 55 per cent respectively. Similarly, in a vote according to regions, the issue would probably be decided favorably in the New England and South Atlantic regions, inasmuch as 50 per cent of the people stated that they were in favor and only 43 per cent and 42 per cent respectively were opposed. In the Middle Atlantic and East South Central regions, the issue would be settled by the 11 and 19 per cent respectively who stated that they were undecided. In the remaining regions, tax support for religious schools was opposed by over half, favored by roughly one third, and the rest were undecided. Of course, the above hypotheses presuppose a 100 per cent turnout at the polls, and no change in attitudes once the issue is referred to the ballot.

One of the results of the renewed popular interest in religion has been the demand for increased religious instruction for youth in public schools. It is rather generally assumed that the public schools themselves are not in a position to give this instruction, inasmuch as most schools include students from a great variety of religious backgrounds and even a very general course in religious instruction would probably not find universal approval. Religious beliefs differ so widely that many teachers feel it would be difficult to establish a basic religious course acceptable to all, though such a solution has sometimes been proposed. Under these circumstances, some communities have made arrangements so that children in public schools are allowed to leave school early on certain days in order to attend classes in religion offered by their respective religious groups.[6]

A glance at the literature on this subject reveals that opinions differ widely concerning the value of released time for religious instruction. Some insist that the family should assume the entire task of instructing children in religion. Some feel that Sunday schools are sufficient and preferable. Others state that the program does not touch the heart of the problem. They believe that too little time is given for religious instructions and, although the program is inadequate, too many parents are using it as a convenient escape from their personal responsibilities in this important matter. Nevertheless, programs of this nature are widespread and they must be enjoying considerable popular support.

What do the American people think of released time programs? The following question was designed to obtain that information: "In some states, children in public schools are allowed to leave school early to attend classes in their own religion, taught by religious teachers of their own faith. Do you think this is a good idea, a bad idea, or don't you think it makes any difference?" Well over half (54 per cent) thought it was a good idea; nearly one out of four (24 per cent) felt that it made no difference; and a little over one out of five (22 per cent) believed that it was a bad idea. Table 16 shows that members of the major religious divisions expressed some differences of opinion on the subject. Of the Roman Catholic group, 76 per cent thought it was a good idea; 10 per cent felt it was a bad idea; and 14 per cent were indifferent. Corresponding percentages for the Protestant groups were: 49, 26, and 25 per cent respectively; for the Jewish group: 43, 31, and 26 per cent respectively, and for the remainder: 39, 21, and 40 per cent respectively.

Agreement on the value of released time ran rather high among the various Protestant bodies. Most inclined to think it was a good idea were the Congregational (60 per cent) and Lutheran (58 per cent) groups. The Baptist (45 per cent),

TABLE 16. *Attitudes of the Major Religious Groups Toward Released Time*

MAJOR GROUPS	VALUE OF PROGRAM			USE OF PUBLIC SCHOOL BUILDINGS			
	Good Idea	Bad Idea	Indifferent	In Favor	Makes no Difference	Opposed	No Opinion
Roman Catholic	76	10	14	31	30	13	2
Protestant total	49	26	25	24	14	10	1
Baptist	45	27	28	26	11	8	0
Methodist	48	26	26	23	15	9	1
Lutheran	58	21	21	25	18	15	0
Presbyterian	50	26	24	19	15	12	4
Episcopal	53	25	22	23	15	12	3
Congregational	60	24	16	26	13	21	0
Others	46	27	27	23	13	9	1
Jewish	43	31	26	18	9	16	0
Other and none	39	21	40	14	11	12	2

"other" denominations (46 per cent), and Methodist (48 per cent) groups held it in somewhat less esteem, and the Presbyterian (50 per cent) and Episcopal (53 per cent) groups were moderately favorable. Among all Protestant bodies, roughly one out of four thought it was a bad idea, and about the same proportion felt that it made no difference.

People between the ages of 18–24 were more likely to be in favor of released time than were those who were 65 and older (62 per cent and 49 per cent respectively). There was no close relationship between educational status and approval of released time. However, a higher proportion of college graduates than those with grade school training or less felt that it was a bad idea (26 per cent and 21 per cent respectively). Among the occupational groups, the professional class displayed the most ambivalence on this subject (55 per cent for; 31 per cent against), while service workers showed the least (60 per cent for, 17 per cent against). Farmers apparently had had less experience with released time, and many consequently had not formed clear-cut judgments, since only 48 per cent thought it was a good idea, another 21 per cent felt it was a bad idea and nearly one third (31 per cent) believed that it made no difference.

There appeared to be a fairly close relationship between income and attitudes toward released time. In the upper income bracket, 50 per cent thought it was a good idea and 28 per cent felt it was bad; whereas, in the lower income class, 56 per cent believed it was a good idea and only 19 per cent felt that it was bad. In cities of 25,000 population and over, between 59 and 60 per cent of the people considered released time a good idea, and only between 16 and 18 per cent felt it was not good. In cities below 25,000 and in rural areas, only between 50 and 54 per cent felt it was a good idea, and between 21 and 26 per cent believed that it was bad. Most favorable attitudes were expressed by people in the Middle Atlantic (67 per cent), New England (64 per cent), East North Central (56 per cent), and West North Central (55 per cent) regions. Less favorable were people in the East South Central (43 per cent), West South Central (45 per cent), Mountain (48 per cent), Pacific (51 per cent), and South Atlantic (52 per cent) regions.

The introduction of released time programs generally gives rise to another problem. Where are the classes in religious instruction to be held? Since the children are already assembled in the public school buildings, and such buildings are commonly assumed to have been constructed to serve the needs of the public in educating youth, many people feel that it would be more convenient to have the various teachers of the proposed religion classes come to the school rather than to have the students travel to different parts of the community in order to attend the classes. At the time our study was made, the issue had not been decided by the Supreme Court. There were then, and still are, various schools of thought on the matter. Our study reveals how the American public views the situation.

All respondents who stated that they thought released time was a good idea were asked the following question: "Would you be in favor or opposed to holding these religious classes in the public school building, or wouldn't it make any difference to you?" Of the 54 per cent who thought released time was a good idea, 24 per cent were in favor of using public school buildings for such classes; 12 per cent were opposed; and 17 per cent were indifferent. As we see from a study of Table 16, there were some differences of opinion among the major religious divisions and also among the various groups composing the Protestant total, but in most instances these differences were not as marked as on most questions studied.

Of the 76 per cent of the Roman Catholic group who felt released time was a good idea, 31 per cent were in favor of using public school buildings; 13 per cent were opposed; and 30 per cent were indifferent. The corresponding percentages for the 49 per cent of the Protestant total were: 24, 10, and 14 per cent respectively. For the 43 per cent of the Jewish group they were: 18, 16, and 9 per cent respectively. For the 39 per cent of those with some other or no religious preference, they were: 14, 12, and 11 per cent respectively. As the Table reveals, members of the Presbyterian group were least likely to be in favor of this arrangement (19 per cent), although the group was not outstanding in its opposition (12 per cent). The religious group most evenly divided over the issue was the Congregational in which 26 per cent were in favor and 21 per cent were opposed.

Among the various educational classes, all expressed a favorable attitude toward the use of public school buildings for released time instructions except college graduates. Although 56 per cent of this group thought that released time was a good idea, only 18 per cent were in favor of using public school buildings for this purpose, and 20 per cent were opposed. Among the various occupational classes, most favorable attitudes were expressed by members of the service and manual worker classes (25 per cent and 27 per cent respectively). Least favorable (21 per cent) and most opposed (18 per cent) were members of the professional class.

A similar pattern appeared among the different income classes. Whereas 29 per cent of the lower income bracket were in favor and 9 per cent were opposed, only 22 per cent of the upper income class were in favor, and 15 per cent were opposed. It is interesting to note that in the New England and Middle Atlantic regions where 64 per cent and 67 per cent respectively stated that they thought released time was a good idea, only 23 per cent and 26 per cent respectively were in favor of using public school buildings for this purpose, and 18 per cent and 14 per cent respectively were opposed. On the other hand, in the South Atlantic and East South Central regions where only 52 per cent and 43 per cent respectively believed released time was a good idea, 31 per cent and 28 per cent respectively were in favor of using public school buildings, and only 8 per cent and 6 per cent respectively were opposed.

Our investigation of attitudes toward the use of public school buildings for religious purposes naturally suggested the study of a related question, tax exemption of church property. Although there is no established church in this country and religious bodies are treated as voluntary associations of private citizens before the law, it has been customary not to tax church property used for religious purposes. Such properties, together with those used by charitable and educational institutions, have been tax exempt on the theory that they are making a notable contribution to the common good. Inasmuch as these properties have reached sizable proportions in some communities, considerable discussion has developed in recent years concerning the advisability of taxing them.[7] In a sense, this tax exempt status represents an indirect government subsidy to organized religious bodies, and judging from some of the literature on the subject, there are those who feel that this practice should be discontinued.

What is the attitude of the American people on this matter? In order to survey their opinions we asked the following question: "Most states don't tax property owned by church groups. Do you think church property used for religious purposes should be taxed or not?" Roughly four out of five (81 per cent) adult Americans felt that it should not be taxed. Twelve per cent were in favor, and 7 per cent stated that they were undecided. With the exception of the Jewish group, which had a relatively high percentage that was undecided (13 per cent), and the non-preference group (23 per cent opposed and 12 per cent undecided), there was striking agreement among all religious divisions on this issue.

The same uniformity of opinion was manifested by members of the various educational, occupational, and income classes. One exception that appears difficult to explain was the difference in attitude manifested by people with 1–3 years of college and college graduates. Whereas 15 per cent of college graduates were for taxation and only 76 per cent were opposed, only 9 per cent of the 1–3 years of college category were for taxation, and 86 per cent were opposed. In general, our study shows that we are dealing here with a rather universally accepted, firm conviction that church property used for religious purposes should not be taxed.

A closely related question is the advisability of taxing church properties that bring profit to an organized religious group. Some church bodies have acquired ownership of considerable property not used specifically for religious purposes. Although the rent or profit from the use of such property is employed for religious purposes, the property itself is used for purposes that compete with those of property owned by taxpayers. In other words, tax exemption appears in this instance as a direct concession to religious bodies on the hypothesis that whatever profits accrue will be used for religious purposes and will consequently benefit the common good. Thus the basis for tax exemption is the same in both cases, and the present issue raises the question of the extent to which this indirect assistance to religious organizations should be given. Further, it should be recalled that since charitable and educational institutions benefit by a similar exemption, it is highly probable that public attitudes toward the taxation of church property are formed with these wider implications in mind.

How do people feel about such tax exemptions? The question was asked: "Do you think church property which brings rent or profit to the church should be taxed, or not?" Almost half (49 per cent) thought that it should; 41 per cent were opposed; and one out of ten was undecided. There were some differences of opinion among the major religious divisions. Forty-four per cent of the Roman Catholic group thought that it should; 46 per cent were opposed; and 10 per cent were undecided. One half of the Protestant total was in favor; 41 per cent were opposed; and 9 per cent were undecided. Among members of the Jewish group, 57 per cent were in favor; 30 per cent were opposed; and 13 per cent were undecided. Of those who had some other or no religious preference, 63 per cent were in favor; 24 per cent were opposed; and 13 per cent were undecided.

Among the various Protestant groups, members of the Baptist (44 per cent) and Methodist (47 per cent) groups were least favorably inclined toward taxation and most in favor were members of "other" denominations (56 per cent). The percentages in favor for the other Protestant denominations were: Episcopal and Congregational, 54 per cent; Lutheran and Presbyterian, 53 per cent.

There was some relationship between formal educational status and attitudes toward taxation. Only 43 per cent of the people with a grade school education or less were in favor of it, while 53 per cent of high school graduates and 62 per cent of college graduates thought such property should be taxed. Sixty-one per cent of the professional, and 55 per cent of the proprietor or manager classes were in favor, while only 45 per cent of the service and manual worker classes shared this view. The same pattern was revealed among the various income classes. Fifty-five per cent of the upper, 52 per cent of the middle, and only 42 per cent of the lower income classes felt that such property should be taxed.

In general, there was a much greater diversity of attitudes on this issue than on the taxation of church property used for religious purposes. Approximately half the people felt that if church organizations were going to compete with other enterprisers in the economic field, they should pay taxes on property used in this way. On the other hand, more than four out of five believed that church property used for religious purposes should be tax exempt. As we have noted, this whole problem is closely related to the tax status of properties owned by educational and charitable institutions.

The political process in any society clearly involves moral issues of no little significance to organized religion. Because there is no established church, the age-old relationship between religion and state, church and political rulers, has never existed in America. At least in theory, organized religious bodies, as such, are supposed to remain outside of politics. In practice, of course, they have not done so whenever they felt that their particular interests were obviously at stake. The traditional assumption seems to be that religion should affect political life indirectly by elevating the moral standards and practices of men. Direct intervention is not considered part of the "American way" of life. Religious leaders in particular are not supposed to use their influence in swaying the minds of their co-religionists on political issues.[8]

What is the attitude of the American people in regard to the role of clergymen in political affairs? We asked the following question: "Do you think it is ever right for clergymen to discuss political candidates or issues from the pulpit?" A little more than one out of five (22 per cent) thought it was all right; 70 per cent did not; and 8 per cent were undecided. The major religious groups revealed somewhat different attitudes on this issue. Among the Roman Catholic group, 18 per cent felt it was all right; 72 per cent did not; and 10 per cent were undecided. Twenty-three per cent of the total Protestant group believed that it was all right; 69 per cent did not; and 8 per cent were undecided. Members of the Jewish group were even less opposed; 27 per cent thought it was all right; 66 per cent did not; and 7 per cent were undecided. Among the group with some other or no religious preference, only 19 per cent felt it was all right; 70 per cent did not; and 11 per cent were undecided.

Among the various Protestant bodies, members of the Presbyterian and Episcopal groups were most in favor of such action (30 per cent and 28 per cent respectively). Members of the other Protestant bodies registered attitudes quite similar to the national average. There was a close relationship between educational status and attitudes on this point. People with the most formal education were more favorably inclined toward such discussions, the range running from 19 per cent for those with a grade school education or less to 43 per cent for college graduates. A similar pattern was revealed among the occupational and income classes. People with a higher status were more inclined to favor such discussion. For example, 33 per cent of the professional, but only 19 per cent of the manual worker classes were in favor. Following a similar pattern, 27 per cent of the upper income bracket were in favor, as opposed to 20 per cent of the lower income class. The tradition of excluding political discussions from the pulpit appeared to be strongest in the New England region where only 12 per cent were in favor and 83 per cent were opposed. A somewhat similar attitude was manifested in the East South Central region where only 17 per cent were in favor and 73 per cent were opposed. On the other hand, 35 per cent of the people in the Mountain region and 27 per cent in the West South Central favored such discussions.

Although differences of opinion were found to exist among various groups, a solid core of well over two-thirds of the American people stated that they thought it was not right for clergymen to discuss political candidates or issues from the pulpit. Some might interpret this as another indication of the separation between religion and life, yet such an attitude more probably reflects concern for the dignity of the pulpit. American political campaigns are not particularly noted for their dignified oratory or by their respect for the truth. Furthermore, clergymen at church services have a "captive" audience and most Americans resent having to listen to political oratory not of their own choosing.

The statement is sometimes made that the churches do not understand the practical problems facing man in the modern world. The term *church* in this context usually stands for the clergymen in the local congregations. There are several latent assumptions in this accusation. First, it may imply that because clergymen do not have to engage in the competitive struggles characteristic of modern industrialized urban society, they do not understand the problems of the "man in the street." Second, it may imply that through their training clergymen have become imbued with a set of principles and ideals applicable to a former age but scarcely practicable in the modern world. Finally, it may imply that clergymen are failing to interpret the rapidly changing social scene in terms of spiritual or transcendental values. Entire areas of modern life have been allowed to develop without benefit of religion, almost as if they were by their very nature not amenable to a spiritual interpretation.

On the other hand, when people say that their clerygmen are understanding, they may mean no more than that their clergymen are sympathetic and not too critical in judging human weaknesses. Particularly in a culture that stresses activity and optimistically cherishes hope in inevitable progress, an understanding clergy may signify only that religious leaders have learned to swim with the tide. In this context, it does not appear wholly by chance that some of our most popular religious writers have soft-pedaled doctrinal principles and stressed "peace of mind." They urge acceptance, adjustment, and adaptation, while failing to point out that such terms are empty and meaningless outside a framework of ultimate values to which they can be referred. In the words of the modern song, some modern religious leaders appear to be offering "all this, and heaven too!"

Do the American people feel that their clergymen are "understanding?" We asked the following question. "How would you rate the clergyman in charge of your own local congregation on his ability to understand your practical problems—would you say he is very understanding, fairly understanding, or not very understanding?" This question was asked only of respondents who stated that they were church members. In general, local clergymen rated very well with the members of their congregations. Over two-thirds (68 per cent) found them very understanding, one out of five (21 per cent) thought they were fairly understanding, only 3 per cent said they were not very understanding, and 8 per cent offered no opinion.

The clergy were rated rather uniformly high by the members

of all religious groups. For example, among the Roman Catholics, 72 per cent found them very understanding; 21 per cent, fairly understanding; 2 per cent, not very understanding; and 5 per cent were undecided. Among the Protestant bodies, the corresponding percentages were: 67, 21, 3 and 9 per cent respectively; and among those with some other or no religious preference, 66, 17, 0 and 17 per cent respectively. A similar pattern appeared among the various Protestant denominations; although there were some differences in rating between "very understanding" and "fairly understanding," in no group were there more than 4 per cent who found their clergymen not very understanding.

A similar high rating was general among the various educational, occupational and income classes. All registered a vote of approval. Indeed, only among the members of the professional and farming classes did the percentages who found their local clergymen not very understanding reach 5 per cent. Perhaps our findings should not come as a surprise. In the first place, only the 73 per cent of the people who professed to be church members were asked to rate their clergy. This was a logical step since non-members were hardly in a position to pass judgment in this matter. Nevertheless, it is possible that some non-members were no longer members because they had found their local clergymen not very understanding. Further, when there are many sects and denominations existing in the same society, there is a tendency for church members to identify their clergymen with their church, so that a question concerning the adequacy of their clergymen is reduced to a question of the adequacy of their church.

Our findings do not make clear what the term *understanding* may mean to church members. As we have suggested, it may mean that clergymen are offering a spiritually meaningful interpretation of life to the members of their congregation, or it may mean that they are telling people what they wish to hear. There are some indications in our study that it is primarily the latter, but an adequate answer to this question cannot be given on the basis of the present findings.

Preaching, in one form or another, has always constituted a recognized element of church services among organized religious groups in the Western world. Although the function of sermons varies considerably among different denominations, particularly among the Protestant groups the sermon has long been regarded as an essential part of church services. The average church member expects instruction, motivation, and encouragement from the sermons that he hears. To be sure, he may no longer possess the patient endurance in this regard that his ancestors are said to have displayed, but it is a well-known fact that a good sermon can still command the attention of large audiences. Whether the quality of contemporary preaching can compare with that of the past is a highly debatable question. If one may judge from the title of Sunday sermons, it seems clear that the content of sermons has tended to shift from emphasis on Scripture and dogma to discussion of more "practical" issues. This is in line with the change in the climate of religious opinion which we have indicated above.

How do church members rate contemporary sermons? The question was asked: "Do you think his sermons (the clergyman in charge of your own local congregation) in general are excellent, good, fair, or poor?" Clergymen should receive some consolation from our findings. Forty per cent of church members thought that their local clergyman's sermons were excellent; 43 per cent rated them good; 12 per cent said they were fair; only 1 per cent judged them to be poor; and 4 per cent modestly offered no opinion. If the percentages judging ser-

mons excellent or good are lumped together, only slight differences of opinion appear among the members of the major
religious divisions as follows: Protestant total, 82 per cent;
Roman Catholic, 85 per cent; Jewish, 86 per cent. A similar
pattern of general approval appeared among the various
Protestant bodies as follows: Methodist, 78 per cent; Baptist,
80 per cent; "other" denominations, 82 per cent; Lutheran, 84
per cent; Presbyterian and Episcopal, 85 per cent; and Congregational, 90 per cent.

A similar impression is received from a study of the various
educational, occupational, and income classes. Four-fifths or
more judged sermons excellent or good. Deviating somewhat
from this general pattern were college graduates (78 per cent),
members of the professional class (76 per cent), and farmers
(76 per cent). As a whole, church members appear well satisfied with the sermons that they hear, and the fact that well
under one out of five rates contemporary sermons as only fair
or poor suggests that modern clergymen have not lost the
ancient art of preaching.

There is no established church in America, and no organized
religious group that enjoys state support. This is a characteristic of the American way in which we take particular pride.
Each denomination is free to develop and expand, but it must
finance its own endeavors.[9] The excellent church structures
that are found in every section of the country give ample testi-
mony to the continued generosity of the American people in
this regard and church members may take justifiable pride in
their religious institutions. Foreign observers sometimes infer
that Americans tend to stress structure rather than spirit in
their religious striving, yet no unbiased judge can fail to pay
tribute to the effort and sacrifice most Americans are willing to
make in matters that concern their churches. At the same time,

in a society dominated by the spirit of competition, it would be unrealistic to suppose that no emulation has manifested itself in the construction of church buildings. Religious groups, like individuals, may often strive to "keep up with the Joneses."

Under these circumstances, it is reasonable to inquire how church members feel about this sector of church activity. In our survey, we asked: "Do you think your local church is too concerned with money matters, or not?" Three out of four church members felt that it was not too concerned; 17 per cent thought that it was; and 8 per cent offered no opinion. Considering the relatively large expenditures involved in the establishment and maintenance of the average church unit, our findings represent a reassuring vote of confidence and approval by church members.

There were some differences of opinion among the major religious divisions. Members of the Jewish group registered the greatest satisfaction with the current situation. Only one out of ten felt that there was too much concern; and 8 per cent were undecided. The attitude of the Roman Catholic group was very similar, the corresponding percentages being 11, 81, and 8 per cent respectively. Members of the Protestant group were less satisfied. Nineteen per cent felt that their local church was too concerned with money matters; 74 per cent thought that it was not; and 7 per cent were undecided.

Among the various Protestant bodies, the proportion who thought that the church was too concerned with money matters ranged as follows: Methodist, 25 per cent; Baptist, 20 per cent; Presbyterian, 19 per cent; Lutheran, 18 per cent; Episcopal, 14 per cent; Congregational and "other" denominations, 13 per cent. There was a close relationship between formal educational status and attitudes on this issue. Only 14 per cent with a grade school education or less thought that the church was too concerned with money matters, while 20 per cent of college graduates thought so. Members of the professional class were similar to college graduates on this point, but the proprietor or manager class took a more businesslike view, for only 14 per cent stated that too much concern with money matters was shown by the local church. Members of the upper and lower income classes shared similar views on this point (15 per cent), while the middle class registered somewhat less satisfaction (18 per cent).

Our survey made some effort to get at the real sources of the dissatisfaction that had been expressed concerning finances. The 17 per cent of church members who stated that they thought their local church was too concerned with money matters were asked: "In what way does this show up that you especially dislike?" About one third of the dissatisfied group stated that the church or clergymen were always asking for money. Roughly one-eighth felt that there was more interest in money than in spiritual values, and approximately the same proportion complained that there was always some project that kept the church in debt. The remainder cited extravagance in church management or in clergymen's personal spending, too many collections—"they interfere with the services," constant requests for money made it hard on the poor, and so forth. In general, therefore, dissatisfaction appeared to stem from many different sources, but it is not clear whether we are dealing with rationalizations or well-reasoned convictions.

To recapitulate briefly, it appears from our findings that the American people are rather generally well satisfied with the religious *status quo* relating to the teaching, preaching, counseling, and financing functions of the churches. On the other hand, current or proposed programs for settling the vexing problem of the relationship between religion and education continues to divide them sharply. Although the majority did not seem to be directly opposed to private religious or parochial schools, almost half felt that public funds should not be used to supply free transportation or books to private school children, and three out of five were opposed to the use of public taxes for the support of such schools. Released time for religious instruction was received more favorably, however, inasmuch as nearly four fifths approved, and less than one fourth of these were opposed to the use of public school buildings for such programs.

As we have suggested, a variety of fears, misgivings, and convictions are involved in the American people's attitudes concerning the proper relationship between religion and education. The majority hold religion in high esteem and desire religious instruction for their children, but in a pluralistic society many are unwilling to favor any program of public support that might prove advantageous to other religious groups, though they are becoming increasingly aware that a public school system designed to train all youth tends to develop secular rather than neutral outlooks. The growing interest in religious schools, as well as current attempts to develop various types of religious orientation courses for the public schools, indicates that some religious leaders have recognized this tendency and desire to remedy it. According to our findings, they probably will receive considerable support from a good proportion of the American public, with the exception of people in the upper socio-economic class as measured by income, occupation, and formal education. This latter group include a relatively large percentage apparently opposed to any attempts to integrate religion and education.

Notes

1. See "Religious and Education," by Rolfe Lanier Hunt in *The Annals, op. cit.,* pp. 89–100.

2. See R. Freeman Butts and Lawrence A. Cremin, *A History of Education in American Culture,* New York: Holt, Rinehart and Winston, 1953).

3. See "Current Trends in Religion—A Summary," by Richard D. Lambert in *The Annals, op. cit.,* pp. 150–51.

4. For a description of how the controversy takes shape in real situations, see Theodore Powell, *The School Bus Law: A Case Study in Education, Religion, and Politics* (Middletown, Conn.: Wesleyan University Press, 1960).

5. For a discussion of the legal aspects of this question, see "Religion and Law in America," by Wilbur G. Katz in *Religious Perspectives in American Culture, op. cit.,* pp. 54–68.

6. According to Hunt (cf. note 1), the Church of Jesus Christ Latter-Day Saints (Mormon) was the first to become active in this approach.

7. The California electorate recently defeated a threat to withdraw tax exemption from the Catholic schools.

8. For a good summary of the current situation, see "Religion and Politics," by Luke Ebersole in *The Annals, op. cit.,* pp. 101–111.

9. See, "Financing the Local Church," by William H. Leach in *The Annals, op. cit.,* pp. 70–79.

CHAPTER **6** Patterns of Change

IN analyzing the religious beliefs, practices, and attitudes of the American people as revealed in our findings, we discovered that the great majority expressed a preference for one of the three major traditional faiths, Protestant, Catholic, or Jewish, while nearly three out of four professed to be active church members, and somewhat over two thirds stated that they had attended Sunday or Sabbath church services during the previous three months. According to church historians, these figures indicate the high point of religious activity in this country and though opinions may differ concerning the character and significance of such activity, there can be little doubt that religion has become relatively popular in mid-twentieth century America.

But organized religion in our country is represented by a great variety of cults, sects, denominations, and churches, so that an attempt to evaluate the contemporary religious revival necessarily raises several further questions. Are people merely becoming more active participants in the religion of their youth? Is it the conversion of the previously "unchurched" that is swelling religious statistics? Are people shifting from one denomination to another? In other words, how stable are their religious preferences? We may safely assume that when a variety of competing religious groups co-exist, convert-making or proselytizing will be fairly common. What do we know about this process in America?

In the first place, it should be recalled that about 5 per cent of the people stated that they had no religious preference, so that they apparently remained unaffected by the present religious revival. Since many in this category characterized themselves as Protestants but added that they had no denominational preference, the term *Protestant*, as used in this context, probably meant little more than that they did not wish to be identified with the Roman Catholic or Jewish groups. We may justly regard them as the presently "unchurched," for their religious participation had not proceeded to the point of formulating a religious preference.

Were these people "fallen-aways," or had they always been without formal religion? A little over one out of six stated that they had been raised in no religious group while the remainder were "fallen-aways." For example, somewhat over 17 per cent had been raised as Baptists, almost 16 per cent as Methodists, almost 14 per cent as Episcopalians, almost 12 per cent as Roman Catholics, a little less than 8 per cent as Lutherans, a little less than 6 per cent as Jewish, only 2 per cent as Presbyterians, and nearly 10 per cent as "other" Protestants. Thus the majority of the "unchurched" represent "converts in reverse." Their present attitude indicates that people may not only abandon the practice of the religion in which they were trained without adopting another but may lose all sense of identification with it. The fact that relatively few are found in this category, however, suggests that most people tend to identify themselves with a definite denominational group long after they have ceased active participation in its activities.

If people no longer identify themselves with the religious denomination in which they were trained, it generally means that they have shifted their preference to another group.[1] How widespread is this change in denomination? Almost four out of five (79 per cent) stated that they had always belonged to the same denomination. There were considerable differences among the major religious divisions in this regard. Greatest stability was revealed by the Jewish group in which 96 per cent stated that they had always been members. Ninety per cent of the Roman Catholic, and 74 per cent of the total Protestant groups had never shifted their affiliation. The various Protestant bodies differed somewhat in stability of membership as follows: Baptist, 82 per cent; Lutheran, 80 per cent; Methodist, 78 per cent; Presbyterian, Episcopal, and Congregational, 73 per cent; and "other" denominations, 61 per cent. In other words, one out of every four Protestants, and one out of every ten Roman Catholics you meet is a "convert," that is, he did not always hold the religious preference he now professes.

From what religious backgrounds had the converts come? The majority came from other denominations rather than from the "unchurched." For example, among the Jewish group, 1 per cent had been Roman Catholics; 1 per cent were reconverts (Jewish members who had left the group, joined some other denomination, and then reverted to the group); 1 per cent, "other" denominations; and 1 per cent, "unchurched." In the Roman Catholic group, 2 per cent had been Methodist; the Baptist, Lutheran, Presbyterian, and Episcopal groups had each contributed 1 per cent; 2 per cent had belonged to "other" denominations; and 2 per cent were from the "unchurched."

Among the Baptist group, 6 per cent had been Methodist; the Roman Catholic, Lutheran, Presbyterian, and Episcopal groups had each contributed 1 per cent; 1 per cent were reconverts; 4 per cent had belonged to "other" denominations; and 3 per cent were from the "unchurched." In the Methodist group, 6 per cent had been Baptists; 3 per cent had been Presbyterians; the Roman Catholic and Lutheran groups had contributed 2 per cent each; the Episcopal and Congregational groups, 1 per cent each; 1 per cent were reconverts; 4 per cent had belonged to "other" denominations; and 2 per cent were from the "unchurched." Among members of the Lutheran group, 4 per cent had been Roman Catholics, the Methodist and Presbyterian groups had contributed 3 per cent each; 2 per cent had been Baptists; 2 per cent were reconverts; 4 per cent, from "other" denominations; and 1 per cent from the "unchurched."

Converts to the Presbyterian group revealed the following backgrounds: Methodist, 7 per cent; Baptist, 4 per cent; Lutheran, 2 per cent; Roman Catholic and Congregational, 1 per cent each; reconverts, 1 per cent; "other" denominations, 8 per cent; and "unchurched," 3 per cent. The religious backgrounds of Episcopalian converts were: Methodists, 7 per cent; Baptist, 5 per cent; Presbyterian, 3 per cent; Congregational, 2 per cent; Roman Catholic, 1 per cent; "other" denominations, 5 per cent; and "unchurched," 1 per cent. The religious backgrounds of converts to the Congregational group were: Methodist, 7 per cent; Baptist and Presbyterian, 2 per cent; "other" denominations, 7 per cent; and "unchurched," 9 per cent. Finally, the "other" denominations drew their converts from the following: Methodist, 9 per cent; Baptist and Lutheran, 4 per cent each; Roman Catholic, 3 per cent; Presbyterian and Episcopal, 2 per cent each; Congregational, 1 per cent, "other" denominations, 9 per cent; and "unchurched," 5 per cent.

These figures indicate that the process of changing one's religious affiliation is fairly widespread in America. With the exception of the Jewish group and to some degree, the Roman Catholic, converts are exchanged rather uniformly by all denominations. Why do people change denominations? The 21 per cent who had shifted their preferences gave the following reasons. Approximately 28 per cent changed in order to adopt the religion of their marriage partner. Roughly one out of five had moved to a community where their denomination had no church, and another church was more convenient. About 14 per cent changed because they preferred the religious beliefs of another church. In about one out of ten cases, relatives, children, and friends had influenced their choice. The remainder gave various reasons such as loss of satisfaction with religious beliefs of former church, disagreeable experience with clergyman, and so forth.

To the extent that these are the real reasons which motivated the change, this information throws a great deal of light on the meaning of religion in America. Although there is no basis for doubting the sincerity of these "conversions," it is interesting to note that the majority of them were not prompted by a change in basic religious convictions.[2] Apparently, there is some evidence for the statement that a good many Americans believe "one religion is just about as good as another." This attitude in regard to each other appears prevalent among the members of the various Protestant bodies, in which a large percentage of the conversions took place.

We gain some additional information concerning this process of denominational change by investigating the religious preferences of the families in which our respondents' parents were raised. It seems safe to assume that the parents were trained in the denominational faith to which their families belonged. Consequently, if the present religious preferences of our respondents differs from that in which their parents were trained, we can conclude either that their parents have abandoned the religion of their youth, or that our respondents are not following the religion of their parents. In either case, we have some indication of the religious stability of families through two generations.

Since there was some possibility that the religious background of the respondent's mother and father differed, we obtained information on each. Our first question, therefore, was: "What religion or denomination was your mother's family?" Members of the Jewish group revealed the greatest stability, inasmuch as 89 per cent stated that the family background of their mother had been Jewish. Members of the Roman Catholic group were a close second, with 83 per cent reporting that the religious background of their mother's family had been Roman Catholic. The corresponding percentages for the major Protestant groups were as follows: Baptist, 62 per cent; Lutheran, 55 per cent; Methodist, 51 per cent; Presbyterian, 50 per cent; Episcopal, 46 per cent; and Congregational, 38 per cent.

In response to the question: "What religion or denomination was your father's family?" we obtained almost similar results. Among the Jewish respondents, 88 per cent stated that their father's family background had been Jewish, while among the members of the Roman Catholic group, 84 per cent stated that their father's family background had been Roman Catholic. The corresponding percentages for the major Protestant groups were as follows: Baptist, 67 per cent; Lutheran, 58 per cent;

Methodist, 51 per cent; Presbyterian, 47 per cent; Episcopal, 45 per cent; and Congregational, 38 per cent.

These figures indicate the widespread changes in religious preferences that have taken place within two generations. Almost all the respondents who expressed a preference for the Jewish faith stated that the family background of their parents was Jewish or non-religious (8 per cent for the latter), and with the exception of roughly one out of seven, a similar pattern of family backgrounds was revealed by Roman Catholics. On the other hand, changes in denominational preferences among members of the major Protestant groups were much more extensive, so that our findings suggest a refinement of the statement that most Americans believe "one religion is about as good as another." It would probably be closer to the truth to state that a good percentage of American Protestants believe that "one denomination is about as good as another."

It should be possible to form some estimate of the general direction that changes in religious preferences may take by finding out how people rate religious groups other than their own. Although, as we have seen, there are many different factors that apparently motivate people to shift their denominational preferences, changes are most likely to occur among groups that mutually esteem each other. Thus if the situation calls for a change, it is reasonable to assume that one may join the group that rates next highest in preference. Of course there is the further possibility that in a society characterized by high mobility and relatively free interaction, people's religious preferences may undergo change. Religious stereotypes still exist, and in our country there are not lacking cheap demagogues to exploit them, yet they are sometimes dispelled once people get to know each other. Cupid frequently plays an important initial role in this process, although through some strange inconsistency in man, people may still cling to their stereotypes by regarding the person they love as an exception to the general rule.[3]

How do members of the major religious denominations rate other religious groups? We asked them the question: "Which denomination (next to your own) do you like best?" Forty-eight per cent named one of the Protestant bodies; 4 per cent, the Roman Catholic; 1 per cent, the Jewish; 7 per cent, one of the various other groups; and 40 per cent stated that they had no opinion. Among the Protestant groups chosen most frequently were: Methodist (13 per cent), Presbyterian and Baptist (8 per cent each), Lutheran and Episcopal (4 per cent each) and Congregational (1 per cent).

The preferences expressed by the major religious groups differed a great deal. In the first place, a large portion of the Jewish and Roman Catholic groups (71 and 64 per cent respectively) replied that they had no opinion. It is probable that the members of these two groups had never given much thought to the possibility of belonging to a religious group other than their own. Our findings have shown that they display a degree of religious stability that contrasts rather sharply with other groups, so that their reluctance to give an opinion here may merely indicate their negative attitude toward changing their religious preferences. However, among members of the Jewish group who expressed an opinion, the highest preference (8 per cent) was given to Roman Catholics, while another 10 per cent named one of the many Protestant groups. Roman Catholics expressed a special preference for Lutherans and Episcopalians (7 per cent each).

On the other hand, between two-thirds and four-fifths of the Protestant membership expressed a definite preference, and their choice was generally another Protestant denomination.

The Roman Catholic and Jewish groups received relatively few choices, as did the various other (non-Christian) groups. The Methodist group was the most popular of the major Protestant denominations, receiving 17 per cent of the Protestant choices. Next in line of preference were the Presbyterian and Baptist groups (11 per cent each of the Protestant choices), followed by the Lutheran (4 per cent), the Episcopal (3 per cent), and the Congregational (2 per cent) groups. Several Protestant denominations expressed particularly high esteem for each other. For example, 33 per cent of the Baptists chose the Methodist group as the one they liked best next to their own. Approximately one-fourth (24 per cent) of the Presbyterian group expressed a similar preference. At the same time, 19 per cent of the Methodists chose the Baptist group as the one they preferred next after their own, and 17 per cent chose the Presbyterian.

The same pattern of preferences was revealed in answer to the question: "What denomination would you like least to belong to?" Twenty-eight per cent named the Roman Catholic group; roughly 20 per cent, one of the Protestant sects or denominations; 3 per cent, the Jewish group; 6 per cent, one of the non-Christian or non-Jewish religions; and 45 per cent gave no opinion. Among the Protestant sects most frequently mentioned were: Jehovah's Witnesses, Holy Rollers, Seventh Day Adventists, Church of God, and Holiness. The Baptist was the only one of the major Protestant denominations that was named with any frequency, receiving 2 per cent of the least preferred choices.

A review of the major religious divisions shows that again the members of the Jewish and Roman Catholic groups tended to express no opinion (72 and 66 per cent respectively.) Roughly two-thirds (65 per cent) of the total Protestant membership expressed an opinion, and of those who did, 60 per cent designated the Roman Catholic group as the one to which they would least like to belong. In other words, it seems clear that if members of the Protestant groups are going to shift their religious preferences, they will by-pass the Roman Catholic group and the Protestant sects, and change to one of the major Protestant denominations. Although the Jewish group received little mention as the least preferred denomination, short of intermarriage, there will probably continue to be relatively few who shift their preference to it, since it represents a combination of both ethnic and religious characteristics.

Church historians have stated that because the American people have no established religion, they have no concept of a universal church and consequently take religious pluralism very much for granted. The contention of the historians may be correct. With the exception of Roman Catholics among the Christian faiths, the various religious denominations in America may not think of themselves as a universal church; they have no historical precedent for it; the majority of them were originally founded as dissident sects, and there is little in their doctrinal beliefs to foster the growth of such a concept. As opposed to Roman Catholics, therefore, the various Protestant denominations tend to regard themselves primarily as historically diversified expressions or parts of a broader spiritual unity known as Christianity.

On the other hand, it would be erroneous to conclude that lack of this concept of universality precludes zeal for convert-making among church members. As long as people believe that religion represents a value, and their specific set of religious beliefs a special type of value, they will logically endeavor to bring outsiders to an acceptance of their church. In America, their zeal will be extended not only to the 27 per cent who do not actively participate in any church group, but also to the members of other denominations whom they may believe to be in partial or total error. Furthermore, since it is generally conceded that similarity of faiths makes for harmony in marriage, and our modern dating customs tend to facilitate courthip between the members of various religious denominations, marriage becomes the occasion for a considerable amount of convert-making.[4]

There are several reasons why a study of religion should be interested in convert-making. First, and most obviously, it indicates the degree of religious conviction and zeal that church members possess. Second, the ease with which conversions from one denomination to another are made throws some light on doctrinal differences that are thought to exist between these groups. Third, failure to work for the conversion of others may result from one of two attitudes. People may believe that "one religion is just as good as another," and consequently there is little point in convert-making; or they may be overly conscious of their position as a cultural minority, and remembering past bigotry and discrimination, they may be quite content to "live and let live" and to "let sleeping dogs lie." In a given instance, it may not always be easy to uncover the factors at work, though an overall view of the convert-making activities of American church members will at least have the merit of offering fertile grounds for speculation.

In our survey, we asked the following questions: "Have you ever tried to get anyone to join your religious group?" "Did you ever succeed in getting anyone to join?" Approximately half (51 per cent) stated that they had never tried their hand at convert-making. Of the 49 per cent who had tried, 35 per cent had succeeded, 10 per cent had not, and 4 per cent did not know whether they had succeeded or not. Table 17 shows the convert-making activities of the different religious groups. It will be noted at once that members of the Jewish (73 per cent), Roman Catholic (72 per cent), and Congregational (68 per cent) groups were least inclined to engage in convert-making.

Members of the Baptist (67 per cent), "other" denominations (61 per cent), Presbyterian (59 per cent), and Methodist (56 per cent) groups were relatively active. Greatest success in convert-making was achieved by members of the Presbyterian (52 per cent) and Baptist (50 per cent) groups. Members of the Episcopal group (45 per cent) and of "other" denominations (44 per cent) also turned in good scores. Least successful were members of the Roman Catholic (17 per cent), Congregational (19 per cent), and Jewish (24 per cent) groups.

College graduates (53 per cent) were somewhat more zealous than high school graduates (47 per cent) or people with a grade school education (51 per cent). Members of the professional class (53 per cent) were more active than proprietors or managers (47 per cent), but of all the occupational classes, farmers (63 per cent) were by far the most zealous in this regard. If one wishes to steer clear of convert-making zeal, our findings suggest settling in the New England region. Here only 23 per cent stated that they had tried convert-making. On the other hand, they generally got their man, for only 3 per cent admitted that they had not succeeded. Greatest activity was shown in the South Atlantic region where 64 per cent had made the attempt. They were not quite as proficient as their New England cousins, however, since 20 per cent admitted that they had either failed or did not know if they had succeeded.

What is the significance of this information on convert-

TABLE 17. *Convert-Making Activities of Active Church Members*

MAJOR GROUPS	RESULTS OF ATTEMPTS TO CONVERT			Never tried to get any-one to join
	Succeeded	Did not Succeed	Don't know if Successful	
Roman Catholic	17	9	2	72
Protestant Total	43	10	6	41
Baptist	50	10	7	33
Methodist	39	8	9	44
Lutheran	28	19	2	51
Presbyterian	52	5	2	41
Episcopal	45	6	2	47
Congregational	19	10	3	68
Other	44	11	6	39
Jewish	24	3	0	73

making? We can only speculate on its implications. It is probable that the failure of the Jewish and Roman Catholic groups to take a more active part in convert-making is associated with the relative concentration and isolation of a considerable portion of their membership, as well as with the definite differences in doctrinal belief that exist between them and the Protestant groups. The successful activity reported by several of the major Protestant denominations lends itself to various interpretations. First, it suggests that there exists a considerable amount of zeal for convert-making among the members of such groups. Second, it appears to be a further indication that members of the Protestant total pass rather easily from one Protestant denomination to another. Finally, since church historians tell us that the present population includes the highest percentage of church members in the history of the country, this success in convert-making may imply that a good percentage of non-active church members are being attracted to these denominations by the zeal of their members.

This chapter has presented our findings on changes in religious preference and the process of convert-making. We called attention to the fact that roughly 5 per cent of the adult population professed no religious preference. However, only 16 per cent of this group had been raised without any religious training. Almost four out of five of the total population stated that they had always belonged to the same denomination. The Jewish and Roman Catholic group revealed the greatest stability in this regard. With the exception of these two groups, converts were exchanged rather uniformly by all denominations.

By studying the religious preferences of the families in which our respondent's parents were raised, we were able to estimate the religious stability of families through two generations. Our findings indicate that, with the exception of the Jewish and

Roman Catholic groups, the process of changing one's religious affiliation is widespread in America. Apparently, the belief that "one denomination is about as good as another's" is rather generally accepted by members of the Protestant groups.

Further information on this process of change was gathered by studying the scale of denominational preferences. A good proportion of the Jewish and Roman Catholic groups expressed no opinion, suggesting that they had probably given little thought to the matter. The second choice among members of the Protestant groups was generally another major Protestant denomination. Responses to the question concerning which denomination was least preferred revealed a similar pattern. Members of the Jewish and Roman Catholic groups tended to express no opinion. Approximately 60 per cent of the Protestant membership who expressed an opinion placed the Roman Catholic group at the bottom of their list of preferences. A good percentage also mentioned the various Protestant sects in this connection. In other words, when Protestants contemplate a change in religion, they tend to think of one of the major Protestant denominations as the next best choice and the Roman Catholic group or one of the various Protestant sects as the last choice.

Finally, about half the people stated that at one time or another they had tried to get someone to join their religious group. Thirty-five per cent reported that their convert-making efforts had been crowned with success. With the exception of the Congregational group, Protestant denominations were most active in getting others to join their religious group. Almost three-fourths of the Jewish and Roman Catholic groups had not attempted to do so. Looking toward the future, it seems safe to predict that if the present zeal for convert-making continues, the percentage of non-active church members in this country will continue to decrease.

Notes

1. It is generally assumed that transfer of membership is relatively uncommon. See "Social Forces Involved in Group Identification or Withdrawal," by J. Milton Yinger in *Daedalus* (Spring 1961), pp. 247–62. Although he quotes a study of Lenski in support of this thesis, we do not draw the same conclusion from Lenski's published study on Detroit. See Gerhard Lenski, *The Religious Factor* (New York: Doubleday & Company, 1961), pp. 48–50.

2. In our study of Catholic marriage patterns, we found that marriages involving a convert tended to resemble mixed marriages. See *The American Catholic Family*, pp. 260–261.

3. See Robert M. MacIver, *The More Perfect Union* (New York: The Macmillan Company, 1948), pp. 186–207.

4. See *The American Catholic Family*, *op. cit.*, pp. 148–69, for an evaluation of studies on mixed marriage.

CHAPTER 7

Interfaith Attitudes

RELIGIOUS preferences of adult Americans tend to fall into one of the three major divisions that constitute the bulk of formal religious expression in this country. Although we discovered considerable differences in beliefs, practices, and attitudes among the members of these three large religious communities, it is clear that the average American thinks of the major faiths as more or less well-defined religious groups and considers it meaningful to classify people as either Protestants, Catholics, or Jews. This popular classification obviously cloaks some profound doctrinal and practical differences. Among the Protestants, there are groups springing from Calvinist, Anabaptist, Lutheran, Anglican, and other origins. The Jewish group may be divided into Orthodox, Reformed, Conservative, and others. Although the Roman Catholic group is characterized by doctrinal uniformity, its membership, like that of other religious bodies, may well be divided into "practicing" and "nonpracticing" adherents.

Despite such real differences, the broad classification of Protestant, Catholic, and Jew remains operative in the popular mind. Individuals or groups within these major religious communities may openly acknowledge their differences, but in regard to the outgroups, they recognize a mutual solidarity, a "consciousnes of kind," setting them apart as a distinct religious community. We are not interested here in the doctrinal, historical, and even ethnic factors that have entered into the shaping of this mentality. The point we would make is that, notwithstanding their recognized individual and group differences, Americans tend to identify themselves with one of the three major religious communities when defining intergroup relationships; and this identification with one religious community leads them to look upon members of the other two communities as constituting distinct outgroups. Thus they tend to cherish stereotypes of their own group and of the others, and it is such stereotypes, however nondiscriminating and unrealistic they may be, that generally serve as the real basis for the comparative evaluations expressed by group members.

Whether true or false, therefore, such evaluations have practical consequences, inasmuch as the routine interaction of different group members is bound to be affected by them. On first meeting a member of one of the outgroups, one tends to see him in terms of a previously formulated stereotype. Unfortunately, as studies in the related field of race relations have shown, even when the new acquaintance does not conform to the stereotype, one frequently does not question the stereotype, but rather looks upon this individual as an exception from his group.[1] People may associate with outgroup members all their lives, so that through personal experience they should be capable of forming their own judgment about the group, yet the stereotypes persist. The Jews in Germany found it hard to believe that their very neighbors would ignore their personal experience and turn against them on the strength of a stereotype revived by Hitler. The Catholic minority in this country endured the same painful experience when, during the twenties, the viciously anti-Catholic Ku Klux Klan was able to count in its membership an estimated one fourth of the men in the United States eligible to join.

For this reason it is important to find out what members of the major religious divisions think about each other. At a time when we as a nation are earnestly striving to overcome our native provincialism or ethnocentrism and to grasp the significance of a community of nations, it would be a tragedy to imperil the basis of mutual understanding and toleration within our own country. Yet in recent years, several keen observers of the religious scene in America have professed to detect an increase of tension among the major faiths. Knowledge of what people think will not in itself reduce tensions, but it serves as a necessary first step in dealing with the problem. Understanding between groups is promoted by mutual trust and respect, but when such sentiments are lacking, it is relatively easy for the unscrupulous to whip up conflicts and tensions. The questions we are about to discuss were designed to uncover what the major religious groups really think and feel about each other.

The way people feel toward members of an outgroup is conditioned primarily by three factors. First, their personal experience, pleasant or unpleasant, in dealing with members of the outgroup is bound to influence their thinking. Second, they are affected by what they believe other members of their own group think about outgroup members. Third, their attitudes are shaped by what they believe outgroup members think about them and their group. The first factor represents a common tendency to generalize on the basis of a few cases. The second may be interpreted either as a type of "group-think" mentality or, with more subtle analysis, as a projection of one's own feelings on to that of one's group. The third is a reflection of what has been termed the "looking-glass self." If people think they are liked or disliked by members of the outgroup, they tend to react in the same manner.

Data concerning these three factors were gathered during the course of the interviews. People were asked to state what they really felt, rather than what they thought they should say. We shall present our findings in their logical order although for purposes of obtaining more spontaneous answers, a somewhat different sequence was followed during the interview. In gathering information on the first factor, the following question was asked: "Have you or your family ever had any unpleasant personal experience that might have made you dislike (here supply Protestants, Catholics, or Jews, depending on the interviewee's religious preference)?"

Among members of the Protestant group, 9 per cent stated that there had been such experiences when dealing with the Roman Catholic group; 89 per cent replied in the negative; and 2 per cent gave no response. At the same time, 8 per cent stated that there had been such experiences when dealing with the Jewish group; 90 per cent replied in the negative; and 2 per cent gave no response. Among members of the Roman Catholic group, 4 per cent reported such experiences when dealing with Protestants, and 96 per cent replied in the negative. In dealing with members of the Jewish group, 6 per cent reported such experiences; 92 per cent replied in the negative; and 2 per cent gave no response. Among members of the Jewish group, 7 per cent reported such experiences when dealing with Protestants; 90 per cent replied in the negative; and 3 per cent gave no response. In dealing with Roman Catholics, 11 per cent reported such experiences; 85 per cent replied in the negative; and 4 per cent gave no response.

Our findings suggest that cases of unpleasant personal experience involving members of different religious communities are relatively uncommon. People were asked to report any such incidents that had happened either to themselves or to members of their family, yet few found anything to report. Apparently, in the area of religion, as in that of politics, the American people have learned how to subordinate their differences to the task of living together without undue friction. Although feelings may run high and receive open expression within the group, interaction with members of the outgroup is generally carried on according to the commonly accepted norms of social conduct.

What types of unpleasant personal experience were reported? Of the 9 per cent of Protestants who had experienced such incidents with Catholics, almost one fourth stated that they had arisen over conflicts resulting from mixed marriage; almost one fourth from experiences with clergy, nuns, or Catholic institutions; roughly one tenth from arguments over religious doctrine or belief; another one tenth from unpleasant business dealings, and the remainder gave various other reasons. The 8 per cent of Protestants who reported unpleasant experiences with Jews gave the following reasons: over 60 per cent, unpleasant business dealings; one fourth, objectionable individual traits; and the remainder, various other factors.

The 4 per cent of Roman Catholics who mentioned unpleasant experiences with Protestants mentioned arguments over religion (25 per cent), discrimination (25 per cent), and various other reasons. Among the 6 per cent who recalled such incidents arising from their relationships with members of the Jewish group, two-thirds named unpleasant business dealings; one-sixth, objectionable individual traits; and the remainder, various other factors. The 7 per cent of the Jewish group who recalled unpleasant experiences with Protestants named being bullied or called names as a child (30 per cent), discrimination (57 per cent), and various other reasons. The 11 per cent who had experienced such unpleasant incidents with Catholics mentioned unpleasant business dealings (18 per cent), and being bullied or called names as a child (45 per cent), and various other factors.

We stated that people's attitudes toward an outgroup are affected by the thinking of their own group on this subject, or, at least, by what people think the attitudes of the ingroup are. The tendency to accept uncritically the opinions and attitudes of one's group is a normal human weakness. It provides an easy substitute for thinking and frequently serves as a convenient escape from the arduous task of living in conformity with one's basic moral principles. If the group fosters bigotry and ill-will or practices discrimination and exploitation, many members apparently see no contradiction between group conformity and the basic moral premises they profess to hold as individuals. Further, it should be noted that prejudiced persons sometimes rationalize their position by insisting that other members of the group share their attitudes. This attribution of their personal attitudes to their group bolsters up their own opinions and furnishes that sense of security which results from conformity with one's group.

How do members of the three major religious communities characterize the feelings of their group toward outgroup members? We asked: "Do you think there is much ill-feeling toward (here supply Protestants, Catholics, or Jews, depending on the interviewee's religious preference) among most people of your religious preference, or not?" Members of the Protestant group reported the greatest amount of ill-feeling toward outgroup members. In regard to Catholics, 24 per cent felt that there was much ill-feeling; 65 per cent replied in the negative; and 11 per cent stated that they did not know. In regard to Jews, 25 per cent felt there was much ill-feeling; 62 per cent replied in the negative; and 13 per cent said that they did not know.

Members of the Jewish and Roman Catholic groups reported somewhat less ill-feeling toward outgroups. In regard to Protestants, 11 per cent of the Roman Catholics felt that there was much ill-feeling in their own group; 83 per cent answered in the negative; and 6 per cent said they did not know. In regard to Jews, 21 per cent felt that there was much ill-feeling; 67 per cent replied in the negative; and 12 per cent stated they did not know. Among members of the Jewish group, 5 per cent felt that there was much ill-feeling toward Protestants; 81 per cent denied this; and 14 per cent said they did not know. In regard to Catholics, 15 per cent felt that there was much ill-feeling; 79 per cent replied in the negative; and 6 per cent stated they did not know.

These are suggestive findings. Approximately one out of every four of the dominant Protestant group thought that there was much ill-feeling in their group toward the two minority outgroups. Only one out of twenty in the Jewish group and a little over one out of ten in the Roman Catholic group thought that ill-feeling toward Protestants was present in their groups. Some observers claim that religious tension is increasing because the Protestant group feels its traditional dominance is being threatened by the Jewish and Roman Catholic minorities. This insecurity may account for the relatively high percentage of Protestants who reported considerable ill-feeling toward the minorities among the members of their group. On the other hand, we have no basis for comparison, so that it is impossible to conclude from our findings that ill-feeling is on the increase.

Historians offer convincing evidence that mutual suspicion and ill-feeling among the three major religious communities must have run very high in the past. Our findings suggest that such an acute state of intergroup tension is no longer sensed, at least, not by three fourths of the American people.

A third factor affecting attitudes toward the outgroup is what people believe members of the outgroup think of them and their group. As individuals and as groups, the self-image reflected or thought to be reflected in the minds of others is bound to condition attitudes and interactions. Respect and esteem tend to foster like feelings in others. When these are lacking, or are thought to be lacking, people become suspicious of each other's motives. They may react aggressively; they may reciprocate with similar feelings; or they may withdraw into themselves and keep interaction at a minimum. At any rate, to feel despised or looked down upon offers scant basis for mutual understanding and cooperation. Prejudice warps both the holder and his victim, as experience demonstrates all too well.

What is the self-image that members of the major religious communities feel is reflected in the mentality of the outgroups? We posed our question in this way: "Do you think most (here supply Protestants, Catholics, or Jews, depending on the interviewee's religious preference) look down on people of your beliefs, or not?" Members of the Protestant group reported the greatest amount of insecurity in this regard. One-third (34 per cent) felt that most Catholics looked down on them; 48 per cent denied this; and 18 per cent did not know. One out of five (20 per cent) felt that most Jews looked down on them; 55 per cent replied in the negative; and 25 per cent did not know.

Among members of the Roman Catholic group, 22 per cent felt that most Protestants looked down on them; 67 per cent replied in the negative; and 11 per cent did not know. Eighteen per cent felt that most Jews looked down on them; 60 per cent denied this; and 22 per cent did not know. Among members of the Jewish group, 16 per cent felt that most Protestants looked down on them; 68 per cent replied in the negative; and 16 per cent did not know. Thirty per cent felt that most Catholics looked down on them; 55 per cent denied this; and 15 per cent did not know.

Our findings raise several important questions. First, do people distinguish between persons and the religious doctrines they may hold? As we have seen in the last chapter, members of the major religious communities do not generally hold that "one religion is just about as good as another," yet this attitude does not prevent respect and esteem for the persons who conscientiously adhere to these different communities. Our findings suggest that this distinction may not always be kept clearly in mind. Further, although Roman Catholics expressed the greatest degree of security as reflected in their self-image, we found in the last chapter that they were the group to which members of the outgroup least preferred to belong. This suggests that one's self-image may frequently not coincide with reality. Finally, is it possible that the insecurity expressed by members of the Protestant group represents little more than a projection of their own feelings? This is to say, they recognize that both the Roman Catholic and Jewish groups seriously question the varied content of their doctrinal beliefs, and they may jump to the conclusion that they are looked down on as individuals because of the beliefs that they hold.

We have summarized our findings on intergroup attitudes in Table 18. As it reveals, there were relatively few unpleasant personal experiences that might have led people to dislike members of the outgroup. A higher percentage stated that they

TABLE 18. *Sources of Tensions Among the Major Faiths*

SOURCES OF TENSION	MAJOR FAITHS		
	Protestant per cent	Roman Catholic per cent	Jewish per cent
Protestant unpleasant experience with:	0	9	8
Roman Catholic with:	4	0	6
Jewish with:	7	11	0
Protestant ill-feeling toward:	0	24	25
Roman Catholic toward:	11	0	21
Jewish toward:	5	15	0
Protestant feels looked down on by:	0	34	20
Roman Catholic by:	22	0	18
Jewish by:	16	30	0

thought there was much ill-feeling toward members of the out-group among most people of their religious preference. Further, a considerably larger portion expressed the belief that most members of the outgroup looked down on people of their own group. These intergroup attitudes are significant, inasmuch as they depict the "climate of opinion" in which interaction among groups must take place.

Acceptance of the American ideal that people are equal though different has never been uniformly achieved. Although we have done comparatively well in this respect, the history of our nation is stained with widespread and long-standing in-stances of exploitation and discrimination.[2] In some cases this situation has endured for so long that flagrant denials of the American ideal appear sanctioned by tradition, with the result that only the most conscientious give any thought to the diffi-cult task of reform. In other cases, exploitation and discrim-ination remain regionally segregated or carefully concealed, so that the general public find it not too difficult conveniently to ignore this negation of the ideal which they proudly profess. Of course, there is another side to the coin. People sometimes advance the charge of discrimination in order to conceal their own incompetency and lack of initiative. A competitive society such as our own bestows few favors, so that those who are incapable or unwilling to stand the competition may be tempted to rationalize their failure by claiming discrimination.

The ideal of "equal though different" can never be assim-ilated by a certain type of personality, possessing what has been called somewhat loosely the authoritarian mind. People of this character tend to view all differences, whether they be of color, creed, class, or even sex, as marks of inferiority. What is different, is necessarily inferior. This refusal to evaluate dif-ferences in a rational manner implies either stupidity or studied

ignorance. In the latter case it is consciously or unconsciously
fostered as the needed justification for practicing discrimination. This is to say, it is not easy to rationalize discrimination
against persons whom we regard as equals, but if they can be
seen as different and consequently as inferior, our unjust treatment of them may be rationalized as representing a fair adjustment to an unfortunate situation.[3]

Our study sought information concerning people's attitudes
in areas which lend themselves to discriminatory practices.
These were voting, housing, and marriage. Further, we asked
whether people thought that religious beliefs were given a fair
presentation in the outgroup press, and we also wanted to find
out whether people thought that employers would discriminate
against them because of their religion. It was hoped that the
answers to these last two questions would furnish some understanding of what discriminatory attitudes members of the
major faiths mutually attributed to each other.

How do members of the major religious communities feel
about voting for one of the outgroup? We asked: "Other
things being equal, would you just as soon vote for a (Protestant, Roman Catholic, or Jew) for President of the U. S. as
for someone of your own religion or not?" Protestants showed
the greatest reluctance to vote for a member of one of the
outgroups. Slightly over half (51 per cent) said that they
would not just as soon vote for a Roman Catholic for President;
42 per cent replied that they would; and 7 per cent did not
know. Sixty-one per cent stated that they would not just as
soon vote for a member of the Jewish group for President; 31
per cent replied that they would; and 8 per cent did not know.

Among the Roman Catholic group, only 6 per cent said that
they would not just as soon vote for a Protestant for President;
92 per cent stated that they would; and 2 per cent did not

know. Roughly one-third (34 per cent) replied that they would not just as soon vote for a member of the Jewish group for President; 57 per cent said that they would; and 9 per cent did not know. The attitudes of the Jewish group displayed a similar pattern. Only 6 per cent stated that they would not just as soon vote for a Protestant for President; 90 per cent said that they would; and 4 per cent did not know. Thirty-one per cent replied that they would not just as soon vote for a Roman Catholic for President; 59 per cent said that they would; and 10 per cent did not know.[4]

How do people feel about having members of an outgroup for next-door neighbors? We asked: "All other things being equal, would you just as soon have a (Protestant, Roman Catholic, or Jew) for your next-door neighbor as someone of your own religion, or not?" Protestants expressed the greatest unwillingness to have outgroup members for next-door neighbors. Thirteen per cent said that they would not just as soon have Roman Catholics; 85 per cent replied that they would; and 2 per cent did not know. Twenty-seven per cent stated that they would not just as soon have Jews; 67 per cent said they would; and 6 per cent did not know.

Among the Roman Catholic group, only 4 per cent replied that they would not just as soon have Protestants for next-door neighbors; 95 per cent said that they would; and 1 per cent did not know. Fifteen per cent stated that they would not just as soon have Jews; 81 per cent replied that they would; and 4 per cent did not know. Among the Jewish group, 7 per cent said that they would not just as soon have Protestants; 89 per cent answered that they would; and 4 per cent did not know. Thirteen per cent stated that they would not just as soon have Roman Catholics; and 87 per cent said that they would. Discrimination in housing can work some real hardships. Although there is no indication in our findings that actual discrimination would be practiced, it is clear that members of the Jewish group and to some extent, Roman Catholics, would feel that they were not welcome in certain residential areas.

Recent studies have shown that the rate of mixed marriages runs surprisingly high not only among members of the various Protestant denominations but also among members of the major religious communities.[5] In a previous chapter, we noted that three out of four of our respondents felt that people who marry will be happier if they both share the same religion. Attitudes toward mixed marriage are obviously conditioned by basic beliefs concerning the nature of marriage and the family. They are also affected by the desire to maintain group solidarity. At the same time, however, people's attitude toward marriage with a member of the outgroup gives some indication of how they feel about that group.

In order to obtain information on this subject, we asked the following question. "All other things being equal, would you just as soon have a member of your family marry a (Protestant, Roman Catholic, or Jew) as someone of your own religion, or not?" Sixty-three per cent of the Protestant group would not just as soon have a member of their family marry a Roman Catholic, and three out of four expressed the same attitude in regard to marriage with a Jew. Fifty-four per cent of the Roman Catholics would not just as soon have a member of their family marry a Protestant and 72 per cent expressed the same attitude toward marriage with a Jew. Members of the Jewish group showed approximately the same attitudes toward marriage with either outgroup. Sixty-eight per cent were not in favor of marriage with Protestants, and 69 per cent held similar attitudes toward marriage with Roman Catholics. It appears, then, that Protestants and Roman Catholics are almost equally inclined to look with disfavor upon marriage with Jews (75 per cent and 72 per cent respectively). Protestants are less favorably inclined toward marriage with Roman Catholics (63 per cent) than are the latter toward marriage with Protestants (54 per cent). Members of the Jewish group make little distinction between marriage with either outgroup.

Ever since the advent of modern printing, the press has offered a facile means of arousing religious tensions and showing discrimination, as well as combating suspicion and bigotry. People rightly feel that if their religious beliefs are to be discussed, they should be presented fairly. Justice also demands that newspaper reports and magazine articles concerning a specific religious group should not be biased or "slanted." It is patently unfair to report incidents out of setting or to cite quotations out of context. The trick of using half-truths is bound to mislead the average reader, while it cannot fail to arouse the resentment of the group that is being misrepresented. It is perhaps fortunate for the preservation of good interfaith relations that the members of the various religious groups are not avid readers of each other's newspapers and magazines. In religious writing, as in war and love, some people seem to operate on the principle that all is fair, while even with the best intentions, it is frequently very difficult to do justice to all sides in an emotion-loaded religious controversy.

Do people feel that their beliefs are getting fair treatment in the outgroup press? We asked them: "Do you think most (Protestant, Roman Catholic, or Jewish) magazines and newspapers try to be fair to your religious beliefs, or not?" Members of the Protestant group were most inclined to think that their religious beliefs were not fairly presented. In regard to Roman Catholic newspapers and magazines, 31 per cent thought that there was unfairness; 21 per cent replied in the negative; and 48 per cent did not know. In regard to Jewish publications, 14 per cent felt that they were unfair; 21 per cent replied in the negative; and 65 per cent did not know.

Among the Roman Catholic group, nearly one fourth (24 per cent) felt that Protestant newspapers and magazines did not try to be fair to their religious beliefs; 40 per cent thought that they did; and 36 per cent did not know. Fifteen per cent regarded Jewish publications as unfair; 27 per cent did not; and 58 per cent did not know. Members of the Jewish group were least inclined to think that their religious beliefs received unfair treatment. Fourteen per cent felt that Protestant publications were unfair; 45 per cent did not think so; and 41 per cent did not know. In regard to Roman Catholic newspapers and magazines, 17 per cent thought that they were unfair; 40 per cent did not; and 43 per cent did not know.

It should be noted that a relatively high percentage of respondents answered that they did not know in reply to this question, suggesting that they were not accustomed to read outgroup publications. In general, members of the Protestant and Roman Catholic groups were most inclined to question the fairness of presentation in each other's newspapers and magazines. Whether their attitudes were based on fact or fiction, 31 per cent of the Protestants and 24 per cent of the Roman Catholics claimed that the publications of the other group did not try to be fair.

Finally, we gathered information on attitudes toward discrimination in employment. The majority of people living in our modern industrialized society depend almost exclusively on the proceeds of their pay check for their livelihood, so that various types of discrimination in employment can cause serious hardship. People either may be hindered from getting a job because of their religious beliefs, or they may not be promoted on the job for the same reason. There are many ways of concealing this type of discrimination, and, in some cases, it would be difficult to judge whether unjust action had really occurred. However, we were not seeking information on actual discrimination. Rather, we wanted to know if people thought that discrimination would be practiced against them because of their religious beliefs. From the viewpoint of intergroup tensions, attitudes are as important as acts. The social system is composed of patterned sets of mutual expectancies, and if these are tainted with mistrust and suspicion, the stage is set for conflict rather than cooperation.

Our respondents were asked: "Do you think most (Protestant, Roman Catholic, or Jewish) employers would discriminate against you because of your religion, or not?" Members of the Jewish group were most convinced that outgroup employers would discriminate against them, and Roman Catholics felt the least insecurity in this regard. Among the Jewish group, 27 per cent felt that Protestant employers would discriminate against them; 52 per cent did not think so; and 21 per cent did not know. Thirty-one per cent felt that Roman Catholic employers would discriminate against them; 57 per cent did not think so; and 12 per cent did not know.

Among members of the Protestant community, one fifth (20 per cent) felt that Roman Catholic employers would discriminate against them; 63 per cent did not think so; and 17 per cent did not know. Eighteen per cent felt that Jewish employers would discriminate against them; 62 per cent did not think so; and 20 per cent did not know. Among Roman Catholics, only 8 per cent felt that Protestant employers would discriminate against them; 85 per cent did not think so; and 7 per cent did not know. Fourteen per cent believed that Jewish employers would discriminate against them; 74 per cent did not think so; and 12 per cent did not know.

Table 19 summarizes our findings on attitudes toward discriminatory practices. It shows that members of the Protestant community were most reluctant to vote for outgroup members for President of the United States, to have them for next-door neighbors, or to want a member of their family to marry one of them. They were also more inclined to believe that Roman Catholic newspapers and magazines in particular did not try to be fair to their religious beliefs. On the other hand, members of the Jewish group were most likely to feel that outgroup employers would discriminate against them because of their religion. Although the attitudes reviewed here offer wide scope for improvement, the overall picture is more satisfactory than some would lead us to believe.

In a sense, organized religious groups may be regarded as standing in competition with each other.[6] This is particularly true in a nation such as our own where there is no established church. Group competition frequently leads to pressure-group tactics, or to the suspicion thereof. Under such circumstances, people may feel that outgroup members are interfering with their rights, stick together too much for the common good, are trying to get too much power, are too aggressive in making converts, are exerting too much pressure on the press or are using their personal influence to support merely group interests. These suspicions create a social climate in which intergroup cooperation becomes difficult. Our study tried to uncover people's attitudes concerning outgroup activities in these areas.

To what extent do people feel that their rights are being threatened by members of the outgroup? We asked: "Do you think that (Protestants, Roman Catholics, or Jews) as a group try to interfere in any way with your religious beliefs or per-

TABLE 19. *Attitudes of Mistrust Among the Major Faiths*

ATTITUDES	MAJOR FAITHS		
	Protestant per cent	Roman Catholic per cent	Jewish per cent
Protestant would not vote for	0	51	61
Roman Catholics would not vote for	6	0	34
Jewish would not vote for	6	31	0
Protestant would not have for neighbor	0	13	27
Roman Catholic would not	4	0	15
Jewish would not	7	13	0
Protestant disapproves marriage with	0	63	75
Roman Catholic with	54	0	72
Jewish with	68	69	0
Protestant feels press is unfair of	0	31	14
Roman Catholic of	24	0	15
Jewish of	14	17	0
Protestant fears job discrimination from	0	20	18
Roman Catholic, from	8	0	14
Jewish, from	27	31	0

sonal liberties, or not?" Only 4 per cent of the Protestant and Roman Catholic groups thought that the Jews as a group were trying to interfere in this regard. At the same time, only 4 per cent of the Jewish group felt that Protestants were trying to interfere. On the other hand, 12 per cent of the Roman Catholic group thought that Protestants were trying to interfere, while 13 per cent of the Jews and 15 per cent of the Protestants felt that Roman Catholics were attempting to do so. These findings indicate that suspicion of outgroup interference with one's religious beliefs or personal liberties is still harbored by about one out of every six or seven people. Such interference is probably not regarded as a major problem by any of the groups.

How widespread is the belief that members of the major religious communities stick together too much? Only 11 per cent of the Roman Catholic and 19 per cent of the Jewish groups thought that Protestants stick together too much. On the other hand, 46 per cent of the Protestants and 48 per cent of the Roman Catholics felt that members of the Jewish group were too cohesive. Forty per cent of the Protestants and 44 per cent of the Jews leveled the same charge against Roman Catholics. It is difficult to evaluate the significance of these charges. Group solidarity is obviously fostered by sharing religious beliefs and practices. However, in this context the charge of sticking together too much probably implies lack of willingness to cooperate with others, as well as the display of undue favoritism toward members of the ingroup. To the extent that this is true, "sticking together too much" represents a hindrance to good community relationships.

Closely related to the above question is the charge that some groups are trying to get too much power in the United States. It would be difficult to define what is meant by "too much power." Applied to politics in a democracy, it would probably signify that a group's influence was out of proportion to the number of its adherents. In the business world it might mean over-representation of the group in positions of economic power. Likewise, in the occupational structure, it could imply what is thought to be undue concentration of group members in the professions. On the other hand, the charge that one group is trying to get too much power may indicate little more than the recognition that the traditional balance of power is being threatened in some areas. Vested interests readily interpet a competitor's rise as an attempt to get "too much power," forgetting that what the change may call for is a new definition of the situation.

Although we may concede that the term *too much power* is indefinite and equivocal, the fact that people harbor such attitudes is not likely to foster intergroup cooperation. At the same time, knowledge that such attitudes exist can prove helpful to social leaders who would remedy the situation, for they can then define the dimensions of the problem with some degree of realism. Do many people believe that some religious groups are trying to get too much power in the United States? Our findings reveal that only 8 per cent of the Roman Catholics and 11 per cent of the Jews felt that Protestants were trying to get too much power. However, roughly one-third of both Protestants and Roman Catholics felt that the Jews were trying to get too much power (35 per cent and 33 per cent respectively), and a somewhat higher percentage of Protestants (41 per cent) and of Jews (36 per cent) leveled the same charge against Roman Catholics.

As we have suggested, this rather vague charge may be interpreted in two ways. First, some people may feel that a specific outgroup is trying to get undue power in some area of social activity. Second, it may indicate the belief that the traditional (and cherished) balance is undergoing change owing to the upward mobility of hitherto subordinate minority groups. In the latter case, the attitude reflects pained surprise rather than an objective appraisal of what is happening. Whatever interpretation may prove most applicable in a given instance, the attitude itself generally leads to an increase of group cohesiveness, since the real or fancied encroachments of the out-group now offer a common rallying point for group members.

It is rather generally recognized that the popular press represents one of the most effective instruments of propaganda in the modern world. Although there is nothing quite as dead as yesterday's newspaper, the steady, persistent impact of the bits of "news" gleaned from the daily press exercises a considerable influence on even the most superficial reader. Because space is necessarily limited, not only what is to be reported but how it is to be reported calls for careful judgment. Even the goal of printing "all the news that's fit to print" implies a definition of "fit." At the same time, in reporting as in speaking, "it's not what you say, but the way that you say it," that may really count. In the field of labor relations and of politics the press is frequently accused of playing favorites or of giving in to pressure-groups. Such accusations may or may not have a foundation in fact, but no adult living in a democratic society that fosters competition should be surprised that such charges should be made.

Since the major religious communities constitute a type of competitive groups, the question may be raised whether they attempt to influence the press too much in their favor. The question of fact would be difficult to answer. In this area, as in most others, competing groups are not likely to agree on what constitutes "too much." Obviously, all demand a fair hearing in the press, and they will rightly use their influence to obtain it. On the other hand, few people can be objective in judging matters in which their own interests are concerned, for they will not only give themselves the benefit of the doubt, but concentration on their own interests tends to prevent them from giving due weight to the legitimate interests of others. Even when one's interests are not at stake, objective criteria for judging rational programs of action are not easily come by, since criteria normally are formulated in terms of the general framework of values within which one operates.

Fortunately, our study merely attempts to uncover attitudes in this matter. Do people think that some groups are trying to influence the press too much in favor of their religion? Most Roman Catholics and Jews did not think that Protestants were trying to do so. Only 13 per cent of the Roman Catholics and 11 per cent of the Jews believed that they were. Likewise, few Protestants and Roman Catholics thought that the Jews were trying to exercise undue influence on the press (9 per cent and 10 per cent respectively). On the other hand, 30 per cent of the Protestants and 36 per cent of the Jews thought that Roman Catholics were trying to exert undue pressure. Hence the charge was leveled against Roman Catholics almost three times as often as against other groups. It remains for future research to uncover how this pressure is thought to be exerted.

A related question concerns the accusation that people try to use their position in society to build up their own group. Consequently, we asked: "Do you think (Protestants, Roman Catholics, or Jews) try to use their positions as editors, teachers, or entertainers to build up their group, or not?" Among the Protestant group, roughly one-third (35 per cent) felt that Roman Catholics tried to do so, and one out of five thought the same of the Jews. Roman Catholics were less apprehensive in this regard. Fourteen per cent thought that Protestants, and 19 per cent felt that Jews tried to exert such influence in their positions. Members of the Jewish group were more inclined to level this charge against Roman Catholics (33 per cent) than against Protestants (18 per cent).

Finally, we asked whether it was thought that some groups tried too hard to get people to join their church. We saw in the last chapter that convert-making was primarily a characteristic of the Protestant group, since a large proportion of Jews and Roman Catholics stated that they had made no attempt to get others to join their groups. A study of how people regard the convert-making activities of outgroup members, therefore, will throw considerable light on the existence of stereotypes in the popular mind. Are some groups considered too aggressive in making converts? Protestants and Roman Catholics agree that members of the Jewish group are not. Only 2 per cent of the Protestants, and 3 per cent of the Roman Catholics thought that they were. Further, only 16 per cent of the Roman Catholics, and 12 per cent of the Jews felt that Protestants were too aggressive in this matter. On the other hand, 32 per cent of the Protestants, and 43 per cent of the Jews believed that Roman Catholics tried too hard to get people to join their church.

It is difficult to reconcile some of these attitudes with our previous findings on convert-making. Members of the Protestant group stated that they were most active in this area, yet they are not thought to be so by either Roman Catholics or Jews. At the same time, a large percentage of Roman Catholics stated they had made no attempt to make converts, but Protestants and Jews believe that they try too hard. Several explanations of this discrepancy between attitude and fact come to mind. Protestant activity in convert-making may be confined primarily to other Protestant denominations so that the major outgroups are not conscious of it. Further, the insistence by Roman Catholics that their prospective non-Catholic marriage partners either join the church or, at least, have their marriages solemnized in the church may leave the impression of too much aggressiveness in convert-making.

Attitudes toward outgroup pressure are summarized in Table 20. As we have noted, relatively few people feel that members of the outgroup try to interfere with their religious beliefs or personal liberties. However, members of the two minority religious groups were accused of sticking together too much and of trying to get too much power. Roughly one-third of the outgroups felt that Roman Catholics were trying to influence the press too much and were too prone to use their position in society to build up their own group. Opinions about the convert-making activities of Protestants and Roman Catholics revealed a wide discrepancy between facts and attitudes. On the other hand, relatively few members of the Jewish group reported that they had tried to bring others to join their group, and the attitudes of Protestants and Roman Catholics reflected this inactivity.

What do people think of others in comparison with members of their own religious group? We selected eight areas to serve as the basis for comparison. For example, we asked: "Compared with most people of your religious beliefs, would you say most (Protestants, Roman Catholics, or Jews) are about the same, better, or not as good, in—loyalty to their country? living up to their religion? being fair in business?" and so forth. It seems reasonable to conclude that if people think others are about the same or better in such areas as compared to members of their own group, there exists a substantial basis for intergroup harmony and good relationships. People

Table 20. *Attitudes Toward Outgroup Pressure Among the Major Faiths*

SOURCES OF PRESSURE	MAJOR FAITHS		
	Protestant per cent	Roman Catholic per cent	Jewish per cent
Protestant feels rights interfered with by	0	15	4
Roman Catholic, by	12	0	4
Jewish, by	4	14	0
Protestant dislikes cohesiveness of	0	40	46
Roman Catholics, of	11	0	48
Jewish, of	19	44	0
Protestant fears drive for power of	0	41	35
Roman Catholic, of	8	0	33
Jewish, of	11	36	0
Protestant dislikes convert-making of	0	32	2
Roman Catholic, of	16	0	3
Jewish, of	12	43	0
Protestant dislikes pressure on press by	0	30	9
Roman Catholic, by	13	0	10
Jewish, by	11	36	0
Protestant dislikes use of position by	0	35	20
Roman Catholic, by	14	0	19
Jewish, by	18	33	0

can agree to disagree on religious beliefs and practices if they feel that others are sincere and willing to contribute to the common good. On the other hand, at least in judging others, they expect religion to be reflected in general conduct. If they find much to be judged adversely in the actions of an out-group, they are likely to take a critical view of the group's religious beliefs and practices. Group members, of course, feel that this attitude is quite unfair, since it by-passes the necessary distinction between members who try to live up to the requirements of their beliefs and those who maintain only a nominal relationship to the group.

Do people think others are loyal to their country? Four fifths (81 per cent) of the Protestants thought that Roman Catholics were about the same or better than members of their own group in this regard; 6 per cent did not think so; and 13 per cent did not know. In regard to members of the Jewish group, 72 per cent felt they were about the same or better; 11 per cent disagreed; and 17 per cent did not know. Among Roman Catholics, 93 per cent felt that Protestants were about the same or better; 2 per cent disagreed; and 5 per cent did not know. Seventy-nine per cent felt that Jews were about the same or better; 10 per cent disagreed; and 11 per cent did not know. Among the Jewish group, 94 per cent felt that Protestants were about the same or better, and 6 per cent stated that they did not know. Nine out of ten thought that Roman Catholics were about the same or better, 1 per cent disagreed; and 9 per cent did not know. It appears from these figures that relatively few Americans think members of a religious out-group are not loyal to their country, though this accusation has been made against one group or another rather frequently in the past.

What do people think about the way others live up to their

religion? Protestants revealed a favorable attitude toward Roman Catholics and Jews in this regard. Thirty-seven per cent thought that Roman Catholics were better, 47 per cent, about the same; 7 per cent, not as good; and 9 per cent did not know. Thirteen per cent felt that Jews were better; 62 per cent, about the same; 5 per cent, not as good; and 20 per cent did not know. Roman Catholics took a more severe view of Protestants. Only two per cent felt they were better; 66 per cent, about the same; 24 per cent, not as good; and 8 per cent, did not know. Six per cent thought the Jews were better; 70 per cent, about the same; 9 per cent, not as good; and 15 per cent did not know. Jews took a favorable view of Catholics in this regard. Twenty-three per cent felt they were better; 64 per cent, about the same; 2 per cent, not as good; and 11 per cent did not know. Only 2 per cent thought that Protestants were better; 78 per cent, about the same; 3 per cent, not as good; and 17 per cent did not know.

Do people feel that others are being fair in business? Protestants were rather critical of the Jews in this respect. Only 41 per cent felt that they were about the same or better; 39 per cent, not as good; and 20 per cent did not know. Their attitude was less severe toward Roman Catholics. Seventy-six per cent thought they were about the same or better; 6 per cent, not as good; and 18 per cent did not know. Roman Catholics took a highly favorable view of Protestants in business. Eighty-nine per cent felt that they were about the same or better; 3 per cent, not as good, and 8 per cent did not know. They sided with the Protestants in their attitudes toward Jews. Only 52 per cent thought that they were about the same or better; 31 per cent, not as good; and 17 per cent did not know. Members of the Jewish group were very favorable in their attitudes toward both groups. Eighty-nine per cent felt that Protestants were about the same or better, and 11 per cent did not know. Four out of five thought that Roman Catholics were about the same or better; 3 per cent, not as good; and 17 per cent did not know.

How do people feel about the way members of other religious groups treat their families? There was rather general agreement that the treatment was all right. Only 4 per cent of the Protestants felt that Roman Catholics were not as good as their own members in this regard, and 2 per cent thought the same of the Jews. Only 3 per cent of the Roman Catholics thought that Protestant and Jews were not as good in the treatment of their families. Members of the Jewish group were slightly more critical of others. Seven per cent felt that Protestants were not as good, and 9 per cent thought the same of Roman Catholics. The traditional high reputation that Jewish families enjoy received some recognition from our respondents, for 13 per cent of the Protestants and 10 per cent of the Roman Catholics thought that Jews were better toward their families than members of their own groups.

Do people feel that members of the outgroup are just as honest in public office as their own people are? Although members of the Jewish group are somewhat more suspect in this regard than others, there is little in our findings to suggest that the majority of American people associate dishonesty in public office with any specific religious group. Eight per cent of the Protestants felt that Roman Catholics were not as good as their own members, and 16 per cent thought the same of the Jews. Only 2 per cent of Roman Catholics felt that Protestants were not as good, and 12 per cent had the same attitude toward Jews. Among members of the Jewish group only 1 per cent judged Protestants adversely in this regard, and 3 per cent held similar views about Roman Catholics. Obviously, if dishonesty in public office exists, the majority of American people feel it is fairly well distributed among all groups.

How do the major faiths rank in helping people of their own affiliation who need help? Protestants expressed a favorable view of other groups in this regard. One fourth felt that Roman Catholics were better than their own members; 61 per cent, about the same; only 3 per cent, not as good; and 11 per cent did not know. Nearly one-third (32 per cent) thought that Jews were better; one-half that they were about the same; only 1 per cent, not as good; and 17 per cent did not know. Roman Catholics supported this view of the Jewish group. Twenty-nine per cent felt that they were better; 60 per cent, about the same; only 2 per cent, not as good; and 9 per cent did not know. Although only 4 per cent felt that Protestants were better; 81 per cent thought they were about the same; 7 per cent not as good; and 8 per cent did not know. The Jewish group were more conservative in their views. Two per cent felt that Protestants were better; 74 per cent, about the same; 8 per cent, not as good, and 16 per cent did not know. Four per cent felt that Roman Catholics were better; 82 per cent, about the same; 4 per cent, not as good; and 10 per cent did not know.

How do the groups compare in respecting the beliefs of others? Roman Catholics received the most unfavorable vote on this point. Roughly one-third (35 per cent) of Protestants and Jews thought that Roman Catholics were not as good in respecting the beliefs of others as were members of their own religious groups. Only one out of every ten Roman Catholics held a similar judgment in regard to Protestants and Jews. Fifteen per cent of Protestants believed that Jews were not as good in this regard, although only 8 per cent of the Jewish group held this attitude toward Protestants. It will be remembered that a similar pattern of attitudes was revealed by a previous question when we asked people whether they felt that others looked down on members of their group. In both cases, roughly one-third of Protestants and Jews indicated that they felt Roman Catholics failed to show due respect for their religious group.

Finally, how do people rank others in generosity toward public charities? Although attitudes were quite favorable in general, some Protestants were sceptical about Roman Catholics and Jews in this regard. Sixteen per cent felt that Roman Catholics and 15 per cent that Jews were not as good in this regard as were members of their own group. Roman Catholics and Jews thought better of Protestants on this point. Only 3 per cent of the Roman Catholics and 6 per cent of the Jews felt that Protestants were not as good. One out of ten Roman Catholics felt that Jews were not as good, and one out of twenty Jews thought the same of Roman Catholics. These attitudes are interesting, inasmuch as the same groups that were considered not as good in generosity toward public charities were considered better in helping people of their own faith who need help, as we discovered in a previous question. The pattern of attitudes revealed here is in line with the view, expressed by nearly half the Protestants, that the minority religious groups "stick together too much."

This rapid overview of comparative attitudes reveals that, in general, the members of the major religious communities held rather favorable views toward one another. Protestants showed highly favorable attitudes toward Roman Catholics "in living up to their religion," and "in assisting people of their own faith who needed help." They were critical of them "in respecting the beliefs of others," and somewhat sceptical about their generosity toward public charities. They thought well of Jews "in living up to their religion," "in treating their families right," and "in assisting people of their own faith who needed help." They were critical of them "in being fair in business," and were somewhat sceptical of them "in loyalty to their country," "in being honest in public office," "in respecting the beliefs of others," and "in generosity toward public charities."

Members of the Jewish group took a generally favorable attitude toward Protestants in all areas studied. They thought well of Roman Catholics "in living up to their religion," but like the Protestants, they were critical of them "in respecting the beliefs of others." In conclusion, it should be noted that, with the exception of roughly one-third of Protestants and Roman Catholics who felt that Jews were not as good as their own members in being fair in business, and roughly one-third of Jews and Protestants who thought that Roman Catholics were not as good in respecting the beliefs of others, the over-all picture was one of mutual respect and esteem. This need not imply that people feel human relationships are functioning perfectly in our society. Rather it suggests that the majority of Americans are mature enough to make a critical appraisal of the members of their own group and, at the same time, not to blame other groups for the failure of individual members.

Although people may have little personal contact with clergymen of other religious communities, the position of religious leaders in the community is such that most people tend to form some more or less clearly defined attitudes toward them as representatives of a distinct profession and religious organization. It may reasonably be supposed that such opinions frequently represent no more than projections of what outsiders think of the religious group in question. At the same time, when judging the clerical profession, people tend to make the obviously false assumption that all the clergymen of a given denomination have similar characteristics and qualities, and since this image is seldom corrected through personal experience, the stereotype persists unchallenged.

On the other hand, most clergymen, like members of other professions such as medicine and teaching, do acquire through training, custom, and the work they do, some distinctive traits. They are also well aware that society, or at least their specific denomination, cherishes definite expectations concerning their character and conduct that they will do well to recognize, for as leaders of a religious community, they are supposed to exemplify in their lives the practical implications of the beliefs they profess. It is within the framework of such lofty expectations that their conduct is judged, and hence, a vote of confidence from the faithful may normally be taken as a high commendation of their lives.

Eight areas were selected as the basis for probing the comparative attitudes of people toward the clergy. For example, we asked such questions as: "Compared with most clergymen of your religious preference, would you say most (Protestant, Roman Catholic, or Jewish) clergymen are about the same, better, or not as good,—in sincerely living up to their calling? in helping their own people who need help? in living for the next world instead of this one?" and so forth. Again this comparison implied a judgment of one's own religious leaders and of those in other communities. In a sense, therefore, the attitudes uncovered here may be taken as a fair indication of how people regard the clerical profession in itself.

Our findings indicate that the majority of American people think that the clergymen of other groups compare very favorably with their own in regard to the areas studied. Since the percentage of people who thought that they were "not as good" remained below 10 per cent in most cases, it will not be necessary to present our data in any great detail. Hence, we shall point out only the areas in which the adverse attitude of some group reached 10 per cent or more. Percentages lower than this can scarcely be considered to have significant influence on intergroup relationships.

Our first question asked how clergymen compare "in sincerely living up to their calling." The only significant adverse attitude was expressed by Protestants. Fourteen per cent thought that Roman Catholic clergymen were not as good as their own in this regard. The second question asked how clergymen compare "in helping their own people who need help." There were no significant adverse attitudes recorded here. On the other hand, 18 per cent of the Protestants and 14 per cent of the Roman Catholics thought that Jewish clergymen were better than their own, and 14 per cent of the Protestants thought the same of Roman Catholic clergymen. The third question probed attitudes concerning life goals. Thirteen per cent of the Protestants felt that Roman Catholic clergymen were not as good "in living for the next world instead of this one." Eleven per cent of Roman Catholics held similar attitudes in regard to Protestant clergymen. On the other hand, 12 per cent of the Jewish group felt that Roman Catholic clergy were better than their own on this point. Concerning the fourth item, "loyalty to their country," there were no significant adverse attitudes expressed by any group.

How did the clergy compare "in giving intelligent leadership to their followers?" Thirteen per cent of the Protestants felt that Roman Catholic clergy were not as good as their own in giving leadership. How did the clergy rank "in promoting understanding between their group and others?" The Protestants registered strong adverse attitudes here. Thirty per cent felt that Roman Catholic clergy were not as good as their own, and 12 per cent thought the same of Jewish clergymen. Fourteen per cent of the Jews shared the adverse attitudes of Protestants concerning Roman Catholic clergymen. A related question asked how clergymen compared "in cooperating with leaders of other religions for the common civic good." Here again Protestants expressed significant adverse attitudes. Twenty-four per cent felt that Roman Catholic clergymen were not as good as their own, and 10 per cent had the same attitude toward those of the Jewish group. Twelve per cent of the Jews agreed with the Protestants in their adverse view of Roman Catholic clergymen. Finally, we asked how clergymen compare "in setting a good personal example." The only significant adverse opinion was expressed by Protestants. Eighteen per cent thought that Roman Catholic clergy were not as good as their own in setting a good personal example.

The responses to their eight questions indicate that the major criticism of outgroup clergymen centers around what might be called their failure in maintaining good public relations. Protestants feel that Roman Catholic leaders, and to a lesser extent, Jewish leaders, are deficient in promoting understanding between their group and others, and in cooperating with leaders of other religions for the common civic good. This attitude is in line with their contention that minority religious groups stick together too much. Obviously, there is no reason why minority religious leaders cannot cooperate with others in fostering understanding between groups and in promoting the common civic good. At the same time, it is only realistic to suggest that in areas where discrimination and bigotry have been rampant such cooperation will come slowly. As we have indicated, prejudice tends to warp all parties concerned and its adverse social consequences endure long after the incidents that occasioned them have disappeared.

We have presented our findings relative to interfaith attitudes and feelings with a minimum of comment, on the assumption that the sentiments expressed tend to speak for themselves. It was not our intent to attempt to analyze the complex etiology of interfaith prejudice or to construct a general theory of religious group interaction. Our study was designed to discover how members of the major faiths tended to define the situation, for it should be obvious that the existing climate of opinion will determine the nature and quality of subsequent interaction. If religious groups feel threatened, looked down upon, or expect discrimination, they will respond accordingly. In social life, every action represents a reaction to the situation as one sees it, and one sees only what he is prepared or predisposed to see.

Because religious commitments normally involve adherence to a formally organized group with a history, it is extremely difficult in studying interfaith attitudes and feelings to distinguish the associated ethnic, historical, or social factors from the specifically religious. For example, one may strongly disapprove of interfaith marriages out of social rather than religious motives; just as one may conceal religious prejudice under convenient rationalizations concerning efficiency, loyalty, and so forth. At the same time, firm adherence to a particular religious group may involve no profound commitment to its religious beliefs, so that group loyalty rather than religious conviction may dictate one's attitudes toward competing religious outgroups. In other words, interesting as our findings on interfaith sentiments may appear, we must be slow to draw any conclusions from them concerning the current vitality of the traditional faiths.

On the other hand, our findings throw considerable light on the major sources of tension and friction among the traditional faiths. Although the over-all picture that emerges from our study is not one of gloom, there is evidence to suggest that a proportion of the dominant Protestant majority feel some apprehension and fear that their traditional hegemony is being threatened by the aggressiveness of the minorities, particularly the Roman Catholic. Roughly one-third of both Protestants and Jews accuse Roman Catholics of sticking together too much, of driving for power, of putting pressure on the press, of using their positions to benefit their group, and of being too active in making converts. Perhaps as a source of even greater irritation, they feel that Roman Catholics look down upon them and fail to show proper respect for their religious beliefs. There are also indications that they believe Roman Catholic clergymen are uncooperative and remiss in promoting better interfaith understanding. Roman Catholics, of course, express somewhat similar attitudes though to a much less marked degree in most instances.

To determine whether these views reflect actual experience, projections, well-founded fears and apprehensions, or mere cultural residues in the form of stereotypes, does not fall within the scope of the present study. We aimed to investigate the current climate of opinion and since people tend to act on the basis of their definition of the situation, our findings suggest that although the religious pluralism characteristic of the American tradition rests on a substantial foundation of mutual toleration and respect, there remain relatively extensive areas of interfaith tension and stress calling for responsible leadership and cooperation from all the churches.

Notes

1. See MacIver, *op. cit.*, Gordon W. Allport, *The Nature of Prejudice* (Boston: Beacon Press, 1954); T. W. Adorno *et al.*, *The Authoritarian Personality* (New York: Harper & Bros., 1950).

2. See Ray Allen Billington, *The Protestant Crusade* (New York: Rinehart & Co., 1952); John J. Kane, *Catholic-Protestant Conflicts in America* (Chicago: Regnery, 1955); Marshall Sklare, *The Jews: Social Patterns of an American Group* (Glencoe, Ill.: The Free Press, 1958); Gunnar Myrdal *et al.*, *An American Dilemma, the Negro Problem and Modern Democracy* (New York: Harper and Brothers, 1944).

3. See Bruno Bettelheim and Morris Janowitz, *Dynamics of Prejudice* (New York: Harper and Brothers, 1950).

4. Adequate studies on the voting patterns manifested during the last Presidential election are not available.

5. See James H. S. Bossard and Eleanor Stoker Boll, *One Marriage Two Faiths* (New York: The Ronald Press Company, 1957).

6. See J. Milton Yinger, *Religion in the Struggle for Power, A Study in the Sociology of Religion* (Durham, North Carolina: Duke University Press, 1946).

CHAPTER **8** God and the
American People

WHAT does religion mean to the American people? Do
our findings support the charge that our vaunted religious traditions have been reduced to mere cultural residues, serving subordinate though socially useful purposes as "culture religions"? Does this study have any special significance for religious leaders or students of American society? Up to this point we have presented our data with a minimum of discussion, for we wished to describe the various aspects of the total religious situation before presuming to evaluate their significance. In this concluding chapter we shall attempt to reconstruct the total picture emerging from our data and to interpret our findings by viewing them in theoretical perspective. Before proceeding to this task, however, it may prove helpful to restate briefly the major postulates and assumptions with which we began.

In the first place, assuming a high degree of interest in religion, our study was designed to investigate the specific religious beliefs, practices, and attitudes of the average American adult, in the belief that such findings would reflect those aspects of the official doctrines of the churches that appear in their taught tradition, and consequently that we would thus discover the pertinently operative aspects of the major faiths in contemporary society. Several minor assumptions were implied in the questions asked; namely, we expected to find differences in beliefs and practices among the various faiths, denominations, age groups, educational, occupational and income categories, as well as between the sexes.

Second, our study was focused on organized religious systems with a known history, and since such systems include a creed, cult and code of conduct defining their adherents' status or position in the cosmic order, we assumed that our findings would indicate the degree of doctrinal continuity manifested by the major faiths.

Third, the organized religious systems with which we were dealing uniformly promoted various individual and corporate religious practices, and we, therefore, assumed that the measure of fidelity manifested in fulfilling such pracitces would indicate the degree of the participants' commitments to their beliefs.

Fourth, inasmuch as the major hypotheses advanced to explain the current revival of interest in religion tend to imply considerable modification of traditional religious beliefs not only in official teaching but primarily as understood by the faithful, we assumed that our findings relating to actual beliefs and practices would indicate the nature and extent of the implied modification or supply the basis for a more adequate hypothesis concerning the current revival.

Finally, the study of religion in America is the study of religious pluralism, of a series of co-existing, competing, distinct religious groups or subgroups that have displayed considerable intergroup stress and antagonism in the past. On the basis of recent studies, we postulated a minimum of tension among the major Protestant divisions but a significant degree of mutual mistrust and suspicion among Protestants, Roman Catholics, and Jews, though we were not sure what direction such adverse attitudes would take.

With these broad assumptions in mind, let us briefly review the relevant conclusions derived from our findings. One impression emerging clearly from our study is that religion still remains highly respectable and extremely popular among all adult Americans. People feel that a man ought to have some religion. Only one out of twenty stated that religion was not very important in their lives, while almost three out of four considered themselves active members of a church or religious group, and over two out of three had attended some Sunday or Sabbath religious service during the previous twelve weeks. Such findings lend strong support to the frequently expressed opinion that we are a religious people, though they may also reflect the effects of a religious revival.

Moreover, the current popular interest in religion, whatever form and expression it may eventually take, or however we may interpret its significance, is not alien to our national traditions and practices. All but 6 per cent of the adult population stated that they had received religious training in their youth, and considering the effect that early training is assumed to exert on the development of personality, it appears that the current trend is merely tapping a basic national resource. Furthermore, there is little likelihood that this resource will soon be exhausted. The American people express little doubt concerning the need for religion in the formation of character, inasmuch as only one out of fifty stated that they did not want their children to receive religious instruction. To be sure, roughly one out of four appeared seriously confused about the nature of early religious training, expressing the view that children should not be raised as church members but be free of formal religion until they were old enough to make up their own minds; nevertheless, they all reflected the national view that there should be some type of instruction.

The average American's respect for religion appears to be more than an empty tribute, for he is quite willing to make considerable sacrifices to support religion. The relatively high quality and extent of church building and associated religious endeavors in this country are well known, yet three out of four people did not feel that their local church was too concerned with money matters, and over four out of five thought that church property used for religious purposes should not be taxed. Although generosity may be characteristic of the national temperament, it is scarcely conceivable that people would make such continuous and considerable sacrifices for an institution that they regarded lightly.

We may safely conclude, therefore, that religion represents an important aspect of American culture. Contrary to many other nations in the Western world, the American people apparently have been able to reconcile traditional spiritual aspirations and contemporary social endeavors. Their national leaders are expected to show a high regard for religion, since they see no necessary conflict between social progress and religious beliefs. In America, the reformer or the advocate of social change feels no compulsion to be anti-religious; on the contrary, he would probably have little chance for success unless he reflected prevalent religious sentiments and appealed to them in his campaigns. That the religious spirit lies deep in the national culture is shown by the fact that people not only want their children to be trained in religion as they themselves were trained, but they are also willing to make the sacrifices such programs necessarily imply.

To underline the significance of the above findings we would point out again that they are based not on official views but on the expressed attitudes of the faithful. Probably under the impact of the current revival of interest in religion, a series of significant and exciting studies dealing with doctrinal developments or relevant official pronouncements in the various churches and documenting the perennial vitality of their intellectual elites are now beginning to appear, but our study focused on the average American, the average participant and his actual religious involvements. For the personal and social relevance of religion obviously depends on the manner and degree of its general acceptance, while in no other sphere of human activity are the practical implications of speculative doctrinal developments more slowly accepted by general practitioners. In this connection we should note that organized religions tend to be conservative not only because the long and often dead hand of tradition may inhibit creative speculative developments, but also because the faithful in general are reluctant to adopt any innovations that appear to threaten their religious conceptions, formed for the most part in youth and serving as the cognitive means by which they have learned to work out tolerable adjustments to life in their present social environment. In other words, although contemporary theological developments in the various churches may appear highly stimulating, they may neither reflect, nor are they likely to affect, for some time, the viewpoints of the faithful in general.

Granting the high esteem in which religion is held, can we determine what it means to the average participant? Does it represent mere empty "faith in faith," the conviction that some type of religious belief or experience is good for the individual and the social system? Has it become a uniquely American product, pared down and trimmed to fit the national character? Is it, if not the opium of the people, at least their tranquillizer, offering "peace of mind" and a convenient escape from the intolerable burden of serious thought? May we rightly regard it as the legitimate descendant of Western religious tradition growing to maturity in the New World? Each of these claims has been made, and there is probably some foundation in fact for all of them; yet an analysis of our findings indicates that we are dealing with a highly complex phenomenon that does not lend itself to such facile generalizations.

Let us begin our appraisal by considering the religious doctrines people retain, as well as those they de-emphasize or reject, for our findings in this area will define the essential dimensions of the doctrinal foundations upon which contemporary religion is based. As we pointed out in Chapter One, Western religious traditions included a well-integrated set of doctrines, involving a central dogma—belief in God, conceived not only as Creator and loving Father but as the Ruler and Judge of all mankind—and a series of associated beliefs concerning personal accountability, the immortality of the soul, the final judgment, and the existence of Heaven and Hell. Because the essential human situation was defined as separation from God through sin, the basic human problem became the need to be reconciled to God. Formal religion fulfilled this function among Christian communities by presenting Christ as the mediator between God and men, the sacrificial victim for sin, and the model of human conduct. These beliefs were mutually interdependent. When men thought of religion, they thought of it in this integrated frame of reference.

The major conclusion to be drawn from our findings on

religious beliefs is that the American people in general have attempted to retain those traditional religious beliefs that appear comforting and consoling and have rejected or de-emphasized doctrines relating to original alienation from God and its consequences. For example, 87 per cent are absolutely certain that God exists, 79 per cent look upon Him as a Loving Father, 80 per cent believe in the divinity of Christ, and 77 per cent thought that their soul would live on after death. On the other hand, 42 per cent stated that they did not believe there was a Hell to which people who have led bad lives and die without being sorry are eternally damned. Even among people who believe in Hell, only about one out of five regarded eternal damnation as a real possibility.

It seems scarcely necessary to repeat that in the traditional Western religious context, belief in the existence of Hell was a key concept, closely related to belief in the Fall and Man's original alienation from God, and implicit in the whole Christian conception of salvation. It was also regarded as a necessary correlative of belief in the final judgment and in Heaven. Furthermore, belief in the possibility of personal damnation in Hell was felt to be a necessary correlative of belief in free will and in personal accountability to God for one's acts. Consequently in denying de-emphasizing traditional beliefs relating to Hell, our respondents revealed a radical shift in the entire frame of reference within which salvation had formerly been viewed.

That this is no unfounded generalization appeared clearly when people were asked to define the most important function of religion. Only 17 per cent felt that the most important objective of the churches was to convert people to a spiritual belief so that they can earn a happy life after death. Obviously, the human situation is no longer defined in the framework of traditional beliefs, for major emphasis is placed not on man's need to be reconciled to God but on human relations. The churches are to teach people "how to live better every day with all other people." In other words, religion is regarded as an instrument of society rather than as an institution transcending all that is secular because it serves as the means of relating man to God. The majority of people still believe in "God," though there is danger, as Oscar Wilde cynically remarked, that man has made God according to his own image and likeness.

This evaluation of contemporary religion may appear unduly severe. It will be argued that the great majority openly profess their belief in God, and a large percentage claim active membership in one of the traditional denominations. It is well to reflect, however, that a good portion of the American people remain religiously immature, if not illiterate. Although all received some type of early religious training as children, their study of religion apparently ended during this period. Half the people read no religious periodicals and followed no religious programs on radio or television. Fifty-five per cent attended Sunday or Sabbath services only twice a month or less. Two-thirds could not be classified as Bible readers. As a result, a good proportion of the American people apparently go through life with the immature, more or less superficial religious knowledge and conceptions acquired as children. Since religion is uniformly regarded as a good thing, they support it; finding themselves classified in a definite religious community, they experience a certain consciousness of kind, at least in regard to the outgroups; the fact that they make little or no effort to deepen their understanding of religion indicates that it does not rank very high in their scale of important life-values.

Although Americans like to consider themselves a religious

people, our findings indicate that religion is not one of their major preoccupations. Less than one-third attend Sunday or Sabbath church services every week; an equal percentage never attend; and the remaining 36 per cent attend somewhere between once and three times per month. Most profess to believe in God, yet only 38 per cent pray to Him more frequently than about once a day. More than four out of five believe that the Bible is really the revealed word of God, though only one-third find time to read it about once or twice a week or oftener. Finally, 40 per cent admitted that they never think about what will happen to them when they die. On the basis of such findings, it seems fair to conclude that although most Americans have considerable respect for religion, a good proportion are neither haunted by "intimations of immortality," nor allow their religious interests to interfere with their routine pursuit of happiness. This latter group are far from ignoring or rejecting religion, but their basic life-orientations are this-worldly.

The above observations are based on an over-all view of the religion of the American people, and though they are valid as stated, we hasten to point out that they apply only to the total existing religious complex, that is, to the broad aspect of American culture termed *religious*. In other words, these observations are relevant to the interpretation of such general statements as, "We are a religious nation," or, "Americans are a religious people." To the extent that such statements are true, our findings show that they can only mean that the majority of Americans highly esteem a complex cultural phenomenon called *religion*. What this term denotes is no longer clear, for the spectrum of current religious beliefs is very wide, and there is evidence that even when traditional beliefs are integrally retained, emphasis is shifted from an essential awareness of the need for salvation to stress on social service or human relations.

Yet such general observations tend to ignore significant and perhaps decisive differences in our religiously pluralist society. Formal religion in America is expressed not only in three major communities, differing considerably in creed and cult, but even within these major communities, marked differences in beliefs and practices are apparent. Such pluralism is particularly evident among the Protestant and Jewish communities, within which distinct denominations and cleavages have historically arisen, but even within the Roman Catholic group, our study disclosed a startling rejection or misunderstanding of approved moral standards, implying a serious lack of consensus. Hence the pertinent question: Whom are we talking about when we generalize not only about religion as such but even more specifically about Protestants, Roman Catholics, and Jews?

Moreover, when attempting to assess the social significance of religion in contemporary society, it is necessary to recall that inasmuch as Christian conceptions of man and the universe were closely associated with the initial formation of our basic institutions, a whole complex of values essentially religious in origin and content has been built into the very spirit and structure of American culture. Although these values may not be presently associated directly with formal religion, they give American institutions, cultural goals and viewpoints a religious orientation of which many are apparently quite unaware.[1] Thus even when people have ceased active participation in a specific religious group, they may retain norms and continue to observe standards of conduct that have no rational basis if considered apart from their religious foundations. In this sense, a society may be more "religious" than appears from the study of the formal beliefs and practices of its members.

To be sure, moral standards and basic value-orientations founded upon unrecognized or forgotten religious premises may constitute no more than cultural residues, but in a complex rapidly changing society like our own where people are forced to make numerous adjustments and adaptations, they may also indicate mere segmented thinking or lack of serious reflection, so that under adequate challenge, people will renew and rediscover the religious foundations upon which their approved normative structures and basic goals were initially built. As we have pointed out, the majority of people seldom reflect on the relationships between religious beliefs and accepted norms except in times of crisis, that is, when their norms are challenged either by outsiders or by substantial changes in the immediate conditions associated with observance of these norms. Under such circumstances, people tend either to reject the norms or attempt to rediscover the ultimate basis for the specific values the norms embody. If the norms in question embody values derived from religious premises, the situation may stimulate a renewed interest in religion, it may encourage attempts to find other premises of values, or it may generate a sense of alienation—a "schism of the soul," as Toynbee would put it—because people find that their cherished norms no longer "make sense."

Following this line of thought, the current revival of interest in religion may be interpreted as an indication of a widespread growing awareness of the cognitive gap between contemporary secular norms and any underlying system of value-premises. In this case, if it is to constitute a legitimate religious revival, it must generate the renewal and rediscovery of relevant traditional beliefs as it attempts to reintegrate contemporary normative structures with pertinent religious values of the past. On the other hand, the current trend may be interpreted as a search for security rather than significance. Sensing a radical challenge to their newly achieved affluence, and under tension from the cold war, the atom bomb, and the atmosphere of international distrust and suspicion, Americans may be turning to religious beliefs for peace of mind, and to active religious participation for the feeling of solidarity resulting from identity with a respectable group. In this case, we are witnessing not a religious revival but a social movement with religious trappings, springing from the same group needs as many of the revivals of nationalism that took place in several European countries after World War I.

Most of the recent hypotheses advanced to explain the current upsurge in religious interest tend to stress its secular aspects. Prescinding from their non-essential features, we can state their basic thesis as follows. Religion is popular today because the major traditional faiths, through a gradual process of doctrinal modification, borrowing, rejection, watering-down, fusion, syncretization, and so on, have become amalgamated or identified with the democratic way of life to such a degree that they now serve as the major social vehicles for the promotion of democratic values and consequently provide convenient and suitable rallying points for people suffering from "loss of nerve," alienation, or lack of identity resulting from the breakdown of primary group affiliations—familial, ethnic, social class, communal, and so on. Hence modern man, experiencing a loss of identity within his society, and facing a challenge to survival from without, is turning to religious organizations in search of secular security rather than to religion itself for transcendental significance. Obviously this becomes possible only because the major faiths are so thoroughly secularized that they no longer stand outside of and above society but have become a subordinate, integral part of the total social system, historically well adapted to serve its purposes and promote its interests.

Do the findings of the present study lend any support to this general thesis? At first glance, they appear to do so, for they document the extensive gap between professed beliefs and actual practices, as well as the significant shift from emphasis on original alienation and the essential need for divine reconciliation to stress on the more optimistic and consoling aspects of the traditional Christian message. Since we may assume that our findings reflect the taught tradition of the churches, we might be tempted to conclude that the major faiths have tailored their doctrines to fit contemporary secular demands.

But such a conclusion would be based on several assumptions meriting careful examination. In the first place, although most people express a definite religious preference, and almost three-fourths consider themselves to be active church members, we may not assume that the expressed beliefs or attitudes of this total group reflect the taught tradition of their respective faiths. Only a little over one-half attend church services with any regularity and roughly the same proportion apparently had pursued no further religious training after the Sunday school instructions received in their youth. As we have insisted, only the stable central core of active participants reflect what the churches are teaching. Furthermore, it is assumed that the current revival constitutes a massive return to the religion of their forefathers by an originally unchurched generation. There is little evidence in our findings to substantiate such an assumption. The vast majority of adult Americans reported that they had been exposed to religious instruction as children, and a survey of the beliefs and practices of the various age categories, covering a span of several generations, indicated no significant trends. Finally, judged on the basis of actively participating believers, there is no valid basis for concluding that past generations of Americans were either more or less religiously inclined than the present. This is not to deny the evidence of recurrent revivals of interest and practice, past or present, but there are no grounds for assuming that the proportion of what we have called the stable, central core of traditional believers has varied a great deal.

Our findings suggest that the present religious situation in this country is far too complex to be explained adequately by the above hypotheses, though they may throw considerable light on some aspects of the current revival. We feel that the three major religious communities must be analyzed separately. Their past experiences, doctrinal starting-points, and contemporary situations differ so widely that it is superficial to lump them together for analysis on the assumption that they have all become equally secularized, Americanized, or to use Herberg's expression, "Protestantized." Some observers appear to be overly impressed by the similarity in beliefs and attitudes manifested by those whom we have called *fellow travelers*, while they seem insufficiently aware that the current revival of interest in religion affects primarily this group of marginals rather than the central core of traditional believers, and since only this latter group will reflect the taught tradition of the churches, it is among them that we must seek for evidence of assumed secularization.

Implicit in what we are saying, of course, is that organized religious systems fulfill both secular and religious functions and may consequently attract adherents on the basis of either or both.[2] A revival occurring in a society characterized by lack of consensus on basic life-values, by anxiety and a growing sense of alienation may indicate no more than a turning to organized religion as a secular haven of refuge or social solidarity; yet the fact that an organized religion can fulfill this function is no proof that it has become secularized. With the possible exception of some of the smaller sects, no organized religious group at present pretends to constitute a "society of saints." The proportion of marginals, fellow travelers, or casual adherents associated with a given religious group tells us nothing about the vitality of the specifically religious functions it may be fulfilling. Hence we feel that what is taken for the secularization of the churches may represent only the secularization of some of the participants. This can scarcely be considered a new phenomenon unless we assume that in the past all members sought affiliation with the churches for purely religious motives.

If we were to attempt an adequate explanation of the present religious situation as revealed in our findings, we would proceed as follows. First, we would assume as a general principle thoroughly validated by history that the creed, cult, and code of an organized religious system will depend not only on the inherent logic of its dogmas but also on the cultural settings within which they are developed. Thus the beliefs and practices of the American churches will necessarily reflect the influence of American society, together with the special conditions experienced by each group within that society. The relationship between religion and society is a two-way street. The American experience is so interesting because it represents the period in Western history when the traditional faiths were most completely exposed to the influence of modern democratic institutions without benefit of state support. Under such circumstances, the churches were forced to re-examine traditional concepts, as well as long accepted definitions of the situation, since their positions as competing minorities did not permit them to try to put new wine into old bottles.[3]

Because the point is significant for understanding the present situation, let us recall briefly the major factors that helped to shape our past, for, although the American religious experience represents a continuation of the broad stream of Western religious experience, it remains in many ways unique. An essential feature of this uniqueness is related to the relatively recent development of the United States as a nation. Compared to other countries in the Western world, we are a new nation. The all-inclusive, restrictive traditions, accumulated through centuries and built into the very social structure of older nations, were not present to mold the attributes and the outlooks of the American people. They faced the problem of founding a new nation in a stern and stubborn environment where their ability to devise new methods and their willingness to make numerous adjustments constituted the very requisites of survival. The character of all their institutions is colored by these circumstances. To be sure, all immigrants to the New World, whether early colonists or later arrivals, brought with them a cultural mold shaped by Old World traditions, but the demands of their environment, together with their relative isolation from the homeland, soon led to the development of new value-orientations and different institutional patterns.

Man's relationship to God as expressed in formal religion was perhaps least affected by the fact of immigration; yet the task of building a new nation soon worked profound changes even in the way the American people came to define the practical implications of their traditional beliefs. Religious toleration became a necessity, if not an ideal. The bitterness and exclusiveness of early theocratic conceptions, frequently fostered by colonial governments that supported an established church, were gradually mitigated under the impact of more practical concerns. Compulsory religious uniformity is not easily enforced in a country with an open frontier, while some degree of unity was required in fighting the Indians and Frenchmen to the North, as well as in throwing off the yoke of the British. At the same time, the new country needed settlers, and early Americans, like their descendants, were too practical-minded to let religious differences interfere with business.

Further, the constant necessity of dominating and transcending the many natural obstacles they faced led the American people to place great value on effective action. Of what use were theory and speculation when one was surrounded with practical problems requiring immediate solutions if one hoped to survive? A pragmatic outlook has long pervaded the national mind, and American religion has not been unaffected. Indeed, some religious leaders boasted of this fact, pointing out that American churches were characteristically activistic, that is, they preached a "practical theology," one that scoffed at "dogmatic subtleties and philosophical abstractions," and "gets things done." Such lack of rigorous precision in beliefs, so characteristic of what is loosely termed *liberal* Christians, renders it difficult to define just what many did believe.

Americans, moreover, succeeded remarkably well in dominating nature, and this success led to a spirit of optimism that affected even their religious views. Whether we consider the healthy-mindedness described by William James or the undogmatic heartiness promoted by others, the net result was a pervasive youthful confidence in the possibilities of human effort and a corresponding de-emphasis on those doctrinal aspects of the historic faiths presenting a pessimistic view of human nature. This note of optimism, perhaps more than any other, sets American religion apart from its Old World origins and its European contemporaries.[4]

The prevailing spirit of pragmatism and optimism so profoundly affected the whole climate of opinion in America that some were tempted to value religion itself primarily for its social usefulness. This characteristically enlightenment view of religion had always been shared by a limited number of the educated, but the orthodox religious traditions of the West never doubted that the essential function of the churches was to serve as the means of reconciling dependent, sinful mankind to God. They conceived the essential human problem as primarily man's need for salvation, because at the very beginning of its history the human race had been deprived of its friendship with God by a disorder of the will that sacrificed God to self, and spirit to impulse. Viewed in this frame of reference, formal religion appeared not only as an instrument of salvation, but as a strong disciplinary force offering the basis for unifying moral theory and practice in men's lives.

It appears that by the turn of the century many no longer viewed religion primarily in this frame of reference, for they became so preoccupied with the conquest of nature and efforts to adapt social institutions to ever changing needs that they began to define the basic human problem chiefly as the need for adjusting to nature and society. According to their view, organized religion served a socially useful function by promoting the spirit of brotherhood and interpreting man's perennial efforts at the more efficient exploitation of nature as the fulfillment of the Christian ideal. Thus religion continued to be highly esteemed because it promoted cherished cultural goals and reconciled the practical exigencies of traditional religious beliefs with prevailing secular interests.

Finally, American religion, considered as an element of the culture, has been both in origin and actual fact, predominantly Protestant—and a special blend of Protestantism. This is to say, it was initially shaped primarily by the Calvinist and Anabaptist forms of original Protestantism, since both Lutheranism and Anglicanism exerted comparatively little influence in the beginning, while Roman Catholic and Jewish groups were originally received and have remained as tolerated minorities. It may be convenient today to speak of American religion as divided into three, large, equal religious communities, but it would be erroneous to conclude that these three religious groups have exercised a uniform influence on American culture. Whatever the future may hold, up to the present, American religion as a cultural influence has been chiefly Protestant.

These historical factors have conditioned the beliefs and practices of all religious groups in America. Religious pluralism, the acceptance of tolerance, at least as an ideal, respect for efficient action, emphasis on the social utility of religion, and the comparative isolation of the two major religious minorities, are all specifically American phenomena that have drawn comments from numerous foreign and native observers alike. Yet there is relatively little agreement concerning how these factors have conditioned the religion of the American people. It explains nothing to attach the pejorative labels, secularization or Americanization, to all processes denoting change from past conceptions or practices, inasmuch as the processes in question may be related to nonessentials, necessary adjustments, logical doctrinal developments, shifts in emphasis, or radical modifications.

Taking into consideration the historical factors mentioned above, we would interpret our findings as follows. First, there are several reasons why religion is still held in high esteem by the majority. Because there is no established church, religious participation is voluntary; the maintenance of a given organized religious group necessarily encourages the active concern of individual members; and religion itself is not identified with the state, a specific social class, or a quasi-political organization including a good proportion of pseudo-members affiliated to promote secular purposes.

Furthermore, religious pluralism, both as fact and possibility, has served to generate creative competition and rivalry, to strengthen ingroup solidarity, and to provide suitable vehicles of religious expression for those dissatisfied members who, if there were only an established church, might have become either anti-clerical or anti-religious. Under conditions of pluralism, however, religion tends to exert a minimum of influence on social institutions and cultural goals, inasmuch as no single faith or denomination is in a dominating position. As a result, the churches emphasize the personal rather than social implications of their doctrines, and may continue to be highly esteemed precisely because they do not "interfere" with the secular pursuits of their adherents. As it has developed in this country, therefore, religious pluralism has tended to postpone the inevitable confrontation of religion with science or modern social problems, at least, among the majority of the faithful. Since the public schools may not teach religion, many students do not become aware of the need to integrate the implications of their religious beliefs and modern science, while no religious group feels called upon to spell out in any detail the relevance of religion when seeking solutions to modern critical social issues. This separation or compartmentalization of religion and reality enables many to maintain quite inconsistent beliefs and attitudes, though it may also alienate some who seek to develop an integrated philosophy of life.

Second, a quality that we have already noted, and one that may be most important in the long run, is the significant shift in doctrinal emphasis evidenced by the core group of the faithful among all the major Christian divisions and resulting in a modification of the traditional orientation to God as Sovereign Ruler and Judge. Thus in contrast to the past, the faithful manifest minor concern over the possibility of eternal alienation in Hell, just as they no longer regard the salvific and reconciling function of the churches as the most important. In other words, the core groups still adhere to the traditional complex of religious beliefs and practices, but awareness of the implications of the Fall, of the essential need for redemption, and of the inescapable exigencies of divine justice and consequent personal accountability, no longer dominate their approach to God. We might almost state that the transcendental aspects of the traditional Gestalt have receded into the background, while the immediate, human implications of divine relationship have become the objects of major interest and concern. Since we are considering the effects of cultural conditioning, it may be of interest to note that this shift in accent parallels the change in the political order from emphasis on the sovereignty of the monarch or state to stress on the rights of the person.

In this sense, one might maintain that American churches have become "democratized," though it would be less misleading to call it a shift in doctrinal emphasis or a change of accent. On the other hand, we feel that the change is highly significant for several reasons. Emphasis on the human aspects of the divine relationship probably helps explain the perennial attractiveness of religion and the apparent ease with which religious commitments are reconciled with secular pursuits. What is more important, lack of emphasis on divine sovereignty may easily prepare the ground for a convenient rationalization in which divine imperatives are transformed from absolutes into ideals. Thus the traditionally defined moral implications of Christian teaching are retained as important general guides or goals to be aimed at, but they are no longer regarded as universally applicable in all instances; and it is held that exceptions must be provided for, particularly in modern complex, rapidly changing situations. Our findings on beliefs relating to the morality of divorce and contraceptive birth control offer ample evidence of the prevalence of this type of rationalization, and, though its extent among Roman Catholics was most unexpected because of the clear-cut stand of their church, it should be noted, as we have previously pointed out, that the recent permissive official pronouncements of the Protestant churches merely recognized a *fait accompli* among their members.

Although we believe the shift in doctrinal emphasis that we have been discussing is highly significant, and clearly reflects cultural conditioning, we would insist that, as long as the churches include a stable, central core group of participants who retain the ensemble of traditional beliefs and practices, even though a change in accent has occurred, we cannot speak of the secularization of the churches but only of the secularization of some, perhaps even a good proportion, of their members. This distinction is pertinent and crucial, for the core group of believers rather than the fellow travelers reflect the current teaching of the churches and represent whatever vitality or potential for survival they may presently possess.

Are we not overlooking the fact that the churches appear impotent in dealing with the major issues confronting modern man? Have we not dismissed too lightly the evidence of "Americanization" or "secularization" in the churches? These latter terms are generally used so loosely and with such vague referents that they tend to confuse the issues. In our explanation we have tried to define what they would mean in terms of organized religion and to what extent the churches appeared to be affected. On the other hand, we would be inclined to concede the charge that the churches appear currently impotent, though we would deny the implication that this is the result of their fusion with or subordination to the secular values of democracy as expressed in the American system. As we have indicated in Chapter One, since any organized religious system tends to define the status or position of its adherents in the cosmic order, it must remain creative if it is to avoid becoming a mere cultural residue or a subsidiary institution of the ongoing social system; for, unless it continues to provide a relatively consistent, orderly, meaningful interpretation of the total, evolving human situation experienced by its adherents, they will turn to other sources in their attempts to "make sense" of their world. Such creativity, as we have shown, is the function of a religious elite.

The churches in America have not succeeded in producing a religious elite capable of making the doctrines of the traditional faiths relevant to our complex and rapidly changing social order or to the new insights into human nature furnished by modern science. The result has been a gradual withdrawal of religious influence from increasingly extensive sectors of human activity and endeavor, for the majority, even of the faithful, fail to see that religion has any pertinent contributions to make in such areas. Hence through a process of compartmentalization, many Americans continue to adhere to traditional religious beliefs and practices, no doubt finding them psychologically satisfying and perhaps even relevant in their private lives, yet their basic value-orientations, as well as the normative structures that pattern their routine pursuits, are based on premises of values having no recognized relationships to the religious beliefs they profess. As we have suggested, the fact that the religious understanding of many remains at the Sunday school or child-hood level obviously facilitates this segmented approach, while the separation of religion and education in the schools leaves many unaware of the need for integration.

The failure of the churches to produce a creative elite stems from both practical and theoretical sources. Inadequate train-ing, in addition to necessary preoccupation with the immediate needs of the churches in terms of buildings, instructions, and guidance, caused many religious leaders to focus most of their attention on meeting demands of a practical nature. At the same time, the rate of change in both the social system and in science accelerated so rapidly and presented such radical chal-lenges to traditional conceptions of social order and nature that many apparently were quite unable to keep abreast of their times. But there were also problems at the level of theory. A glance at the record shows that religious revivalist leaders uniformly ignored scientific advances and the broader social implications of religious beliefs while stressing conversion, confession of sins, and personal commitments. Many of the more orthodox leaders, because they did not understand the relationships between religious beliefs, values, and normative structures, tended to canonize the past as the most adequate expression of the Christian ideal; and they consequently re-garded most social changes as unhealthy and new scientific theories regarding human nature as a threat to their cherished beliefs. A considerable number, of course, reacted energetically to this sterile conservatism, but they tended to discredit themselves by lacking realism in their enthusiasm for social reform, as well as theological depth in their interpretations of scientific advances.

As a result, the religious situation in America has become extremely complex. Within the Protestant community, a substantial, energetic block of primarily fundamentalist persuasion appears little concerned about coming to terms with the modern world, while the more intellectual, neo-orthodox leaders of the remaining bodies, little disposed to accept moral absolutes derived from religion, are apparently finding it increasingly difficult to demonstrate the relevancy of traditional religious beliefs to the critical issues confronting modern man. Within the Roman Catholic community, the situation is somewhat different because of the church's organizational structure and minority status. There is ample evidence that the traditional system of religious instruction and indoctrination, relying heavily on simple acceptance of authority, no longer adequately prepares the faithful to withstand the full impact of secular pressures in an affluent society. At the same time, the lack of a creative elite is painfully reflected in the failure to rethink traditional positions or to make explicit the functional exigencies of accepted moral imperatives. Perhaps because of their quasi-segregation and minority status, Roman Catholics have not yet grasped the full implications of religious pluralism in a secular culture.

The major problems faced by all religious minorities under conditions of pluralism stem primarily from two sources: intergroup tensions and the very nature of the social system itself. An understanding of these sources involves several theoretical considerations. Let us begin by attempting to evaluate the significance of our findings relating to these areas and then proceed to develop the needed theoretical considerations.

Religious pluralism has been so characteristic of our nation that the ideal of toleration, though seldom examined, has seldom been called into question in recent times. This does not mean that there have not been outbursts of bigotry and intolerance. Churches and convents have been burned by angry mobs, powerful organizations have been formed under the banner of bigotry, cheap demagogues have never hesitated to exploit the ignorance and intolerance of some groups; but such actions have always been regarded by serious Americans as a desecration of a sacred ideal. Historically, America is a "nation of nations" in which unity became possible because mutual respect and tolerance formed an essential part of the national ethos. Temporary deviations from the ideal have occurred, but the American conscience has never been at rest until the ideal was restored.

Some contemporary observers feel that they can detect an increase of tension among religious groups, though pertinent comparative data in this area are not easily obtained. At the same time, it should be noted that the popular discussion of current political issues bearing on religion may lead to an increase of critical literature in the religious press without necessarily indicating an increase of tension or intolerance among the American people in general. The main impression derived from our study of intergroup attitudes is that the average American is not overly conscious of tension among members of the major religious communities. However, we discovered some attitudes that could supply the basis for tension should the proper occasion arise.

Let us explain. Relatively few people reported that they or any members of their family had ever had any unpleasant personal experience that might have caused them to dislike members of the outgroup. Relatively few felt that the outgroups tried to interfere in any way with their religious beliefs or personal liberties. On a comparative basis, people thought very well of each other in regard to loyalty, living up to their religion, fairness in business, treating their families right, honesty in public office, helping people of their own faith, and generosity toward public charities. The one exception was the roughly one-third of Protestants and Roman Catholics who considered members of the Jewish group to be less fair in business than the members of their own religious beliefs. Most people also expressed a uniformly favorable attitude toward each other's clergymen in regard to living up to their calling, helping their own people, living for the next world, loyalty to country, and setting a good personal example. A considerable percentage of Protestants and Jews, however, felt that Roman Catholic clergy were deficient in cooperating with others and in giving intelligent leadership to their followers. In general, these attitudes indicated that people wanted to be fair, understanding, and tolerant toward what might be termed the specifically religious traits of other groups.

On the other hand, we discovered some attitudes that offered a poor basis for good intergroup relationships. For example, a considerable percentage in each group thought that people of their beliefs were looked down on, that some groups did not show due respect for the beliefs of others, and that they would be discriminated against by outgroup employers because of their religion. Such attitudes imply a definition of outgroup feelings that may or may not be correct, but they indicate a sense of insecurity and suspicion that render good intergroup relations more difficult. Further, particularly among members of the dominant Protestant community, there appeared considerable concern over what they thought was the tendency of the minority groups to be uncooperative, to stick together too much, to be too aggressive in making converts, to use their positions to build up their group, and, in short, to attempt to get too much power in the United States. As we have indicated, such insecurity may be interpreted in various ways, but it clearly offers fertile ground for the growth of intergroup mistrust and tension.

These intergroup attitudes are quite in line with our other findings. The American people are not deeply concerned about differences in religious beliefs and practices, for they apparently accept them as part of the American Way. Organized religion, however, represented in a specific social group and considered under its specifically social aspects as a group capable of competing with others for prestige and power, is obviously not regarded with indifference. In this connection, the historically developed patterns of intergroup relationships become highly pertinent, inasmuch as there are indications that some people feel the traditional "balance of power" is being threatened by aggressive, cohesive, mobile minorities. Whether or not the pattern may be changing, is not pertinent here, but as long as such attitudes persist, religious intergroup tensions will remain part of the American scene.

Let us now consider the second source of religious minority problems developing under conditions of pluralism. There are two major reasons why the social system itself tends to generate problems for religious minorities. First, in any ongoing social system, values and behavioral patterns tend to be integrated, that is, the values of the dominant culture tend to be embodied in the normative structures regulating accepted conduct. Hence religious minorities within such a society will face serious problems to the extent that the values they cherish differ from the values promoted by the dominant culture, since minority members actively participate in the ongoing social system. Such problems would not arise, of course, if a minority isolated itself from the influences of the dominant culture, as a few small sects such as the Mennonites, Hutterites, Dukhobors, and so on, have attempted with some apparent success.

Second, because the major institutions in an ongoing social system are interrelated, a change in one institution has widespread repercussions leading to readjustment in others. Hence when change occurs, it is gradually "geared into" the entire system, so that relevant social relationships and normative structures are modified in terms of it, that is, it gradually becomes "institutionalized." For example, the introduction of a change like contraceptive birth control has wide repercussions throughout the total social system. Thus early age at marriage need not lead to large families, for pregnancies can be controlled. Children can be "bunched" in the early years of marriage, because family size can be planned. Young wives may enter the work force or remain at school if they choose, because first pregnancies can be postponed. The maintenance of living standards, the "keeping up with the Joneses," in dress, entertainment, and the accumulation of material goods in general, becomes possible to the extent that the couple choose to limit their offspring when competition appears to require it. On the other hand, members of religious minority groups whose value systems prohibit the use of this key cultural solution, are thrown out of balance with the total system and consequently must either develop some workable form of social equilibrium in terms of their own distinctive values or encounter conflicts and frustrations at every step.[5]

Hence a minority's problem is not that it must deal with individual objectionable acts, but with what it considers a morally pathological system. From the minority's viewpoint, many culturally "normal," institutionalized practices must be regarded as morally pathological. It is this normalcy of the pathological in the dominant system that makes the achievement of minority values so difficult. In short, a religious minority cherishing distinctive values must participate in a social system geared to goals they may not accept, and which has achieved some type of working equilibrium or balance by institutionalizing practices they may consider morally pathological. All participants of a complex, technically advanced, urban environment must work out a suitable *modus vivendi* by constantly adjusting to changing situations, but religious minorities face the additional problem of developing adjustments within a framework of values judged consonant with their distinctive religious beliefs.

Our analysis of the social sources of minority problems involves a conception of the relationship between religion and society that merits further clarification. Let us begin with an analysis of the pertinent aspects of a social system. As we use the term *social system* here, it includes the total patterned regularity or structure of social interaction observable in an organized group or society. In an ongoing social system, the essential structure through which human social activities are directed, ordered, and integrated is constituted by the accepted sets of obligatory norms centering around the fulfillment of man's basic social needs—sexual, economic, political, and so on. These norms may be viewed as directives for action, since they define the acceptable ways of doing things in a given society.

What is the source of the obligatory quality of such norms? Social norms imply values, that is, goals or objectives that are considered worth striving for and to which the norms are related as means to ends. People usually act directly on the basis of the norms they have learned, inasmuch as short of crisis situations, during which a specific norm may be brought into question, the majority seldom reflect on the meaning of their actions, that is, on the values implicit in the norms they are following.

What is the source of the values embodied in the norms? Values are related to the beliefs concerning the nature of man and his world as held by the group. In this context, beliefs represent statements about the nature of reality. In an integrated system of action, beliefs furnish the ultimate rationale for the values or ends embodied in the system's obligatory normative structure.

It may help to clarify our understanding of the relationships between beliefs, values, and norms, if we analyze a specific social institution like the family. Such analysis reveals three elements of primary importance. First, we discover a set of social relationships or recurrent interaction patterns describing the mutual orientations to each other of husband and wife, parents and children, conjugal unit and extended family, family and society. These relationships are regulated by a set of accepted norms or institutionalized means judged necessary for, or at least considered consonant with, the practical fulfillment of the group's sexual needs. Hence these norms have meaning, that is, they "make sense," only in terms of the sexual values, or family objectives, held by the group.

Second, further analysis reveals the major characteristics of these institutionalized sexual objectives or values. Broadly speaking, they represent the culturally devised sets of goals, preferences, or ideals defining the meaning of sex, marital union, parenthood, and kinship. Since these values deal with human needs, they are ultimately related to the conceptions of human nature and society held by the group. Of course, as a given culture endures and evolves, some of these objectives, or the values associated with them, may receive symbolic expression, and in time, these vaguely defined, symbolically expressed values may acquire a quasi-autonomous existence, so that they remain operative in a culture long after the conception of human nature from which they were initially derived has been rejected, reformulated, or no longer recognized as pertinent by the members of society.

Third, inasmuch as institutionalized values or objectives deal with human needs, it follows that their ultimate rationale or basis is the set of beliefs concerning the nature of the human agent and society held by the group. What is man? What is his origin? What is his nature, individual and social? What is his destiny? The preferences, values, or goals related to the satisfaction of men's sexual needs will be defined in terms of the answers people give to these questions. At least in their initial formulation, family norms, representing the culturally approved means by which human sexual needs are to be fulfilled, embody values or goals based on a set of shared beliefs about the nature of man and society. Indeed, as we have indicated, all obligatory social norms embody values based on beliefs about the nature of reality.

Let us now review briefly some of the pertinent elements of a religious system as outlined in Chapter One. We used the term *religious system* there to include the complex of creed, cult, and code constituting the participants' total conception of their relationship to God and the practical consequences they believe derive from these relationships. We also pointed out that beliefs about the sacred or divine never appear as segmented, relatively isolated phenomena. They are always part of a more extensive system that includes the past religious experiences of the group, together with a more or less distinct image or conception of the human agent. Considered in its broadest extension, this image involves a set of beliefs concerning man's origin; his relationships to space and time; the essential qualities of his nature and consequently his orientation toward his fellowmen, society, and the world of nature; and finally, his life purpose or destiny, that is, the desirable terminus of his development or fulfillment in the cosmic order.

The content of a religious creed is expressed in dogmas, myths, and symbols. The cult, including religious festivals, ceremonies, and rites, guarantees the continuity and purity of doctrine through successive generations of the faithful. The code defines the actions prescribed, proscribed, or permitted by creed and cult. Moreover, since a religious system also includes a conception or image of man, it furnishes the basic beliefs underlying the group's major value-orientations and obligatory normative structure.

This latter observation is highly pertinent to the present discussion, for it indicates a significant aspect of the relationship between religious and social systems. In this connection, it should be noted that we are here concerned with the social impact of religion considered as a set of beliefs, conceptions, or ideas, and not as an organized community of the faithful. Viewed from this perspective, religious beliefs affect a social system and its major institutions by furnishing the conception or image of man held by the participants. We have already pointed out the basic role played by such conceptions in the development of a society's normative structures. Thus to the extent that a religious system furnishes essential elements in the group's conception of man, it supplies the indispensable foundation or rationale for the system of values, goals, ends, or objectives embodied in their obligatory norms and consequently in their practical programs of action.

There are several reasons why the significance of this relationship between religious and social systems tends to be overlooked. Over time, organized religious systems tend to become identified with sets of prescribed or proscribed attitudes, norms and actions related to cult or code, and assumed to be based on revelation and/or tradition. A perennial danger inherent in such systems is to further identify a given cultural attempt to implement an abstract value with the value itself. Thus cultural implementations, that is, the historical institutions and associated patterned relationships embodying accepted premises of values, are thought to be as sacred as the values themselves and are defended against change accordingly. For example, feudalism, monarchy, traditional social class distinctions, systems of private property, and so on, have been mistakenly identified with religious values, though they represented only more or less adequate attempts to embody abstract values in concrete institutional norms.

Further, the relevance of religion to society has remained obscured, owing to the reluctance of many modern social scientists to acknowledge the pertinence of values in their analysis. Yet logic would require that they content themselves with the mere description of social phenomena if they refuse to consider values, for rational social programs, like practical judgments, are conclusions based upon the application of premises of values to sets of pertinent social facts. To deny that a practical program involves premises of values is to deny it rationality; and it is well to reflect that one does not eliminate values from a program merely by refusing to discuss one's basic assumptions. Once the premises of values implicit in practical judgments and social programs are made explicit, their relationships to an underlying conception of man becomes evident. Ultimately, an essential element of all definitions of human values is derived from some conception, some image of the human person.

Up to this point we have discussed only the essential point of contact between religious and social systems. But the location of this "point of insertion" does not tell us why religious systems apparently differ widely in their "contributions" or practical relevance to social systems. To answer this question we must consider how various religious systems envisage what we have called the ethical process, that is, the determination of the right ordering of man's individual and social life on the basis of his religious beliefs. It should be obvious that such basic beliefs as the brotherhood of man, the equality of all under God, Christian stewardship of earthly goods, and so on, acquire normative significance in the practical order primarily only when applied to specific social institutions and definite human relationships in concrete social situations. Exhortations to practice social justice or maximize love can have little social relevance unless one can determine the specific demands of justice in real life situations or define the manifold, relative exigencies of charity in current complex relationships.

We pointed out in Chapter One that there are several ways of conceiving the process by which relevant values are derived from religious beliefs and translated into society's normative structure. For example, one may follow a system of casuistry and seek for precedents or directives in traditional religious documents regarded either as revealed or as the inspired *dicta* of great religious leaders; one may maintain that the order of creation was so vitiated by the Fall that, outside of explicit directives in the Bible, the patterns of ethical ideals and normative structures we currently formulate must be regarded as relative, culture-bound products having no essential direct relationship of origin to religious beliefs conceived as absolutes; or finally, one may hold that the Creator's law can be discovered by reason in the natures of things, and thus the ethical process is considered dynamic and existential in the sense that human reason, supplemented by principles drawn from revelation and tradition, formulates relevant systems of values in terms of natures and the changing exigencies of the situation.

Although the major faiths we have been discussing may conceive the ethical process somewhat differently, they all maintain that religious beliefs have personal and social implications. Such implications would seem fairly obvious in a tradition-oriented, relatively integrated culture, but the churches in America are subjected to rapid and extensive change under conditions of pluralism, and consequently face the persistent challenge of re-examining and reformulating the implications of their specific beliefs if they are to offer their adherents a religiously meaningful interpretation of the world in which they live. We contend that it is the failure of the churches to meet this challenge adequately that is frequently mistaken for secularization. A substantial core group of the faithful still maintain traditional beliefs and practices, but the churches have not been able to develop a creative elite capable of spelling out the practical implications of these beliefs in current situations. As a result, traditional beliefs are retained, while the faithful tend to follow the norms and standards established by the dominant secular culture.

This indictment of the churches may appear somewhat exaggerated to readers who recall the extensive efforts of some of the churches to develop social programs and specific directives for conduct. Commendable as such efforts surely are, they constitute, for the most part, only the first step in the process. It should be obvious from our discussion that sets of premises of values, ideal goals, or social objectives do not constitute a practical program of action. Socially relevant values have functional exigencies or requisites, that is, they can be actualized by participants only if related institutional structures and implementing patterns of conduct are designed to make this achievement possible. Broadly speaking, such functional requisites stand in relation to ultimate goals as means to ends; yet they are not specifically predetermined by these goals except in the rare cases in which there is only one means available for achieving a given end. When this necessary relationship between means and ends does not exist, the institutional forms and behavioral patterns (means) required to implement a desired goal cannot be deduced *a priori* from the goal or from the conception of human nature held by the group but must be developed in terms of related institutions, the past experience of the group, and their available resources. We need only call attention to the varied types of political, economic, or family systems that have existed in different Christian communities to demonstrate the point.

In this connection, it appears that the churches have not been sufficiently aware of, or have not been able to produce a creative elite capable of dealing with the unending, arduous task of developing, modifying, and adjusting means that would adequately assure the realization of their desired goals. This task constitutes a perennial challenge to the faithful, for at best, their efforts will represent no more than "cultural approximations" of their ideals. They will be approximations because their very relatedness to a given social milieu limits them to being but one expression of the ideal. They are subject to modification, for changes in the total social system may render ineffective some established patterns and call for the substitution of others. Hence, not Americanization or secularization but failure to meet this challenge adequately has caused the churches to confine their message to general principles and has drawn the charge of irrelevancy from modern critics.

Our remarks do not imply that the churches are responsible for the construction and maintenance of secular society; yet they must be concerned with formulating in the temporal order the practical implications of the religious beliefs that they teach. The quality of such concern manifested by the traditional faiths will reflect their current vitality, for each generation of the faithful must reformulate and attempt to reapply the personal and social implications of its religious commitments if it is to bear witness to the truths that it professes. In this sense, the churches may never rest satisfied with the *status quo*. Although the transcendental values they cherish can never be adequately embodied in any temporal order, they must continue to attempt to develop workable approximations that respect the functional requisites of these values in a given society, or admit that their beliefs involve values that are unattainable.

As we have suggested, it is precisely this need of the churches to define and implement the practical implications of their specific beliefs that constitutes the major challenge they face in a religiously pluralist society. We may also add that it becomes the chief source of interfaith tensions and conflicts. Under conditions of pluralism, therefore, the traditional faiths may serve both as divisive and integrating factors, while in a purely secular society, they inevitably challenge the basic assumption of the dominant culture, for it is unthinkable that they could ever accept as a permanent settlement one law for themselves and another for the world.

As we conclude this study of religion in mid-century America, we are fully aware that some questions remain unanswered. How does one estimate the depth and vitality of a people's religion? We have documented the complexity and diversity of contemporary religious beliefs, practices, and attitudes. We have shown that religion still constitutes a pervasive element in American culture and will probably remain so in the future. We have uncovered a substantial, stable core group of traditional believers in all the churches and suggested that they be carefully distinguished from the fellow travelers currently swelling the recorded membership. We have noted the spirit of relative tolerance and mutual acceptance among the major faiths though they differed considerably in their attitudes toward some practical programs. Yet the real nature of religion in America remains open to conjecture.

Contrary to some contemporary observers, we maintain that the traditional faiths have not been secularized, or become so fused with American democratic values that they may now be classified as culture religions. Although the attitudes of the faithful were found to reflect some shift in doctrinal emphasis, we contend that what has been taken for secularization is the failure of the churches to remain adequately creative. The implications of the extensive developments in science and social organization have not been interpreted in terms of value premises derived from traditional religious beliefs, while the functional requisites of professed religious ideals have received scant attention from religious leaders. As a result, the modern believer tends to find himself living in a world of which an increasing portion no longer "makes sense" in terms of his religion, and committed to values that frequently appear unattainable under current circumstances.

The popularity of religion is no necessary indication of its vitality. The traditional faiths face a radical challenge in our affluent, secular society, for unless they can define the pertinent personal and social implications of the specific transcendental beliefs and values they profess, they will lose not only their identities but forfeit their claims to the attention of the sincere. The churches must not be reduced to being *comfort stations* for the worried or *morale builders* for the culture, but neither must they become pious assemblies of *moral eunuchs.* Either they continue to interpret life within a framework of values extending above civilization and outside of human history or they will fulfill no *irreplaceable* function.

Notes

1. Americans tend to forget that they are products of the broad Western cultural stream and consequently view man and his universe in Judaic and Christian frames of reference. Many values that they assume to be "self-evident" are not such to men raised outside of these traditions. In this connection, experience with the United Nations has been a maturing, if sobering process for the American people.

2. Historically acquired, nonessential organizational aspects or identifications may also repel.

3. See "Tradition and Experience in American Theology," by Daniel B. Williams in *The Shaping of American Religion, op. cit.,* pp. 443–495.

4. The effects of this cultural conditioning are least apparent among the primarily rural or small town fundamentalist bodies.

5. See John L. Thomas, S.J., *Marriage and Rhythm* (Westminster, Maryland: The Newman Press, 1957), pp. 57–65.

Sampling Methods Used

THE following information on the sampling methods used in the survey on religion in the United States was prepared by Ben Gaffin and Associates, a Chicago marketing and opinion research firm. It contains complete details regarding the planning and execution of the sample.

PART 1. PLANNING THE SAMPLE

How the Sample Size Was Arrived At

Our aim in determining the sample size was two-fold: to keep the sample as small as practicable in order to operate within an obtainable budget, and to have it sufficiently large to give reasonably reliable information for the major subgroups by which we plan to cross tabulate. On the basis of estimates for the major religious groups, and the U. S. population distribution by Census regions, three thousand cases seemed to be the minimum adequate number. This was the number we recommended in our proposal on the project.

Reverend Paul Bussard, Editor of the *Catholic Digest*, to

whom the proposal was submitted, took it to Dr. George Gallup for review. Gallup concurred in our recommended sample size and also went along with our basic sampling methods as outlined in the proposal.

Stratification of Sample by City Size and Census Region

The proposal recommended that the 3,000 interviews be distributed throughout the nine Census regions of the U. S. in the same proportion as the 1950 U. S. population, and that they be distributed within each Census region by city size and urban-rural breakdowns, in the same proportions as the 1950 population within that region.

To avoid the excessive travel costs of sending interviewers to places where none of our 1150 resident interviewers lived, we decided to select the actual interview points on a judgment basis rather than by purely random methods.

The assumptions we used in constructing the sample were given in the job proposal as follows:

"Assuming that there is no correlation between the distribution of our interviewers and the religious affiliations of U. S. citizens, it seems safe to select the cities in which to interview on the basis of interviewer coverage. The number of interviews per city will be determined on the basis of distribution of U. S. population. Our interviewer distribution by Census region, state, and city-size is given in an appendix.

"It is important that selection of the blocks within the city wherein interviews are to be made, the selection of the households within the block and the individuals within the household to be interviewed, should not be left to the discretion of the interviewers.

"These selections, therefore, will be based on purely random methods which will be worked out later."

PART II. CONSTRUCTING THE SAMPLE

STEP 1. *Decision to Use a Cluster Sample*

Since one of the major costs in field interviewing is the travel time and travel expense involved in the interviewers going from one interview location to another, we decided to use a cluster-type sample for greater efficiency. This type sample seemed particularly suited for this survey, since observation indicated that, except in certain neighborhoods in the largest cities, people of different religious persuasions tend to intermingle to a large extent in their residences.

We decided that a cluster-size of six interviews would represent a full day's work for an interviewer. Having the interviewers begin work in the early afternoon, and work on in the evening, would enable them to interview men as well as women at their homes in the proper proportions.

Having decided on the use of clusters of six interviews, the sample design then became a problem of selecting 500 interviewing points throughout the country.

STEP 2. *Stratifying the Sample by Census Region and City Size*

The 500 interview-units were then distributed by the nine Census regions, and by ten city-size-and-rural categories within each Census region, in the same proportions as the 1950 Census estimates.

STEP 3. *Selection of Specific Interviewing Spots*

In those Census regions where there was only one city within a city-size category, the interviews were necessarily assigned to that particular city.

Where there were a number of cities within a Census region

and a city-size category, the specific interviewing location was selected by judgment.

Since the budget was limited, and since our field organization was large (1,150 interviewers) and well distributed (representatives in all 48 states) and since there was no relation between religion and the distribution of our interviewers (at the time of assigning the interviews, we did not know the religion of the interviewers selected) and since it seemed reasonable to assume that the religious preference of the interviewers would probably be representative of the predominant preference of the area in which they lived, we felt that the selection of individual interviewing points would be better made by selecting our better interviewers (achieving as wide a geographical distribution within any Census region as possible and observing, of course, our original stratifications) than by selecting the interviewing points strictly at random and then trying to get interviewers to cover these points.

The basic rules followed in the spot-selections were: that not more than five clusters (in the smaller spots, as few as one) would be assigned a single interviewer; that a wide geographic distribution would be maintained, with interviews distributed roughly by state by city size as nearly as practicable; and that the basic stratification be adhered to strictly.

Step 4. *Selection of Blocks and Households*

After selecting the specific cities, towns and rural areas which would be used, the next step was the selection of the specific households from which interviews would be taken.

The interviewing points were accordingly divided into six groups: (1) urban areas for which Census tract information and block statistics were available; (2) urban areas with

Census tract but no block statistics; (3) urban areas for which no Census information was available but for which there were current city directories; (4) urban areas for which there were current telephone books on file at the Illinois Bell offices in Chicago; (5) urban areas for which there were no telephone directories available in Chicago; and (6) rural areas.

(1) Urban areas for which both Census tract and block statistics were available.

The Census tract in which a cluster of interviews was to be made was selected on the basis of probability proportionate to the total dwelling units, with a systematic selection of tracts after a random start.

For example, in Boston, Massachusetts, there were six clusters to be selected. The sampling interval was determined by dividing the total number of the Boston 1950 population by six. The census tracts were numbered in a continual sequence, and a table of random numbers was used to select the first sampling point. The actual block within the selected tract was picked by interpolation. The second sampling point was selected by going down the continuum the distance of the sampling interval. This procedure was followed until all of the six blocks in Boston in which interviews were to be made had been selected. This gave us six specific blocks distributed geographically over the entire city of Boston in proportion to the distribution of the 1950 Boston population.

The southwest corner of the selected block was designated as the "key address" or starting point. Proceeding around the block clockwise, the first interview attempt was made at the first household past the southwest corner.

(2) Urban areas with Census tract but no block statistics.

The procedure followed in selecting the Census tracts within which a cluster of interviews was to be made was the same as that for Group 1 above.

The blocks within the Census tract were numbered, and the specific block to be used for the key address was selected using a table of random numbers. From there on, the procedure was the same as that for Group 1.

(3) Urban areas for which no Census information was available but for which there were current city directories.

Census information was available for practically all cities over 50,000 population. Where no Census information was available, we used Polk or the other city directories wherever current ones existed.

Specific addresses were selected from the directory by a two-step method: the page was selected by a systematic method using a proportionate sampling interval, and with the first page selected by the use of a table of random numbers; and the specific address on the page was selected at random.

This method did not give as consistently widespread geographical distribution as that obtained in the two preceding groups, since the streets were listed alphabetically. It did, however, give a completely random selection of households within the city.

The specific address was considered as the key address, instead of the southwest corner of the block as in the other two groups.

The subsequent procedure, however, was the same as for the first two groups, as is indicated in the "Instructions to Interviewers."

(4) Urban areas for which there were current telephone books on file at the Illinois Bell offices in Chicago.

Where neither current city directories nor Census information was available, current telephone books on file at the Chicago office of the Illinois Bell were used wherever possible.

The same two-step method used with the city directories was followed.

While the key addresses selected in this group of cities were in all cases telephone homes, the homes where the interviews were conducted were not necessarily homes with phones.

It is doubtful, therefore, that any appreciable amount of bias was introduced by using this method of selecting interview-households.

The subsequent interviewer procedures were the same as for the preceding groups.

(5) Urban areas for which there were no current telephone directories available in Chicago.

In these towns, the interviewers selected the key addresses from current telephone books locally available. The methods which they followed were given in the "instructions to Interviewers" as follows:

"Take the telephone directory in which the town or suburb is listed. You will use the name 'Baker' for the first cluster you have to complete in that town, 'Jones' for the second, 'Roberts' for the third, 'Smith' for the fourth, and 'Williams' for the fifth.

"Look in the telephone book for the name which you are to use. If there are one or more people of that name listed, take the FIRST RESIDENT OF THE TOWN WHERE YOU ARE SUPPOSED TO INTERVIEW FOLLOWING THIS NAME. The actual address of this resident is then written down on the card, and becomes the key address.

"If the name you are supposed to use is not listed, take the FIRST RESIDENT OF THE TOWN YOU ARE SUPPOSED

TO INTERVIEW IN, WHICH FOLLOWS WHERE THE NAME *WOULD* HAVE BEEN, *HAD* IT BEEN LISTED."

After selecting and writing the key address on the cluster card, the interviewer then proceeded in the same manner as in Group 1.

(6) Rural areas.

The interviewers selected the rural households to be interviewed, using a three-step method outlined on Pages 6 and 7 of the "Instructions to Interviewers"—they learned the number of rural routes going out of the town from the local postmaster and selected the route for the "key address" using a sampling interval method with a random start; picked as the key address the farm which was about half way out on the swing of the route out from town; and using this farm as a key address, they followed the same procedure as for blocks in town, using a road in the place of a street. They then followed the same procedure as for other groups.

STEP 5. *Selection of Individuals to be Interviewed*

We decided to interview only people 18 years of age or over, since we felt that those under 18 would generally only reflect the opinions of the older people in the household.

Each interviewer was given a sex and age quota for the total number of interviews he was assigned. These quotas were breakdowns of the overall sex and age stratifications for the Census region in which they were to be made. By keeping a tally of the sex and age of the persons they had interviewed as they went along, the interviewers were able to end up with the proper number of interviews for each category.

PART III. CONCLUDING REMARKS

After determining the sampling methods to be used in the survey, we discussed the reasonableness of our approach with several of our research expert friends. All of them concurred that the method would produce a satisfactorily representative sample.

The final sample figures as given in Appendix B "Technical Information on Research Methods Used in the *Catholic Digest* Study of Religious Beliefs, Attitudes and Practices of U.S. Adults" show a comparison of the figures achieved with the Census Bureau estimates.

The only factor in which there was considerable variance between sample and estimates was amount of education. The sample contained 7 per cent more people with only a grade-school education than the Census estimates for the population in the group.

We do not as yet have any satisfactory explanation for this variance. It is our understanding that the Census estimate was also based on sample survey methods, and therefore is also subject to sampling error. Furthermore, though we may be considered brash for suggesting it, we feel that the Census' respondents might have been more apt to inflate the amount of education they claimed to have received than our respondents, who had been, at the point in the interview where they gave us this information, conditioned by reflections on God, Heaven and Hell.

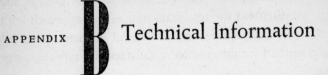

ON RESEARCH METHODS USED IN THE CATHOLIC DIGEST STUDY OF RELIGIOUS BELIEFS, ATTITUDES AND PRACTICES OF U. S. ADULTS

This study is based on 2,987 personal interviews with a representative cross-section of U. S. adults 18 years of age and over. The interviews were made during June and July, 1952.

Purpose of the Study

The objectives of this study were to measure quantitatively (we believe for the first time), some of the religious beliefs and practices of American adults, and some of the attitudes of members of the three main religious groups toward each other.

We hope that this knowledge will help Americans to better understand each other, and, respecting each other's religious convictions, work together better for the common social good.

The Questionnaire

The questionnaire used in the study was prepared independently by Ben Gaffin and Associates, a Chicago marketing and opinion research firm. It was developed through a number of informal interviews with people of various religious affiliations, and revised on the basis of extensive pretests. Great care was exercised to avoid bias in question wording or slant.

The final questionnaire was reviewed by Dr. George Gallup, prior to the inception of the field work.

The Sample Determination

The sample was initially stratified proportionately to the distribution of the U. S. population by census region, and by city size within census region. The specific interviewing points were selected and the quota assignments were made in accordance with this stratification.

The household units to be contacted within these points were selected by accepted systematic sampling methods in accordance with population distribution. Selection of the specific individual to be interviewed within the household was based on sex and age quotas for the area.

Interviewing Technique

The interviews were conducted in person by experienced interviewers of the Ben Gaffin and Associates resident interviewer staff, after instruction on standard sampling and interviewing methods. Interviewers were instructed to ask the questions exactly as written in the questionnaire, without introducing any variations in question-wording, or in the transitions from one section of the questionnaire to another.

Representativeness of the Sample

The following comparisons between 1950 Census estimates

and the sample, indicate its representativeness. Since region and city size were used as a basis for stratification, and sex and age were assigned as quotas to the interviewers, differences between the census estimates and the sample are the result of variations in the field.

None of the other categories, however, were used as controls in any way and the resemblances are strictly the result of the laws of chance which govern operations of large samples.

	1950 CENSUS (Estimates) per cent	Sample per cent
CENSUS REGION		
New England	6	6
Middle Atlantic	20	20
South Atlantic	14	14
East South Central	8	8
West South Central	10	10
East North Central	. 20	20
West North Central	9	9
Mountain	3	3
Pacific	10	10
CITY SIZE		
1,000,000 and over	12	14
100,000–1,000,000	18	18
25,000–100,000	12	10
10,000–25,000	8	7
Under 10,000	34	36
Rural Farm	16	15
SEX		
Men	49	48
Women	51	52
AGE		
18–24	11	11
25–34	23	25
35–44	22	21
45–54	19	18

	1950 CENSUS (Estimates) per cent	Sample per cent
55–64	13	14
65 and over	12	11

RACE

White	90	94
Negro	10	6

EDUCATION

0–8th grade	24	31
1–3 years high school	19	19
High school graduate	38	32
1–3 years college	7	9
College graduate	12	9

OCCUPATION

Professional	9	8
Proprietor or manager	9	13
White-collar worker	19	16
Service worker	10	8
Manual worker	40	42
Farmer	12	8
Other	1	5

INDUSTRY

Agriculture	13	9
Mining	2	2
Construction	6	8
Manufacturing	25	27
Transportation and Communications	8	11
Wholesale and Retail Trades	18	13
Service Industries	22	25
All other	6	5

There are no comparable census figures for income and religious groupings. The sample figures for these are as follows:

	Sample per cent
INCOME	
Upper	17
Middle	51
Lower	32
RELIGIOUS PREFERENCE	
Roman Catholic	23
Protestant total	69
Baptist	17
Methodist	15
Lutheran	8
Presbyterian	8
Episcopal	3
Congregational	2
Other Denominations	16
Jewish	3
Other and None	5

C Religious Survey Questionnaire

Prepared by
BEN GAFFIN & ASSOCIATES
141 West Jackson Blvd.
Chicago 4, Illinois

I'm working on a public opinion survey that is being made all over the United States, to find out what Americans think about religion. I would appreciate it very much if you would tell me your own personal opinions—not what you think you *should* say, but just what *you yourself* REALLY believe.

1a. Do you think people in general today lead as good lives—as honest and as moral—as they used to?

Yes 5-1   Qualified .... -3
No .... -2   No Opinion .... -4

b. Do you think that young people today have as strong a sense of right and wrong as they did, say, fifty years ago?

Yes 5-7   Qualified .... -9
No .... -8   No Opinion .... -0

2a. How important would you say religion is in your own life—*very* important, *fairly* important, or *not very* important?

Very Important 6-1   Qualified .... -4
Fairly Important .... -2   No Opinion .... -5
Not Very Important .... -3

b. Do you think children should be raised *as church members,* or do you think they should be free of formal religion *until they are old enough to make up their own minds?*

Raised as Church		Qualified	-9
Members	6-7	No Opinion	-0
Free to Make up Own			
Minds	-8		

3a. Some religious denominations support their own schools, to which members prefer to send their children rather than to public schools. Do you think these religious schools are *good* or *bad* for the country or don't you think it makes any difference?

Good	7-1	Qualified	-4
Bad	-2	No Opinion	-5
Makes no Difference ...	-3		

b. How would you rate the quality of the general education given in *religious* grade schools as compared with the public grade schools—about the *same, better,* or *not as good?*

Same	7-6	Qualified	-9
Better	-7	No Opinion	-0
Not as Good	-8		

4a. Public funds are used in some states to give free bus service and free books to children in the *public* schools. Do you think public funds should also be used to give free bus service and free books to children in *religious* schools, or not? ....

Yes	8-1	Qualified	-3
No	-2	No Opinion	-4

b. People who send their children to religious schools pay taxes for the support of the *public* schools, as well as paying for the support of the religious schools. Do you think public taxes should be used to support the *religious* schools also, or not?

Yes	8-7	Qualified	-9
No	-8	No Opinion	-0

5a. In some states, children in public schools are allowed to leave school early to attend classes in their own religion, taught by religious teachers of their own faith. Do you think this is a *good* idea, a *bad* idea, or don't you think it makes any difference?

Good Idea .... SP	Qualified .... -2
Bad Idea 9-1	No Opinion .... -3

(IF "GOOD IDEA" ON 5a, ASK):

b. Would you be *in favor* or *opposed* to holding these religious classes *in the public school building*, or wouldn't it make any difference to you?

In Favor .... -7	Makes no Difference ... -9
Opposed .... -8	No Opinion .... -0

6a. Did you yourself happen to receive any religious training as a child?

Yes .... SP	No 10-1

(IF "YES" ON 6a, ASK):

b. What was it—Sunday School; religious or parochial school; or instruction by your parents at home?

Sunday School .... -2	Instructions at Home .... -4
Religious or Parochial	Other .... -5
School .... -3	

7a. In looking back, is there anything about your own religious training that you wish had been different?

Yes .... SP	DK .... -2
No 11-1	

(IF "YES" ON 7a, ASK):

b. What?

☐

8a. Would you want a child of yours to receive any religious instruction?

Yes .... SP	DK .... -2
No 12-1	

(IF "YES" ON 8a, ASK):

b. What kind—Sunday School, religious or parochial school, or instruction at home?

Sunday School .... -3   Instruction at Home .... -5
Religious or Parochial   Other .... -6
    School .... -4

9a. Did you happen to attend any Sunday or Sabbath church services during the last 12 weeks?

Yes .... SP   DK .... -1
No 13-0

□

(IF "YES" ON 9a, ASK):

b. About how many times would you say you attended Sunday services during the last 2 weeks?

About .... Times

Now I'd like to ask you a few questions on some of the things you believe. This is being asked to get a picture of what Americans believe today. Please answer just what you yourself *really* believe, not what you think you *should* believe.

10a. Do you believe in a God?

Yes .... SP   Qualified .... -2
No 14-1   DK .... -3

(IF "YES" OR "QUALIFIED" ON 10a, ASK):

b. How strong would you say this belief is? Are you absolutely certain there is a God—fairly sure there is—not quite sure, but like to think there is—or, not at all sure, but not sure there isn't.

Absolutely Certain ..... -4   Not Quite Sure .... -6
Fairly Sure .... -5   Not at all Sure .... -7

c. How do you think of God—as a loving *Father* who looks after us; as *some kind of supernatural power* but don't know what; or how?

Loving Father 15-1   Other .... -3
Some Kind of Power.... -2

d. Do you believe in the Trinity—The Father, Son and Holy Ghost?

Yes 15-8   DK .... -0
No .... -9

11a. Do you believe that Jesus Christ ever actually lived?

Yes .... SP   DK .... -2
No 16-1

(IF "YES" TO 11a, ASK):

b. Do you think He was God; or just another religious leader like Mohammed or Buddha?

God .... -3   DK .... -5
Another Leader .... -4   Other .... -6

12a. Do you believe the Bible is really the revealed word of God; or do you think it is only a great piece of literature?

Word of God 17-1   DK .... -3
Great Literature .... -2   Other .... -4

b. Do you ever read the Bible?

Yes .... SP   No 18-1

☐

(IF "YES" ON 12b, ASK):

c. About how many times would you say you read it during the last 12 weeks?

About _____ Times

(IF "NO" ON 12b, ASK):

d. Is there any particular reason why you don't read it? (Why?)

13a. Do you ever pray to God?

Yes .... SP   Other .... -2
No 19-1

(IF "YES" ON 13a, ASK):

b. Which of the following prayers do you usually say—short

prayers during the day—night prayers—morning prayers—grace before meals—occasional prayers in emergencies?

Short Prayers During Day	-4	Occasional Prayers in	
Night Prayers	-5	Emergencies	-8
Morning Prayers	-6	Other	-9
Grace Before Meals	-7		

c. Why do you pray?

20-☐
20-☐

d. About how many times would you say you prayed during the last seven days?

About .... Times

14a. Do you think your soul will live on after death?

Yes	SP	DK	-2
No	21-1	Other	-3

(IF "YES" OR "OTHER" ON 14a, ASK):

b. Do you think there is a Heaven, where people who have led good lives are eternally rewarded?

Yes	-6	DK	-8
No	-7	Other	-9

c. Do you think there is a Hell, to which people who have led bad lives and die without being sorry are eternally damned?

Yes	SP	DK	-2
No	22-1	Other	-3

(IF "YES" ON 14c, ASK):

d. Do you think there is any real possibility of *your* going there?

Yes	-6	DK	-8
No	-7	Other	-9

15a. When are your religious feelings strongest—when everything is going well, or when the going gets rough?

When Going Well	23-1	No Difference	-3
When Going Gets Rough	-2	DK	-4

b. Do you ever think about what may happen to you after you die?

Yes 23-7   DK .... -9

No .... -8

16a. Which do you think you yourself *are* most serious about—trying to live comfortably; or preparing for a life after death?

Trying to Live Com-   Both .... -3

fortably 24-1   DK .... -4

Preparing for Life after   Other .... -5

Death .... -2

b. Which do you think you *should* be most serious about—trying to live comfortably; or preparing for a life after death?

Trying to Live Com-   Both .... -9

fortably 24-7   DK .... -0

Preparing for Life after   Other .... -X

Death .... -8

Now I'd like to ask you some less personal questions. Again, I would like to know what *you yourself* think, not what you think you *should* say.

17. *All other things being equal*, do you think that people who marry will be happier if they both have the *same religion*, or don't you think it makes any difference?

Happier with Same Re-   DK .... -3

ligion 25-1   Other .... -4

No Difference .... -2

18a. Some religions hold that divorced people who remarry are living in sin. Do you agree or disagree with this stand?

Agree 25-5   DK .... -7

Disagree .... -6   Other .... -8

b. Some religions forbid married couples to use mechanical birth control methods. Do you agree or disagree with this stand?

Agree 25-9   DK .... -X

Disagree .... -O   Other .... -Y

19. Do you think it is ever right for clergymen to discuss political candidates or issues from the pulpit?

Yes 26-1   DK .... -3
No .... -2   Other .... -4

20a. Most states don't tax property owned by church groups. Do you think church property used for *religious purposes* should be taxed, or not?

Yes 26-5   Qualified .... -7
No .... -6   DK .... -8

b. Do you think church property *which brings rent or profit* to the church should be taxed, or not?

Yes 26-9   Qualified .... -X
No .... -0   DK .... Y

21. Which do you think is most important for the church to do— to *convert people to a spiritual belief* so that they can earn a happy life after death; or to *teach people how to live better every day* with all other people?

Convert to Spiritual   Both .... -3
  Belief 27-1   DK .... -4
Teach How to Live Better -2   Other .... -5

Now here are a few questions we just ask people who happen to be church members.

22. Do you happen at the present time to be an active member of a church, or of a religious group?

Yes, Am Member 28-1   Other .... -3
No, Non-Member ...... -2

(IF "NO" ON QUESTION 22, SKIP TO QUESTION 26a)

23a. Have you ever tried to get anyone to join your religious group?

Yes .... SP   DK .... -2
No 29-1

(IF "YES" ON 23a, ASK):

b. Did you ever succeed in getting anyone to join?

Yes .... -3   DK .... -5
No .... -4

Now let's talk in terms of your local congregation or the *local church* at which you attend services.

24a. How would you rate the clergyman in charge of your own local congregation on his ability to understand your practical problems—would you say he is *very understanding, fairly understanding,* or *not very understanding*?

Very Understanding ....30-1 Not Very Understanding -3

Fairly Understanding ... -2 DK .... -4

b. Do you think his sermons, in general, are *excellent, good, fair* or *poor*?

Excellent ....30-6 Poor .... -9

Good .... -7 DK .... -0

Fair .... -8

25a. Do you think your local church is too concerned with *money matters,* or not?

Yes, Too Concerned .... SP Qualified .... -2

Not Too Concerned ....31-1 DK .... -3

(IF "YES" ON QUESTION 25a, ASK):

b. In what way does this show up that you especially dislike?

                ▢

NOW, SKIP TO QUESTION 27

(ASK ONLY NON-MEMBERS FROM QUESTION 22)

26a. Were you ever in the past an active member of a church?

Yes .... SP Refused .... -2

No 32-1

(IF "YES" ON QUESTION 26a, ASK):

b. How long ago were you active?

           ....Ago ▢

c. What denomination was it?

                33-▢

d. Would you mind telling me why you happened to drop your membership?

34-☐

e. Any other reasons why you dropped?

(ASK EVERYBODY) :

27. Now, I'd like to ask you some questions about what you think of some other denominations than your own.

a. Which denomination (next to your own) do you *like best*?

35-☐

b. Which denomination would you *like least* to belong to?

36-☐

28a. By the way, what is your religious preference—*Protestant, Catholic, Jewish* or what?

Protestant	37-1	Other	.... -5
Catholic	.... -2	None	.... -0
Jewish	.... -4		

(IF "PROTESTANT" ON 28a, ASK) :

b. What *denomination* do you belong to? (Baptist, Presbyterian, etc.)

(IF "NONE" ASK 28e)

38-☐

(IF "CATHOLIC" ON 28a, ASK) :

c. Is that *Roman* Catholic, or what?

Roman Catholic	38-1	Other	.... -3
Anglican	.... -2		

(IF "JEWISH" ON 28a, ASK) :

d. Is that *Orthodox, Reformed, Conservative*, or what?

Orthodox	38-1	Conservative	.... -3
Reformed	.... -2	Other	.... -4

(IF "NONE" ON 28a or 28b, ASK) :

e. In what denomination were you raised?

38-☐

(IF "NONE" ON 28a, SKIP TO QUESTION 54;
ASK EVERYONE ELSE) :

29a. Have you always been a (mention denomination—Baptist, etc.)?

    Yes ....39-Y   No .... SP

(IF "NO" ON 29a, ASK):

b. What were you before?

39-☐

c. How did you happen to change?

40-☐

PART I

Now, I have to ask one more group of questions on your feelings toward the two main religious groups in the U.S. other than your own. Again, please tell me what you really feel, not what you think you should say.

(IF "PROTESTANT" ON 28a, SKIP TO PART II (Q. 38)
ASK EVERYONE ELSE):

These are about your *feelings toward Protestants.*

41-1

30a. Do you think there is much *ill-feeling toward Protestants* among *most* people of your religious preference, or not?

    Yes 42-1   DK .... -3

    No .... -2   Other .... -4

b. Do you think *most Protestants* look down on people of your beliefs, or not?

    Yes 42-5   DK .... -7

    No .... -6   Other .... -8

c. Do you think that Protestants *as a group try to interfere* in any way with your religious beliefs or personal liberties, or not?

    Yes 42-9   DK .... -X

    No .... -0   Other .... -Y

31 Compared with most people of your religious beliefs, would you say *most* Protestants are *about the same, better,* or *not as good,* in—

a. Loyalty to their country?

    Same....43-1   Better....-2   Not as Good....-3   DK....-4

b. Living up to their religion?
   Same....43-5   Better....-6   Not as Good....-7   DK....-8
c. Being fair in business?
   Same....43-9   Better....-0   Not as Good....-X   DK....-Y
d. Treating their families right?
   Same....44-1   Better....-2   Not as Good....-3   DK....-4
e. Being honest in public office?
   Same....44-5   Better....-6   Not as Good....-7   DK....-8
f. Helping people of their own faith who need help?
   Same....44-9   Better....-0   Not as Good....-X   DK....-Y
g. Respecting the beliefs of others?
   Same....45-1   Better....-2   Not as Good....-3   DK....-4
h. Generosity toward public charities?
   Same....45-5   Better....-6   Not at Good....-7   DK....-8

32a. Would you just as soon vote for a Protestant for President of the
   U.S. as for someone of your own religion, or not?
   (PROBE: All other things being equal?

   Yes 46-1   DK .... -3
   No .... -2

b. Would you just as soon have a Protestant for your next-door
   neighbor as someone of your own religion, or not?
   (PROBE: All other things being equal?)

   Yes 46-4   DK .... -6
   No .... -5

c. Would you just as soon have a member of your family marry a
   Protestant as someone of your own religion, or not?
   (PROBE: All other things being equal?)

   Yes 46-7   DK .... -9
   No .... -8

33a. Do you think *most* Protestant employers would discriminate
   against you because of your religion, or not ?

   Yes 47-1   DK .... -3
   No .... -2

b. Do you think Protestants stick together too much, or not?

Yes 47-4   DK .... -6

No .... -5

c. Do you think the Protestants are trying to get too much power in the U.S., or not?

Yes 47-7   DK .... -9

No .... -8

34. Compared with *most* clergymen of your religious preference, would you say *most* Protestant clergymen are *about the same, better,* or *not as good,* in—

a. Sincerely living up to their calling.

Same....48-1   Better....-2   Not as Good....-3   DK....-4

b. In helping their own people who need help?

Same....48-5   Better....-6   Not as Good....-7   DK....-8

c. In living for the next world instead of this one?

Same....48-9   Better....-0   Not as Good....-X   DK....-Y

d. In loyalty to their country?

Same....49-1   Better....-2   Not as Good....-3   DK....-4

e. In giving intelligent leadership to their followers?

Same....49-5   Better....-6   Not as Good....-7   DK....-8

f. In promoting understanding between their group and others?

Same....49-9   Better....-0   Not as Good....-X   DK....-Y

g. In cooperating with leaders of other religions for the common civic good?

Same....50-1   Better....-2   Not as Good....-3   DK....-4

h. In setting a good personal example?

Same....50-5   Better....-6   Not as Good....-7   DK....-8

35a. Do you think Protestants try too hard to get people to join their church, or not?

Yes 51-1   DK .... -3

No .... -2

b. Do you think Protestants try to influence the press too much in favor of their religion, or not?

Yes 51-4   DK .... -6
No .... -5

c. Do you think Protestants try to use their positions as editors, teachers, or entertainers to build up their group, or not?

Yes 51-7   DK .... -9
No .... -8

36. Do you think most Protestant magazines and newspapers try to be fair to your religious beliefs, or not?

Yes 52-1   DK .... -3
No .... -2

37a. Have you or your family ever had any unpleasant personal experience that might have made you dislike Protestants?

Yes .... SP   DK .... -5
No 52-4

(IF "YES" ON 37a, ASK):

b. What was it?

☐

PART II

(IF "CATHOLIC" ON 28a, SKIP TO PART III (Q. 46);
ASK EVERYONE ELSE):

These are about your *feelings toward Catholics*.   41-53-2

38a. Do you think there is much *ill-feeling toward Catholics* among *most* people of your religious preference, or not?

Yes 42-54-1   DK .... -3
No .... -2   Other .... -4

b. Do you think *most Catholics* look down on people of your beliefs, or not?

Yes 42-54-5   DK .... -7
No .... -6   Other .... -8

c. Do you think that Catholics *as a group try to interfere* in any way with your religious beliefs or personal liberties, or not?

Yes 42-54-9   DK .... -X

No .... -0   Other .... -Y

39. Compared with most people of your religious beliefs, would you say *most* Catholics are *about the same, better,* or *not as good,* in—

a. Loyalty to their country?

Same...43-55-1   Better...-2   Not as Good..-3   DK...-4

b. Living up to their religion?

Same...43-55-5   Better...-6   Not as Good...-7   DK...-8

c. Being fair in business?

Same...43-55-9   Better...-0   Not as Good...-X   DK...-Y

d. Treating their families right?

Same...44-56-1   Better...-2   Not as Good...-3   DK...-4

e. Being honest in public office?

Same...44-56-5   Better...-6   Not as Good...-7   DK...-8

f. Helping people of their own faith who need help?

Same...44-56-9   Better...-0   Not as Good...-X   DK...-Y

g. Respecting the beliefs of others?

Same...45-57-1   Better...-2   Not as Good...-3   DK...-4

h. Generosity toward public charities?

Same...45-57-5   Better...-6   Not as Good...-7   DK...-8

40a. Would you just as soon vote for a Catholic for President of the U.S. as for someone of your own religion, or not?
(PROBE: All other things being equal?)

Yes 46-58-1   DK .... -3

No .... -2

b. Would you just as soon have a Catholic for your next-door neighbor as someone of your own religion, or not?
(PROBE: All other things being equal?)

Yes 46-58-4   DK .... -6

No .... -5

c. Would you just as soon have a member of your family marry a Catholic as someone of your own religion, or not ?
(PROBE: All other things being equal?)

Yes 46-58-7   DK .... -9
No .... -8

41a. Do you think *most* Catholic employers would discriminate against you because of your religion, or not?

Yes 47-59-1   DK .... -3
No .... -2

b. Do you think Catholics stick together too much, or not?

Yes 47-59-4   DK .... -6
No .... -5

c. Do you think the Catholics are trying to get too much power in the U.S., or not?

Yes 47-59-7   DK .... -9
No .... -8

42. Compared with *most* clergymen of your religious preference, would you say *most* Catholic clergymen are *about the same, better,* or *not as good,* in—

a. Sincerely living up to their calling?
Same...48-60-1   Better...-2   Not as Good...-3   DK...-4

b. In helping their own people who need help?
Same...48-60-5   Better...-6   Not as Good...-7   DK...-8

c. In living for the next world instead of this one?
Same...48-60-9   Better...-0   Not as Good...-X   DK...-Y

d. In loyalty to their country?
Same...49-61-1   Better...-2   Not as Good...-3   DK...-4

e. In giving intelligent leadership to their followers?
Same...49-61-5   Better...-6   Not as Good...-7   DK...-8

f. In promoting understanding between their group and others?
Same...49-61-9   Better...-0   Not as Good...-X   DK...-Y

g. In cooperating with leaders of other religions for the common civic good?
Same...50-62-1   Better...-2   Not as Good...-3   DK...-4

h. In setting a good personal example?

Same...50-62-5   Better...-6   Not as Good...-7   DK...-8

43a. Do you think Catholics try too hard to get people to join their church, or not?

Yes 51-63-1   DK ....-3
No ....-2

b. Do you think Catholics try to influence the press too much in favor of their religion, or not?

Yes 51-63-4   DK ....-6
No ....-5

c. Do you think Catholics try to use their positions as editors, teachers, or entertainers to build up their group, or not?

Yes 51-63-7   DK ....-9
No ....-8

44. Do you think most Catholic magazines and newspapers try to be fair to your religious beliefs, or not?

Yes 52-64-1   DK ....-3
No ....-2

45a. Have you or your family ever had any unpleasant personal experience that might have made you dislike Catholics?

Yes ....SP   DK ....-5
No 52-64-4

(IF "YES" ON 45a, ASK):

b. What was it?

PART III

(IF "JEWISH" ON 28a, SKIP TO QUESTION 54a;
ASK EVERYONE ELSE):

These are about your *feelings toward Jews*.   53-3

46a. Do you think there is much *ill-feeling toward Jews* among *most* people of your religious preference, or not?

Yes 54-1   DK ....-3
No ....-2   Other ....-4

b. Do you think *most Jews* look down on people of your beliefs, or not?

Yes 54-5   DK .... -7

No .... -6   Other .... -8

c. Do you think that Jews *as a group try to interfere* in any way with your religious beliefs or personal liberties, or not?

Yes 54-9   DK .... -X

No .... -0   Other .... -Y

47. Compared with most people of your religious beliefs, would you say *most* Jews are *about the same, better,* or *not as good,* in—

a. Loyalty to their country?
   Same....55-1   Better....-2   Not as Good....-3   DK....-4

b. Living up to their religion?
   Same....55-5   Better....-6   Not as Good....-7   DK....-8

c. Being fair in business?
   Same....55-9   Better....-0   Not as Good....-X   DK....-Y

d. Treating their families right?
   Same....56-1   Better....-2   Not as Good....-3   DK....-4

e. Being honest in public office?
   Same....56-5   Better....-6   Not as Good....-7   DK....-8

f. Helping people of their own faith who need help?
   Same....56-9   Better....-0   Not as Good....-X   DK....-Y

g. Respecting the beliefs of others?
   Same....57-1   Better....-2   Not as Good....-3   DK....-4

h. Generosity toward public charities?
   Same....57-5   Better....-6   Not as Good....-7   DK....-8

48a. Would you just as soon vote for a Jew for President of the U.S. as for someone of your own religion, or not?
   (PROBE: All other things being equal?)

Yes 58-1   DK .... -3

No .... -2

b. Would you just as soon have a Jew for your next-door neighbor as someone of your own religion, or not?
(PROBE: All other things being equal?)

Yes 58-4   DK .... -6
No .... -5

c. Would you just as soon have a member of your family marry a Jew as someone of your own religion, or not?
(PROBE: All other things being equal?)

Yes 58-7   DK .... -9
No .... -8

49a. Do you think *most* Jewish employers would discriminate against you because of your religion, or not?

Yes 59-1   DK .... -3
No .... -2

b. Do you think Jews stick together too much, or not?

Yes 59-4   DK .... -6
No .... -5

c. Do you think the Jews are trying to get too much power in the U.S., or not?

Yes 59-7   DK .... -9
No .... -8

50. Compared with *most* clergymen of your religious preference, would you say *most* Jewish clergymen are *about the same, better,* or *not as good,* in—

a. Sincerely living up to their calling?
Same....60-1   Better....-2   Not as Good....-3   DK....-4

b. In helping their own people who need help?
Same....60-5   Better....-6   Not as Good....-7   DK....-8

c. In living for the next world instead of this one?
Same....60-9   Better....-0   Not as Good....-X   DK....-Y

d. In loyalty to their country?
Same....61-1   Better....-2   Not as Good....-3   DK....-4

e. In giving intelligent leadership to their followers?

Same....61-5   Better...-6   Not as Good....-7   DK....-8

f. In promoting understanding between their group and others?

Same....61-9   Better....-0   Not as Good...-X   DK....-Y

g. In cooperating with leaders of other religions for the common civic good?

Same....62-1   Better...-2   Not as Good....-3   DK....-4

h. In setting a good personal example?

Same....62-5   Better....-6   Not as Good....-7   DK....-8

51a. Do you think Jews try too hard to get people to join their church, or not?

Yes 63-1   DK .... -3

No .... -2

b. Do you think Jews try to influence the press too much in favor of their religion, or not?

Yes 63-4   DK .... -6

No .... -5

c. Do you think Jews try to use their positions as editors, teachers, or entertainers to build up their group, or not?

Yes 63-7   DK .... -9

No .... -8

52. Do you think most Jewish magazines and newspapers try to be fair to your religious beliefs, or not?

Yes 64-1   DK .... -3

No .... -2

53a. Have you or your family ever had any unpleasant personal experience that might have made you dislike Jews?

Yes .... SP   DK .... -5

No 64-4

(IF "YES" ON 53a, ASK) :

b. What was it?

☐

BACKGROUND QUESTIONS—(ASK EVERYBODY)

This has been a long interview, I know, but I'm almost done. These are just a few more questions to help me keep track of the people I interview. They will be used only for statistical purposes—nothing personal.

54a. What religion or denomination was your *mother's* family?

65-☐

b. What religion or denomination was your *father's* family?

66-☐

55a. Do you happen to read any religious magazines or newspapers regularly?

Yes .... SP   DK .... -2

No 67-1

(IF "YES" ON 55a, ASK):   ☐

b. Which ones?

c. Do you happen to listen to any religious programs on the radio (or television) regularly?

Yes .... SP   DK .... -2

No 68-1

(IF "YES" ON 55c, ASK):   ☐

d. Which ones?

56a. Would you mind telling me exactly what kind of work you do?

(IF RESPONDENT IS A HOUSEWIFE, WIDOW, STUDENT, OR IS EITHER RETIRED OR UNEMPLOYED, ASK):

b. What kind of work does the chief wage earner in your family do?

69-☐

57. What kind of business is that—what do they make or sell?

70-☐

58a. What is the last grade or class you completed in school?

No schooling 71-1	High School Graduate .. -4
Grammar (1-8 Grade) .. -2	College, 1-3 Years ...... -5
High School, Incomplete	College Graduate .... -6
(9-11 Grade) .... -3	Refused .... -7

(IF "COLLEGE," ASK):

b. What type of college?

59a. Has any member of your family been in the armed forces since 1941?

    Yes 72-1   No Answer .... -3
    No .... -2

  b. Do you or any members of your immediate family happen to belong to a labor union?

    Respondent Belongs 72-7   No One Belongs .... -9
    Family Member Belongs . -8   DK .... -0

60a. Did you happen to be home yesterday at this time?

    Yes 73-1   DK .... -3
    No .... -2

  b. Were you here the day before yesterday at this time?

    Yes 73-7   DK .... -9
    No .... -8

61a. How many people are there living here at the present time, *including yourself?*

    ....

  b. How many of them happen to belong to a church at present?

    ....

  c. Would you mind telling me to which denomination each of them belongs?

        (DENOMINATION)   (NO. BELONGING TO)

    ....
    ....
    ....

  d. Let's see—that leaves................that don't belong to a church at present. Would you mind giving me the *sex* and approximate *age* of each of these, and tell me what *denomination* (if any) *they used to belong to?*

          Sex
        (M or F)   Age   Denomination

        ....
        ....

....
....
....
....

62. HEAD OF HOUSEHOLD IS RESPONDENT'S..............................

Respondent .... SP

63. RESPONDENT'S SEX: 64. AGE:

Man 74-1   18-24 75-1
Woman .... -2   25-34 .... -2
                            35-44 .... -3
                            45-54 .... -4
                            55-64 .... -5
                            65 & Over .... -6

65. RACE: 66. STATUS:

White 76-1   W 77-1
Negro .... -2   AV+ .... -2
Other .... -3   AV .... -3
                            P+ .... -4
                            P .... -5

RESPONDENT'S NAME ....

ADDRESS ....

CITY .... STATE ....

CLUSTER NO. .... INTERVIEW NO. ....

INTERVIEWER .... DATE ....

TIME .... M.   CITY SIZE   CEN REG

78-☐   79-☐   80-☐

Index

Siegfried, André, on significance of religion in America, 2

Sin, American concepts of, 50–51

Social system, definition of, 251

Society, relevance of religion to, 254–256

Solidarity, group, survey of attitudes of, in voting, 195–196; in neighbor preferences, 196; in marriage, 197; in the press, 198

Sperry, Willard L., on "unresolved contradiction" in American religion, 15

Stability, religious, survey of evidence of, 172–174

T

"Taught tradition," 90

Tax-exemption, for Church property, attitudes toward, 154–157

Tax support, for religious purposes, attitudes toward, 146–148

Taylor, revivalist, 24

Television, survey on religious programs on, 119–120

Tension, intergroup, American consciousness of, 247–249; sources of, among major faiths, 193

Theology, Protestant, William James on, 89

Toleration, religious, American need for, 237–238; tradition of, 247–249

Toynbee, Arnold, on schism of soul, 232

Transcendent, relation of, as primary element of religious system, 5–6

Trinity, belief in among Americans, according to age, 81; according to education, 83; according to size of community, 86; among major Protestant sects, 79; various concepts of, 54–55

U

"Unchurched," 169, 170, 171

Understanding, clergy rated for, 159–162; survey of attitudes toward outgroup clergy concerning, 216–218

Urbanization, as challenge to Protestantism, 87; degrees of, in major faiths, 36–38

V

Value-orientations, basic principles of, in religious system, 6, 9; and role in Churches, 87–93; relation of, to religious system, 251–258; segmentation of, 90–91

W

Wilde, Oscar, on man's concept of God, 229

Z

Zeal, in convert-making, 177–181

Imprimi potest:

    LINUS J. THRO, S.J.

    Provincial

    Province of Missouri

Imprimatur:

    JOSEPH CARD. RITTER

    Archibishop of St. Louis

    January 23, 1963

A NOTE ON THE TYPE
IN WHICH THIS BOOK WAS SET

This book has been set in Weiss, an interesting face created by E. R. Weiss of Germany, who prefers to be called a painter. While he has studied almost every known letter in the world and copied inscriptions from Roman monuments, Renaissance capitals and fantastic baroque letter-forms from gravestones, he still remains a painter. The Weiss types, while traditional letters, are the product of our own time. Lines of text take on a gracious air—an easy, limpid flow when set in this modern type design. Weiss types have good color and create dignity whenever one sees them, either in a book or advertisement. This book was composed and printed by the York Composition Company, Inc., of York, and bound by Moore and Company of Baltimore. The design and typography are by Howard N. King.